20.X.2004

Kochana Nineńko!

W dniu Imienin
samych pomyślności
i uśmiechów
życzy Ci

Cludzio

FORTRESS AMERICA

FORTRESS AMERICA

ON THE FRONT LINES OF HOMELAND SECURITY—
AN INSIDE LOOK AT THE COMING SURVEILLANCE STATE

MATTHEW BRZEZINSKI

BANTAM BOOKS

New York • Toronto • London • Sydney • Auckland

FORTRESS AMERICA:
On the Front Lines of Homeland Security—
An Inside Look at the Coming Surveillance State

A Bantam Book / September 2004

Published by
Bantam Dell
A Division of Random House, Inc.
New York, New York

Book design by Robin West Morrau / Ox and Company

Library of Congress Cataloging in Publication Data is on file with the publisher.

ISBN: 0-553-80366-2

Manufactured in the United States of America
Published simultaneously in Canada

10 9 8 7 6 5 4 3 2 1

BVG

To the twins to be named later

CONTENTS

ACKNOWLEDGMENTS

This book grew out of a series of articles originally commissioned by the *New York Times Magazine*. Without the early vision of Adam Moss, Gerald Marzorati, Kathy Bouton, and Hugo Lindgren, it would not have seen the light of day.

At Bantam I am indebted to Irwyn Applebaum and Nita Taublib for taking the baton and running with it; and most of all to John Flicker, truly the best editor and sparring partner a writer could ask for. Aside from John, Scott Waxman, agent and friend, has championed this project from the very beginning.

No work of nonfiction is possible without the generosity of its subjects, who give their time and knowledge so that others can benefit from their experiences. To all those quoted in the book, thank you for letting me into your secretive world and allowing me to see the important work you do.

Closer to home, in my own little universe, I have been helped by a number of behind-the-scenes players. Natalia Feduschak took time off from a Fulbright scholarship to assist with research. My daughter Lena provided a steady stream of sanity-preserving work breaks. And my wife, Roberta, as always, led the way.

"A FAILURE OF IMAGINATION"

Manila, January 1995

THE CALL CAME IN SHORTLY AFTER 11:00 P.M.: A ROUTINE fire alarm, some smoke spotted on the top floor of a six-story building just down the street from Police Station No. 9. Aida Fariscal, the watch commander, had just come on duty that Friday night. She always got stuck with the graveyard shift on weekends and pulled administrative assignments her male colleagues didn't want. The discrimination had stopped bothering her. It came with the territory.

Fariscal peered out of the precinct house window, but couldn't see any sign of a blaze on Quirino Avenue. Still, she dispatched Patrolman Ariel Fernandez to check it out. "Nothing to worry about," he reported when he returned a few minutes later. "Just some Pakistanis playing with firecrackers."

Fariscal wasn't so sure. She hadn't earned her senior inspector stripes by sitting down on the job; she'd risen in the male-dominated ranks of the Manila police force by trusting her "female intuition." And her instinct that night told her something was wrong. "The pope was coming to the Philippines, and we were worried about security," she recalls. The senior inspector decided to walk the five hundred yards to the Doña Josefa Apartments to see for herself. She barely had time to change out of her civilian clothes, a flower-patterned dress and sandals, and she didn't think she needed her gun. But just in case, she ordered Patrolman Fernandez and another officer to tag along. Backup in tow, she picked her way past the uprooted trunks of palm trees and scattered debris from a typhoon that had hit several days earlier. Cleanup was always slow during the monsoon season, while city workers waited out the storms.

The Doña Josefa apartment building was a well-kept but not luxurious residence, with an open lobby and an airy feel. It was often used for short-term rentals by Middle Eastern tourists, who came to Manila's neon-lit Malate nightclub district to get away from the strict mores back home. It was also a block away from the papal nunciature, where John Paul II would be staying. "What's happening here, boss?" Fariscal asked the Doña Josefa doorman in Tagalog, a native tongue of the Philippines. Two men, he said, had fled their sixth-floor apartment, pulling on their pants as they ran in the smoky corridor. "They told me everything was under control, just some fireworks that accidentally went off." Fariscal didn't like the sound of that, but she faced a quandary. She couldn't legally enter the apartment without a search warrant, now that there was no longer an imminent danger of fire. But she couldn't simply walk away, either. She was stubborn that way. It was one reason why in 1977, after seventeen years as a homemaker raising four children, she had decided to follow in her husband's footsteps and enroll in the police academy. He had been a problem cop: violent and trigger-happy, predisposed to drinking on the job. Eventually it had cost him his life.

"Open it up," she instructed. Suite 603 was a cluttered one-bedroom bachelor pad. The first thing Fariscal noticed was four hot plates, still in their packing crates. Bundles of cotton lay scattered around the room, soaked in some sort of pungent beige solution, next to clear plastic containers of various sizes and shapes bearing the stamps of German and Pakistani chemical manufacturers. And loops of electrical wiring: green, yellow, blue, and red. Just then the phone rang, causing Fariscal to jump. "I'd just seen a movie with Sylvester Stallone where the telephone was booby-trapped," she recalls now. "Everybody out," she ordered. They scrambled back downstairs, where the doorman appeared to be in a high state of agitation. "That's one of them," he whispered. "He's coming back."

Patrolman Fernandez grabbed the suspect. He was young, in his mid- to late twenties, Fariscal guessed, and handsome in a rakish sort of way. He said his name was Ahmed Saeed, that he was a commercial pilot, and that he was just on his way to the precinct house to explain any misunderstanding over the firecracker smoke. "There's the other one," interrupted the doorman, pointing to a thin, bearded individual standing outside. Fariscal set off in his direction. He was calmly talking on his cell phone, smoking a pipe and watching her. For a brief instant their eyes met. Fariscal had no idea she was looking at the man who had tried to bring down the World Trade Center in 1993.

The sound of gunfire froze Fariscal in her tracks. She had been wounded a few years back when a bullet ripped through her left arm and torso to lodge an inch from her spine, and the memory left her skittish. But she whirled around just in time to see Patrolman Fernandez aiming his service revolver at the fleeing Saeed's back. As the cops gave chase, Saeed suddenly lurched forward, sprawling; he had tripped over the exposed roots of a tree toppled by the typhoon. Saeed was now in custody. But his accomplice had taken advantage of the confusion to melt into the gathering crowd of street peddlers and gawkers.

Neither Fariscal nor the two officers with her had any handcuffs, so they improvised with rope from a clothesline and hauled Saeed to his feet. "I'll give you $2,000 to let me go," he pleaded. Most Manila police officers don't make that in a year, and Philippine officials, like those in many developing nations, have a history of accepting under-the-table payments. But Fariscal refused. Concerned that the suspect would try to bolt again, she radioed the precinct for a squad car. As usual, none was available. One of the cops tried to hail down a passing jeepney, the converted World War II–vintage U.S. Army Jeeps pressed into service as cheap, if not always reliable, public transportation. Finally Fariscal commandeered a minivan taxi and conscripted two burly pedestrians to help watch Saeed during the short ride to the precinct station.

By now the senior inspector had an inkling that she had stumbled onto something big. She couldn't know, however, just how big her discovery would turn out to be; that amid the clutter of the chemicals and cotton at the Doña Josefa apartment, investigators would unearth a plan that, with the benefit of hindsight, would look alarmingly like an early blueprint for the September 11 attack on America. All Fariscal knew for the moment was that she had just nabbed some sort of a terrorist—and, in the Philippines, that could mean anything: Abbu Sayyaf, Moro Islamic National Liberation Front, Mao-Marxists, Secessionists—the list was perilously long.

At the precinct, Saeed signed a handwritten statement in which—according to police records—he again claimed to be a simple tourist visiting a friend in the chemical import-export business. But, perhaps sensing that the game was up, he complained to Fariscal that there are "two Satans that must be destroyed: the pope and America." The senior inspector had already surmised that Pope John Paul II was a target of assassination, a suspicion that was borne out when she returned to Suite 603 at 2:30 A.M. with the bomb squad and found a photograph of the pontiff tucked into the corner of a bedside mirror, near a new crucifix, rosary, and Bible. There were street maps of Manila, plotting the papal motorcade's route; two remote-control brass pipe bombs; and a phone message from a tailor saying that the cassock Saeed had ordered was ready for a final fitting.

By 4:00 A.M. the situation was deemed serious enough that the first generals had started showing up on the scene, and a judge was soon rousted out of bed to sign a belated search warrant. "It was obvious they had planned to dress someone up as a priest and smuggle the bomb past the Holy Father's security detail," Fariscal recalls. But the sheer magnitude of the chemical arsenal Fariscal found in Suite 603 also made it clear that the conspirators had other, possibly even more ambitious, targets. The four new hot plates seem to suggest that the extremists were gearing up for mass production. It took days for the bomb squad to draw up a complete inventory of the apartment's contents, which included a cornucopia of explosive ingredients—sulfuric, picric, and nitric acids; pure glycerin; acetone; sodium trichlorate; nitrobenzoyl; ammonia; silver nitrates; methanamine; and ANFO binary explosive, among others. Funnels, thermometers, graduated cylinders and beakers, mortars and pestles, various electronic fusing systems, timers, circuit breakers, batteries, and a box of Rough Rider lubricated condoms rounded out the home laboratory, which included chemistry reference manuals and a recipe written in Arabic on how to build powerful liquid bombs.

The formula, part of more than 200 pages of classified Philippine and U.S. intelligence documents Fariscal allowed me to copy, was chilling in its simplicity. Step 1: "Put 0.5 g of sodium hydroxide with 30 ml of warm water. Add to them 3 g of picric acid." Step 6: "By using an eye dropper, very slowly add sulfuric acid to the liquid until its color is changed to orange, then to brown." Step 11: "Leave the mixture for 12 to 14 hours to allow the acetone peroxide to precipitate, then wash on filter paper until pH level = 7." Final Step: "Put them in a dark place to dry." That dark place turned out to be the cupboard under the apartment's kitchen sink, where technicians found a foot-long finished bomb with a Casio wristwatch timer. "The guys in the bomb squad had never seen an explosive like this before," says Fariscal. Neither had many U.S. investigators. "The particularly evil genius of this device was that it was virtually undetectable by airport security measures," says Vincent Cannistraro, the former head of the Central Intelligence Agency's counterterrorism center. But what were the targets? And who were the conspirators? A clue to the identity of the suspects emerged when Fariscal found dozens of passports in different names hidden in a wall divider. Saeed apparently had many aliases, including Abdul Hakim, student, age twenty-six, Pakistani passport No. C665334, issued in Kuwait. His real name, investigators would eventually discover, was Abdul Hakim Murad. According to transcripts from his interrogation, he was the Pakistani-born son of a crane operator for a Kuwait petroleum company. He had graduated from high school in Al-Jery, Kuwait, before attending the Emirates Flying School in Dubai and moving on to flight schools in Texas, upstate New York, and North Carolina, where after completing the required 275 hours of flight time, he received a commercial pilot's license from Coastal Aviation Inc. on June 8, 1992.

The plot clearly had the makings of a larger, global conspiracy, so Philippine investigators decided to call in their American counterparts for help. Both the CIA Manila station chief and the resident Federal Bureau of Investigation legal attaché were notified. A team of intelligence agents flew in from Washington. Murad, as Senior Inspector Fariscal now thought of Saeed, was indeed a suspect in the 1993 World Trade Center bombing. So, it turned out, was his accomplice at the Doña Josefa Apartments, the thin, bearded man who had given Fariscal the slip. He had registered under the name Najy Awaita Haddad, purporting to be a Moroccan national. But the United States already had a thick file on him, and that was just one of his twenty-one known aliases. Sometimes he passed himself off as Paul Vijay, Adam Sali, or even Dr. Richard Smith. He was in fact Ramzi Ahmed Youssef, mastermind of the 1993 World Trade Center bombing, a fugitive with a $2 million bounty placed on his head by the U.S. government. Fingerprints lifted at the apartment helped give Youssef away; a lifetime spent assembling bombs had left his fingers burned and distinctively deformed from mishaps mixing tricky chemical concoctions. He had learned his deadly skills, Philippine officials said, in Afghanistan, at a training camp for Osama bin Laden's followers, and had taught Murad the art of bomb making in Lahore, Pakistan. Apparently Murad had not learned his lessons well, for it was his mistake that set off the fire in the kitchen sink that alerted the Manila police. In his haste to flee the apartment, Youssef had left behind many clues. Some, like contact lens solution and a receipt from a pharmacy, seemed innocuous. But others would give the FBI and the CIA a chilling preview of what the terrorists had in store for the United States.

The most damning information was gleaned from Youssef's notebook computer and four accompanying diskettes. The data were encrypted and in Arabic, but Philippine technicians eventually deciphered the code and translated the texts. One of Youssef's translated documents—stamped SECRET by Philippine intelligence—spells out the terrorist cell's broad objectives. "All people who support the U.S. government are our targets in our future plans and that is because all those people are responsible for their government's actions and they support the U.S. foreign policy and are satisfied with it," it declared. "We will hit all U.S. nuclear targets," the manifesto continued. "If the U.S. government keeps supporting Israel, then we will continue to carry out operations inside and outside the United States to include—" Here the text terminated ominously.

A list of cell phone numbers was also found on the computer hard drive. It led authorities to stake out another apartment in Manila, this one on Singalong Street. There they apprehended a third conspirator in the terrorist cell, a stocky Afghan by the name of Wali Khan Amin Shah. Like Youssef, Shah carried many passports under various aliases—Norwegian, Saudi, Afghan, and four Pakistani, all filled with travel visas and entry stamps from Europe, the Middle East, and Asia. Shah also had mangled hands, and was missing two fingers. Both his legs were heavily scarred with shrapnel and he had a large surgical scar on his stomach.

Shah turned out to be the operation's unlikely finance officer. To launder incoming funds, Shah used bank accounts belonging to his live-in Filipino girlfriend and a number of other Manila women, one of whom was an employee at a Kentucky Fried Chicken outlet, and others who were described as bar hostesses. Most of the transfers were surprisingly small—$500 or $1,000 handed over at a Wendy's or a karaoke bar late at night. Under interrogation at Camp Crame, a military installation on the outskirts of Manila, Shah admitted that most of the funds were channeled to Adam Sali, an alias used by Ramzi Youssef, through a Philippine bank account belonging to Omar Mahmoud Abu Omar, a Syrian-born man working at a local Islamic organization known as the International Relations and Information Center that was run by one Mohammed Jalal Khalifa, who was none other than Osama bin Laden's brother-in-law.

Already intelligence officials had gleaned an almost unparalleled treasure trove of information on the inner workings of bin Laden's international terrorist network, later to become known as al Qaeda. Cell members did not appear to even know one another's real names. Duties were divided and compartmentalized, and none of the conspirators stayed in the same place for any length of time. But more frightening revelations were still to come. Yet another file found on Youssef's computer consisted of a printout of U.S. airline schedules, which initially baffled investigators. The file listed the travel itineraries of eleven long-haul flights between Asia and the United States, mostly on United and American Airlines. All the flights had several legs and were grouped under five headings bearing code names of accomplices such as Zyed, Majbos, or Obaid. Each accomplice would leave the bombs on the first leg of the flight and eventually return to Lahore, Pakistan. Obaid, for instance, would fly from Singapore to Hong Kong on United flight 80, which continued as United flight 806 to San Francisco. Under the flight plan, Youssef had written: "SETTING: 9:30 PM to 10:30 PM. TIMER: 23HR. BOJINKA: 20:30–21:30 NRT Date 5." Zyed would take Northwest Airlines flight 30 from Manila to Seoul, with continued service to Los Angeles. "SETTING: 8:30–9:00. TIMER: 10HR. BOJINKA: 19:30–20:00 NRT Date 4," the accompanying instruction read. The repeated use of the word "TIMER" concerned investigators, who by then had made the connection between the dozens of Casio wristwatches found in Suite 603 and one discovered a few weeks earlier on a Philippine Airlines flight from the Philippine town of Cebu to Tokyo's Narita International Airport. The watch had detonated a blast that ripped through the Boeing 747, killing a Japanese passenger and forcing the plane to make an emergency landing.

Philippine intelligence put the screws to Murad. In Camp Crame, he was subjected for sixty-seven days to what Philippine intelligence reports delicately refer to as "TI," or tactical interrogation. By the time he was handed over to the Americans, interrogators had extracted everything they thought they needed to know. Youssef, Murad confessed, had indeed been responsible for the blast aboard the

Philippine airliner, which was actually a dry run to test the terrorists' new generation of nitroglycerin explosive, known as a Mark II bomb. Youssef had deposited his device—lethal liquid concealed in a contact lens solution bottle with cotton-ball stabilizing agents and a harmless-looking wristwatch wrapped around it—under seat 27F on the Manila-to-Cebu leg of the flight to Tokyo. He had gotten off in Cebu after setting the watch's timer for four hours later. The same plan, code-named Operation Bojinka (which is pronounced bo-GIN-ka and means "loud bang" in Serbo-Croatian), was to be repeated on the eleven American commercial jetliners, with the timing devices synchronized to go off as the planes reached midocean. U.S. federal prosecutors later estimated that four thousand passengers would have died had the plot been successful. The enormity of Bojinka also frightened U.S. officials. "We had never seen anything that complicated or ambitious before. It was unparalleled," recalls Vincent Cannistraro, the former CIA counterterrorism head.

But the Bojinka operation called for a second, perhaps even more ambitious, phase, as Philippine interrogators discovered when they pressed Murad about his pilot's license. All those years in flight school, he confessed, had been in preparation for a suicide mission. He was to buy, rent, or steal—that part of the plan had not yet been worked out—a small plane, preferably a Cessna, fill it with explosives, and crash it into CIA headquarters. There were also secondary targets the terrorist cell wanted hit: Congress, the White House, the Pentagon and possibly some skyscrapers—Youssef had made it clear that they had unfinished business with the World Trade Center. The only problem, Murad complained, was that they needed more trained pilots to carry out the plot.

Three terrible weeks had passed since the tragic events of September 11, 2001. The cleanup at the World Trade Center and the Pentagon was only just beginning. Rescuers were still pulling bodies out of the rubble, and the death toll was fast approaching three thousand.

Anger welled in every corner of the land. People were frightened and confused. How could this have happened? many wanted to know. What were we going to do about it? others demanded. "Kill the bas-tards" was a common refrain, bomb Afghanistan into the Stone Age. Teach the Taliban and al Qaeda a lesson they would not soon forget. In Washington, amid emergency sessions of the National Security Council, the finger-pointing had already begun. The CIA and the FBI bore the brunt of the blame, accused by some of being out of touch with the times, stuck in a Cold War mind-set that ignored new perils at the nation's risk.

Like many Washingtonians in those anguished and anxious days, when ominous National Guard Humvees were parked on my quiet block in Georgetown and frazzled neighbors gingerly handled their mail with gloves for fear of anthrax, I, too, was more preoccupied with the how of 9/11 than the why. It was an easier journalism subject to wrap my arms around—to investigate how the world's most sophisti-cated intelligence-gathering apparatus had missed the early warning signals—rather than to tackle the more historically complex and cumbersome subject of why so many in the Middle East seemed in-tent to do us harm. I wasn't sufficiently schooled in the subtleties of Arab culture, oil interests, Palestinian-Israeli conflicts, or postcolo-nial corruption to take on that weighty topic. That was best left to learned historians like Bernard Lewis.

I approached the intelligence failure issue with mixed feelings. On one hand, it was not patriotic to assail America's leading coun-terterror agencies while 9/11's wounds were still so fresh. The men and women at the FBI and the CIA had already felt the sting of re-sponsibility without my heaping further criticism on them. And their services would be desperately needed now that Osama bin Laden had declared war on the United States. On the other hand, if there was something structurally wrong with these vital organs of state, if they were indeed out of touch with reality, the country was at considerable risk. If an overhaul of the system was needed, it would come only from outside pressure and scrutiny. And the more information the public and congressional panels had at their disposal, the better prepared they would be to judge what, if anything, needed to be fixed. Plus, I desperately wanted to be part of the story. From a journalistic point of view, it was the biggest story in decades, perhaps since Pearl Harbor. So I boarded a virtually empty plane and flew to the Philippines to examine claims by the embattled U.S. intelligence establishment that al Qaeda's aerial attack had been completely unpredictable, that it had come quite literally out of the blue.

As I quickly learned, that wasn't the feeling in Manila. General Avelino "Sonny" Razon, one of the lead investigators in the Bojinka case, had experienced such a shock of recognition at what he saw on September 11 that he had immediately jumped on a plane in Cebu, where he was now police chief, and had flown to the Philippine capital to convene a hasty press conference. "We told the Americans about the plans to turn planes into flying bombs as far back as 1995," he complained to reporters. "Why didn't they pay attention?" His candid remarks had earned him an official rebuke from President Gloria Macapagal Arroyo, who was clearly anxious not to embarrass Washington, the Philippines' staunchest ally and patron, and all senior officials had been put under a gag order to prevent any further compromising details from leaking out. "I'm sorry," Razon apologized when I called him. "I would like to talk to you, and there is much to say. But the president has forbidden me to speak publicly on the subject of Bojinka."

Only Fariscal would meet me to discuss the U.S. intelligence failure. She had insisted on meeting at a chicken rotisserie in a busy mall, and would sit only at a corner table, so she could keep an eye on the other patrons and the shoppers beyond the restaurant's greasy glass partition. Old habits, she explained, die hard, and, after a life of fighting crime, she always took security precautions, especially now that she was off the force, a widowed grandmother living off a police pension in a small one-bedroom apartment. Her brother, in fact, was supposed to swing by—just to make sure I was who I said I was.

As we spoke, she seemed bitter and surprisingly fragile in her hoop earrings and bright pink lipstick. She was bitter that the generals in the Philippine high command hogged all the credit for Bojinka, while all she received was a $700 bonus and a free trip to Taiwan. She was angry that the Americans apparently hadn't taken the foiled plot seriously enough. But most of all, she was angry that, in the end, her hunch didn't save thousands of lives after all. "I can't get those images," she said of the World Trade Center wreckage, "out of my mind.

"It's so chilling," said Fariscal. "Mohammed Atta and those kamikaze pilots trained in America, just like Murad. The FBI knew all about Youssef's plans. They'd seen the files, been inside 603. The CIA had access to everything, too. Look," she added, fishing into a plastic shopping bag for one of her most prized possessions, a laminated certificate of merit bearing the seal of the Central Intelligence Agency. "Awarded to Senior Inspector Aida D. Fariscal," it read. "In recognition of your personal outstanding efforts and co-operation."

Fariscal chalked up the intelligence failure to hubris, the unwillingness of arrogant American investigators to listen to their poor, ill-equipped Filipino counterparts. I wasn't so sure. The best explanation I had heard had come from a retired CIA officer from the Directorate of Operations, the agency's clandestine field service. He was a veteran of many Middle Eastern intrigues and a published novelist. "September 11," he said, "was not a failure of intelligence, or security. It was a failure of imagination. We didn't make the intellectual leap from flight schools and dynamite-filled Cessnas to box cutters and fuel-laden Boeing 767s."

Hindsight, he pointed out, is 20/20. I have made enough blunders in my life to readily agree with him. Yet one couldn't fault Fariscal for being angry or frustrated, either. After all, she was personally invested in the failure. Foiling Bojinka had clearly been the crowning glory of her career. She remembered every detail as if it were yesterday. And now it had all been for nothing. "All those people dead," she kept repeating over and over again. "Those poor, poor people. Dead."

We had talked for four hours. Our food had long grown cold, and even the waiters were starting to become impatient and wonder what we were up to. While Fariscal spoke, my eyes occasionally wandered to uniformed security guards searching every patron entering the mall, not for stolen merchandise, but for bombs and weapons. A strange and exotic sight for anyone accustomed to walking into Wal-Mart without the need for airport-style security. The procedure was much the same at the hotel where I was staying: Men with M16s and metal detectors guarded the entrances and searched the trunk of every car parking in the underground garage. They'd been doing this in the Philippines well before anyone had ever heard of bin Laden, yet I couldn't imagine such draconian counterterror measures ever being introduced in the United States.

Fariscal was not hampered by such a failure of imagination. Just as she blamed analysts at the CIA and FBI for dropping the ball, she chided me for not seeing the far-reaching implications of 9/11. "This should have never, ever been allowed to happen," she repeated angrily. "I hope," she added, "that you learned your lesson. That the American government will now take whatever steps are necessary to make sure this never happens again."

It took a while for the full force of her words to hit me. It wasn't until I had returned home to Washington that I began to think about what she had said. A complete outsider, she had nonetheless recognized that homeland security would emerge among the central issues driving America's domestic and foreign policy in the years, if not decades, to come. Which raised a whole host of questions: What were the steps necessary to safeguard America from terror? Did anyone even know? Conventional wisdom said it could never be done; that the United States was simply too big, too unwieldy to protect properly; that the American people were too inherently independent to accept restrictions on their liberties. There were, of course, no easy answers. The United States was probably the world's most open society, its citizens accustomed to unparalleled freedom of movement and minimal government interference. Would that now change? Would America fundamentally *need* to change, trade liberty for security, and become more like the Philippines or other terror-prone places such as Israel? Would we drop our guard with the passage of time? Or overreact wildly? And if we did, what would it be like living in a country bristling with advanced technology and obsessed with security? Would we even want to live in such a place? In the end, would the trade-offs be worth it?

I decided to try to find out.

FORTRESS AMERICA

I

THE MAXIMUM SECURITY STATE

TERRORISTS COULD BE HIDING
AMONG US, ESPECIALLY AT WORK.

—Background investigation firm Pre-employ.com, Inc.

IMAGINATION UNBOUND

Baltimore Harbor, November 2002

WATCH YOUR STEP," SAID SERGEANT GEORGE MCCLASKEY. The police launch strained against its tether, grinding on the tires and rubber padding that had been slung along the dock. It was an old craft, dating back to the 1960s, and much weathered. The blue paint on its patched hull was faded. Its gunwales were pockmarked from countless collisions, and soot from its old diesel engine caked the icy stern. But its partially enclosed wheelhouse offered some protection from the biting wind. "Hope you're wearing long underwear," cracked McClaskey, as the deck shuddered and the launch slipped its moorings.

Baltimore's Inner Harbor spread out before us. On the south side, below the grassy slopes of Federal Hill Park, the marina slips were filled with white, gleaming motor yachts, and halyards and shackles beat noisily on the aluminum masts of expensive sailboats. In the innermost center, against the backdrop of the convention center and the retro brick baseball stadium beyond, floated the big charter boats and wooden skipjacks that took vacationers out on day cruises. And to the north, beneath the skyline, loomed the marine tourist attractions that anchored the Pratt Street Pavilions: a vintage submarine, painted gray and black with red shark's teeth on the bow, and a full-size replica of a Civil War–era frigate, the USS *Constellation*.

"That," said Sergeant McClaskey, craning his football player's neck toward a water taxi landing next to the *Constellation*, "is where I'd strike if I were a terrorist." I followed his gaze to the landing.

Other than a few angry seagulls squabbling on the bulkhead, the place was deserted. But in summer, up to a quarter of a million people congregated on the Inner Harbor's piers and brightly painted promenades each weekend, catching a show at the waterside amphitheater, dining on crabcakes after an Orioles game, or taking the kids to see the dolphins at the National Aquarium.

"If I wanted to create a big bang," McClaskey continued, "I'd pack a small boat with explosives"—relatively easy-to-find nitrate fertilizers or dynamite, he later elaborated, plus plenty of nails, screws, and other building materials that can double as shrapnel—"and crash it right here." The police launch slowed to an idle, sinking back into its own wake. For a moment we drifted, and I stared at McClaskey. Cops weren't supposed to say things like that, to plot like al Qaeda. At least, they never had before. But McClaskey wasn't being irresponsible or tipping off terrorists to what they probably already long knew. (After all, for any organization that could have dreamed up 9/11, smashing a boat into a wharf was the creative equivalent of child's play.) No, McClaskey was on the right track. He was adapting to the times. Imagining terrorist scenarios was part of any public safety official's job description post-9/11.

The launch bobbed in the choppy waters. McClaskey paused long enough for me to envision the gruesome consequences of a strike on the pier. "It'd be a catastrophe," he finally declared. "It would take forty-eight hours just for the tide to flush out the bodies from under the boardwalk."

This nautical factoid he had learned from experience, from nearly twenty years on the force fishing out dead drug dealers, drowning victims, and the occasional jumper from the Fort McHenry Bridge. But the big Irishman made it clear with an uncharacteristic sigh that his new counterterrorism assignment was truly uncharted territory. In the war on terror, he and most of his fellow officers were mere rookies, suddenly forced to play catch-up to the rest of the world. "Before 9/11," he said, "it never even occurred to us to consider the waterfront as a source of danger." Now perceived dangers lurked around every wharf. "Look at that barge," he added, nodding toward a tug hauling a barge full of diesel fuel off in the distance. "A beautiful weapon."

More grisly details followed. Ram the promenade with the fuel barge, said McClaskey, and deaths would not be the only tragedy. There would be dire economic repercussions, as well. Baltimore had spent more than $1 billion revitalizing the tourist district. Thousands of jobs had been created in the effort, and the project was a national showcase for urban renewal. But just one suicide bomber could undo all of that good work, sow panic, sink the whole town. Such was the nature of terrorism; the damage was never isolated, as the attacks on New York and Washington had so painfully demonstrated. By some reports, 9/11 had cost the U.S. economy anywhere from $75 billion to several hundred billion. The collateral damage was immeasurably higher when one considered how stock exchanges around the world had plunged—the Nikkei, the DAX, the CAC 40, the TSE. No one was immune to the carnage, and for cities like Baltimore, the stakes were now exponentially higher than anything the police department had ever faced before. And that was saying a lot, given Baltimore's unenviable distinction as America's drug capital. Ten percent of the city's residents, by police department estimates, were heroin addicts. In the week prior to my visit, four police officers had been shot, including one executed point-blank for testifying against a local gang. The police department here had enough on its plate without having to worry about where and when extremists might strike next. But worry it did. The department's Criminal Intelligence division, which before 9/11 devoted virtually all its efforts to the war on drugs, now spent upward of three-quarters of its time chasing down terrorist leads. The division's head, a polished and urbane young major by the name of John Skinner, was even sent to Israel to bone up on the basics of counterterrorism. And the police department's eleven-man maritime unit, whose main responsibilities until recently had included ticketing speeders and enforcing no-drinking-and-boating rules, now had far more daunting responsibilities.

Other big urban centers faced similar dilemmas. The NYPD diverted three hundred officers to a special counterterror unit. The city of Los Angeles went so far as to create its own department of homeland security, appointing ABC News terror expert John Miller as civic security czar, largely on the strength of an interview he had once conducted with the elusive Osama bin Laden. Nationally, every state followed L.A.'s lead and set up homeland security departments, and the FBI reassigned a quarter of its eleven thousand field agents to counterterror duties.

We rounded Locust Point, steamed past the towering steel hulls of thousand-foot-long Navy LMSR transport ships that would soon take tank brigades to Iraq, and entered the industrial sector of the port. Here the list of potential terrorist targets multiplied: oil terminals flying BP's and Shell's corporate colors, unprotected liquid natural gas storage tanks, exposed coal-fired power stations, and large petrochemical facilities with flimsy chain-link fences. Even the Domino sugar refinery, with its sticky-sweet flammable dust, posed a potential security threat: "Most people don't think about it," said McClaskey. "But that's a giant bomb."

Across Curtis Bay and the exposed trusses of the Fort McHenry Bridge, under which all freighters and tankers pass before docking, thick white plumes rose from smokestacks of the CW Grace chemical plant. "They make some really nasty stuff there. Highly toxic," said McClaskey's colleague, Sergeant Ed Coleman, a squat, muscular man who headed the maritime unit. According to the Environmental Protection Agency, there were fifteen thousand facilities just like it around the country that produced, stored, or used toxic chemicals. "It's mind-boggling," he added, as a wave sent salt spray over the bow and drenched his black paratrooper boots. "I pretty much see targets wherever I look." And every one of those targets could set in motion an ever-broadening ripple effect. Should al Qaeda frogmen, for instance, manage to blow up an oil terminal, the nearby I-95 tunnel ventilation systems would have to be shut down. Shut down the tunnels, and the interstate highway must be closed. Close down a section of I-95, and traffic along the entire Eastern Seaboard snarls to a stop, to say nothing of what such an attack would do to disrupt oil supplies and prices in the mid-Atlantic region or to insurance premiums of ships docking on the East Coast.

Sergeants Coleman and McClaskey were not the only public servants fretting about suicide bombers following 9/11. All across the country, officials at virtually every level of government were rushing to take stock of America's vulnerabilities, starting with the White House, which commissioned the Central Intelligence Agency to identify the 100 most likely terrorist targets in the United States. The governors of every state were asked to identify 150 of the most visible targets in their jurisdictions and another 180 secondary targets. The grim surveys were known in bureaucratese as risk assessments, and for the most part they were not made public, for obvious reasons. But they were extremely important and constituted the opening phase of the domestic war on terror. Just as environmental impact studies are required before ground is broken on major construction projects, the risk assessments would form the foundation on which the security state was built. Priorities needed to be identified, the most pressing vulnerabilities addressed. The results of the assessments would form the basis from which scarce resources would be diverted and billions of dollars of federal, state, and local funding would be allocated to shore up homeland security. The problem, of course, was that the list of targets, to quote Sergeant Coleman, was mind-boggling. Subways, sewers, shopping centers, even our food processing and drinking water systems were all now fair game to terrorist plots. Anything could be turned into a weapon: the postal service, an air-conditioning unit, a truck or train hauling hazardous materials. Passenger ferries from Staten Island, seven thousand commuters on board, could be sent careening into a passing oil tanker. Viruses could be spread, industrial facilities sabotaged. Cyberattacks could be launched, financial networks disrupted. All you need is a little imagination.

In the new threat environment, the United States has 600,000 bridges to protect and 14,000 small airports from which terrorists can wreak havoc. There are 4 million miles of paved roadways and 95,000 miles of coastline for extremists to escape on. Eighteen thousand separate law enforcement bodies need to be synchronized in any counterterror response. In addition to Baltimore Harbor, there are 361 other ports just as exposed. The United States boasts a network of 260,000 natural gas wells and 1.3 million miles of pipeline that terrorists can blow up. In New York City alone, the subway system has an astonishing 1.2 billion riders annually. Seventy-seven million passengers use its three airports annually. More than 16 million commercial cargo containers arrive by air, sea, and land every year, and all it would take for a catastrophic disaster would be for one of the steel crates to conceal a nuclear device. If we can't even put a dent in the flow of thousands of tons of illicit drugs smuggled past customs, how can we hope to stop a fifty-pound suitcase filled with fissionable material from getting through?

The list goes on and on. A four-thousand-mile open border with Canada runs through villages, homes, golf courses, and even a public library, where the stacks are in Quebec and the reading room is in Vermont. Ninety-one million foreign nationals enter the country by air every year. And any one of them could be hell-bent on unleashing tularemia or botulinum toxin. No one even knows how many million illegal immigrants are already in the country, and al Qaeda sleeper cells in Detroit, Omaha, Coral Gables, or anywhere else may already be in place, biding their time.

The list of terrorist opportunities is literally limitless: movie theaters, department stores, feedlots, resorts, stadiums, and arenas—you name it. That is the drawback of living in the world's most open society, America's Achilles' heel. And the targets are by no means limited to the East Coast terror corridor between Washington and New York. Places like Cleveland or Tuscaloosa, Memphis or Minneapolis are vulnerable precisely because any attacks on Middle America would sow panic in Iowa or Indiana the way another strike in D.C. or Manhattan never could. Many people in Wisconsin or Louisiana still do not see the immediacy of the terror threat the way New Yorkers do. But after a chemical plant is blown up in, say, Tennessee, no one would feel safe, regardless of where they lived.

The grim task of cataloging the nation's vulnerabilities was the necessary first step toward ensuring that our imagination would never fail us again and that we would not find ourselves in a predicament where even residents of a small Midwestern town would fear for their safety. As former assistant FBI director Stephen Pomerantz explained to me: "We have to acknowledge our weaknesses to take corrective action. And we have to recognize that we are far behind other countries in this regard."

That meant adopting the mind-set of the terrorists and drawing up lists of potential targets. Targets generally can be grouped into three broad categories: soft, medium, and hard. Of least concern are those that have a minimal impact on the national psyche. A bomb in a mailbox in a residential area, for instance, is unlikely to create a nationwide panic. It is virtually impossible to defend against, and not worth the effort. Medium-impact targets up the ante in the angst and damage they cause. Cyberterrorism can, for example, disrupt communications or financial networks. But as CNN terrorism expert Peter Bergen noted, such an attack lacks a key ingredient: drama. "Al Qaeda wants to see blood and smoke," he said. Other medium-intensity targets might include throwing a grenade on a bus or leaving a bomb in a department store. While these fulfill bin Laden's gory criteria, they are likely to be seen by the general public as localized events, unless repeated simultaneously a half dozen times in different parts of the country, which requires considerably more planning and personnel to pull off. The third category is what really keeps officials up at night: a strike that would sow fear across the land. This usually involves, but is not restricted to, an assault on critical infrastructure, on something we all use regardless of whether we live in Tucson or Tampa Bay. Statistically, an insignificant percentage of Americans worked at the World Trade Center or the Pentagon. But we all fly, relying on air travel perhaps more than any other nation on earth. And al Qaeda has made us all think twice about flying. We all drink water. A lethal contamination of the water supply in any U.S. city would make us all think twice about that, too. As Pomerantz put it: "If there's a chemical attack on the subway in Chicago, you think people are going to risk riding the Metro in New York, or Washington, or anywhere else?" The most dangerous targets do not necessarily produce the biggest body counts. Rather, they have a built-in psychological component: They spread the most terror.

To compound the problem, protecting the homeland against any and all such assaults was an entirely new area for the U.S government in 2002. The nuclear umbrella that had served so well during the Cold War was useless against this unconventional new adversary. NORAD radar stations can give no early warning of this enemy's strikes. Nor can the squadrons of F-16 fighter jets that now buzz over Washington with maddening frequency be easily scrambled to prevent them. This enemy keeps too low a profile: Hiding among us, they might live next door, or sit next to us in business class. This enemy uses freedom as cover, turning the American way of life into his most potent weapon. To fight this foe you need an entirely new approach, along with a new technological and legal arsenal, one that stands at the ready for deployment at a moment's notice in every major city and county in the country.

No easy task. Combating terror is likely going to rank among the biggest, costliest, and most daunting domestic challenges in U.S. history, up there with the New Deal and the war effort that followed the attack on Pearl Harbor. As in the case of most ambitious government undertakings, there was no clear consensus in 2002 on how to go about it or even where to begin. Some of the most glaring weaknesses, such as the stricken commercial aviation sector, were being addressed with the hiring and training of 53,600 federal airport screeners. Emergency laws—the Uniting and Strengthening America by Providing Appropriate Tools Required to Intercept and Obstruct Terrorism Act, more popularly known as the USA Patriot Act—greatly enhanced surveillance, search, and seizure powers. Thousands of mostly illegal Muslim immigrants were detained and deported. Suspected al Qaeda assets of $34 million were frozen in the United States, bringing the total to $124.5 million worldwide by November 2002. Canada had been pressured to tighten its immigration policies and to beef up border security, and Saudi Arabia had been pressed to clamp down on charities that could be used as fronts to fund terror. U.S. Special Forces had been dispatched to sixty-five countries to hunt down al Qaeda surrogates such as the Abbu Sayyaf, Jemaah Islamiyah, Harakat al-Mujahideen, and the Islamic Movement of Uzbekistan, to name a few. On the home front, a color-coded five-tier terror threat advisory system was established in March 2002, along with joint counterterrorism task forces in every state to coordinate responses to the different danger levels.

Throughout the country, the FBI, the Immigration and Naturalization Service, and the Justice Department are working hand in glove to track down potential sleeper cells using their expanded Patriot powers. In New Jersey alone, sixty-two terrorist indictments had been brought down by the U.S. Attorney's Office, thanks to the new laws. (Mind you, sixty of the sixty-two terrorist indictments were filed against Middle Eastern students for paying people to take their English proficiency exams.)

Of all the new initiatives, the most ambitious, however, revolved around plans for the creation of a new superagency to coordinate the entire counterterror effort, the Department of Homeland Security. But its responsibilities and staff were still vague in 2002, and it did not even have a headquarters. The truth was that no one knew exactly what to do. Antiterror measures, like the targets they were intended to defend, were so numerous that this new agency would need a stack of documents a dozen phone books thick simply to catalog them.

Many countermeasures were simply physical barriers: checkpoints at tunnels, new fences, extra guards or concrete barricades outside government installations. Some relied more heavily on tested technology: motion sensors on bridges, biometric locks on restricted areas at airports, and giant gamma ray machines at ports capable of scanning forty-foot-long containers. Still others took technology to the cutting edge: vast database-mining programs created by the military, face-recognition software, unmanned surveillance drones, radio-frequency identification transponders, and complex computer models of air currents in subways.

In 2002, few government officials were aware of all these counter-measures, since terrorism historically had never been a high priority in the United States. America, after all, had been remarkably terror-free prior to 9/11. In the 1970s, the Weathermen and the Symbionese Liberation Army had wreaked some havoc. Occasionally a pro-life group blew up an abortion clinic or environmental protesters set fire to a ski resort or SUV dealership. Sometimes white supremacists shot it out with the Bureau of Alcohol, Tobacco and Firearms, or a lone crazy like Unabomber Ted Kaczynski struck by mail. Organized acts of terror on the scale of the 1997 Oklahoma City bombing have been, however, mercifully rare. Most of the more violent attacks on the United States have occurred abroad, at embassies and military barracks in distant and messy places like the Middle East or Africa. At home, in Middle America, terrorism had ranked low among all the issues facing law enforcement, somewhere between crystal methamphetamine production and automobile-insurance fraud. The United States, in fact, was and continues to be the only industrialized country in the world not to have a domestic intelligence agency specializing in counterterrorism like the British MI5, Germany's GSG-9 Grenzschutzgruppe, the Israeli Shin Bet, or France's Secretariat Generale de la Defense Nationale. Even blissfully peaceful Canada had its domestic spooks, the Canadian Security Intelligence Services.

Attorney General John Ashcroft did not even include terrorism among the top seven priorities of the Strategic Plan he outlined on August 9, 2001, for the Justice Department. On September 10, 2001, he proposed slashing funding for the FBI's meager counterterror division. This would later strike observers as somewhat ironic, for the deeply devout and conservative attorney general quickly became the personification and chief lightning rod for the excesses of the new security state. To be fair, his predecessors in the two Clinton administrations hadn't exactly made counterterror the number one priority, either. Ashcroft's reasoning at the time was based on budgetary concerns. The United States didn't need a vast counterterror apparatus. It was a waste of time and money to develop expensive expertise in a fringe area that had so little impact on American everyday life.

September 11 changed all that. For perhaps the first time in the nation's history, Americans were feeling vulnerable. After the shock wore off, people began to fly again, returned to work on the top floors of skyscrapers, and went back to watching reality TV. Yet there was a lingering sense of unease, of trepidation, that al Qaeda could strike again—anywhere, at any time. The paranoia at times bounded on the absurd. Baking soda or coffee creamer left in a corporate cafeteria was immediately taken for anthrax. People were wearing gloves to open their mail. Unscrupulous companies took out full-page ads in newspapers hawking dubious home air filtration systems that supposedly would protect people in the event of biochemical release.

Higher in the threat-laden atmosphere, planes were making emergency landings because a passenger who looked Middle Eastern spent too long shaving in the toilet. Just looking like an Arab could get one thrown off a commercial flight. One member of President Bush's Secret Service detail was even turned away from a flight because he was of South Asian descent. In Florida, the interstate highway was closed and a huge manhunt launched when a waitress at a roadside diner in Georgia thought she overheard several "olive-skinned" customers discussing something suspect, probably the quality of the food. In Texas, one misguided and obviously none-too-bright vigilante shot a turbaned Sikh shopkeeper, not realizing that he was not even Muslim, much less in cahoots with bin Laden. In Washington, some immigrant cabdrivers were so terrified of being taken for terrorists that they festooned their taxis with so many American flags that you could barely see out the window.

Suddenly we were seeing plots and enemies, both real and imagined, everywhere. On the I-66 in Virginia, the electronic message boards usually reserved for construction or traffic updates flashed the 1-800-492-TIPS number of a terrorist hotline, along with exhortations for motorists to report any and all suspicious activity.

Our imagination was truly running wild. Security risks were now everywhere, threatening the very foundations of an open society. Asking questions about a mysterious new white box installed in the Mall near Congress could get you arrested by overzealous Park Police, as a curious *Washington Post* columnist discovered. Ph.D. dissertations, once the stuff of dry academic conferences, now needed to be classified if they dealt with infrastructure grids that could prove useful road maps for al Qaeda planners. Secrecy was the order of the day in the White House, which could invoke national security to keep media and inquiring watchdog groups at bay.

The media themselves helped sow the seeds of paranoia. The cable news networks became particularly adept at purveying fear twenty-four hours a day. You couldn't watch CNN or Fox without being certain that you were going to die. In fact, according to studies by legal scholar Jeffrey Rosen, 17 percent of Americans suffered some form of post-traumatic stress disorder following 9/11, even though the vast majority lived hundreds if not thousands of miles from Ground Zero. The psychological disorders were most acute, Rosen found, not in New York City, but among those who watched the most TV.

In this climate of fear, it was easier to push for the implementation of invasive laws like the Patriot Act that most Americans would never accept otherwise. The Islamic scare even created a market niche that wedded the newfound paranoia to old-fashioned American entrepreneurial instincts. "IS YOUR EMPLOYEE A TERRORIST?" asked a press release from a background investigation firm I came across in one issue of *Harper's Magazine*. "According to the FBI, terrorists could be hiding among us, especially at work," warned the company, Pre-employ.com Inc. of Redding, California. "An FBI bulletin says industry officials should check out their current employees in an effort to root out any terrorists who have been working there for years, waiting for the signal to strike.... if you are concerned about terrorists among your employees you can take measures to uncover the operatives. Pre-employ.com Inc. completes 2,000 background checks each day for clients nationwide. For as little as $10..."

To add to the hysteria, the United States was desperately short on counterterror experts to make sense of it all. Fortunately not everyone was guided by profit-driven cynicism. There was a truly inspiring spirit of volunteerism following 9/11, with thousands of people making real sacrifices to help shore up the nation's defenses. In one case, a professional football player with the Arizona Cardinals, Pat Tillman, walked away from a multimillion-dollar paycheck to join the Army. (He would later be killed in action in Afghanistan.) Similarly, a bigshot Wall Street stockbroker put his career on hold to sign up for active duty. Within the military, a deputy assistant secretary of defense gave up his post to join his National Guard unit. On the West Coast, a Drug Enforcement Administration agent in San Diego took a year off to become a Coast Guard sea marshal. The whole country seemed to be wearing NYFD baseball caps. It was a remarkable period of solidarity, during which even Democrats and Republicans put aside their differences for the good of the wounded nation.

Moving as all these outpourings of patriotism were, good intentions don't always translate into better counterterror preparedness. Applications for positions at the CIA in the year following 9/11 spiked from the typical several thousand to several hundred thousand. Unfortunately, lamented a spokeswoman, most of the applicants were "severely lacking" in even the most basic qualifications. It was the same story over at the J. Edgar Hoover Building at FBI headquarters. Prior to 9/11, the Bureau averaged seven thousand applications for the 200 to 300 vacancies it filled yearly. In 2002, according to Joe Bross, who was in charge of recruiting at the Bureau, over 100,000 equally unsuitable people applied for 923 open slots. Bross told me that the ideal recruit in the post-9/11 era was "someone who can deal with people well, can speak a foreign language, and has a sciences degree." To attract applicants with those skills, Bross even dropped the FBI's mandatory three-year work experience requirement and lowered the minimum age for agents. But still it will take years before the pool of new recruits can be trained and elevated to positions where they can have a significant impact in the war on terror.

None of this meant that we were completely helpless in those early days. There had been many successes in the struggle against terror abroad. Some three thousand al Qaeda members had been killed or captured in the year that followed the October 2001 retaliatory invasion of Afghanistan, according to the U.S. State Department. Al Qaeda's Taliban protectors had been routed, driven from their strongholds of Kandahar and Kabul into the mountains and lawless tribal belts on the Pakistani border. Several of bin Laden's most senior lieutenants had been apprehended, most notably Khalid Sheik Mohammed, his pudgy chief of operations, and Ramzi bin al-Shibh, the gaunt and ghoulish coordinator of the 9/11 strikes. Under interrogation Mohammed, whom American officials referred to as KSM, was unusually voluble. He had been in Manila with his nephew, Ramzi Youssef, in 1995. Bojinka, he confessed, had indeed been the genesis of 9/11, and the operation had been five years in the planning. Other post-9/11 plots had also been in the works, KSM said. In Baltimore, an al Qaeda operative named Majid Khan was given the responsibility of blowing up a dozen gas stations simultaneously. He had family in Maryland in the retail gasoline business, which gave him inside knowledge on where to place the explosives for maximum destructive effect, and had hoped to recruit several African American Muslims to do the job. But, fortunately, he was arrested in Pakistan before he could pull off the plan, according to *Newsweek*.

Some 660 Taliban and al Qaeda luminaries picked up in raids in Afghanistan and Pakistan had been shipped off to Guantánamo Bay, Cuba, where they languished in a Navy brig. Their cave network in the Afghan mountains had been bombed to rubble and then sifted, like an archeological find, for intelligence data. Computers discovered in the debris netted a treasure trove of international terror contacts in Germany, France, Spain, Yemen, Saudi Arabia, and Malaysia. Financial statements found among the detritus left scores of promising money trails for the CIA and FBI to pursue. Other seized documents hinted at a multitude of disrupted diabolical plans: blueprints of U.S. nuclear plants, water distribution systems, maps of the Washington Metro, manuals for crop dusters, videos of caged animals being poisoned by gas, sundry bioweapons formulas, and recipes for radioactive dirty bombs.

But despite the inroads against the network, tens of thousands of extremists—the estimates ranged as high as seventy thousand—from dozens of countries had, over the years, passed through the terror training camps in Afghanistan. They are all still out there somewhere. The six-foot-six terrorist leader himself remains at large (at least as of June 2004, along with Ayman al-Zawahiri, and Mullah Omar, the one-eyed chief Taliban cleric). Rumors swirled that the Tall One, as he is reverently known by his followers, was in Pakistan, that he had taken refuge in the Pankisi Gorge in Soviet Georgia, that he had had plastic surgery and was living in Somalia or Sudan. There remains a $50 million bounty on his head, but so far no one has come forth to claim the prize money. How many other extremists have escaped the U.S. dragnet is not publicly known. Nor did anyone in 2002 know for sure if al Qaeda had successfully regrouped, attracted new recruits to replenish its decimated ranks, or found other safe havens from which to operate. One thing was fairly certain following the deadly bombings in Bali, Karachi, and Mombasa: Al Qaeda was still in business, and the United States had not heard the last from Osama bin Laden and his band of fanatical cohorts. There remain other, equally pressing, concerns. Would some like-minded lunatic take his place, a Stalin to bin Laden's Lenin? Would the remnants of al Qaeda forge alliances with the North Koreans or Iran? Would the scattered and decentralized terror network prove even more difficult to corral? Would it drastically change its tactics and modus operandi to foil further detection? And what nightmare scenario could the next generation of al Qaeda schemers dream up to upstage 9/11, to one-up themselves?

"So what about counterterror measures?" I asked McClaskey and Coleman as we chugged past the white, windowless hull of the USN *Comfort*, a 900-bed Navy hospital ship that last saw service in September 2001, treating victims and first responders from the World Trade Center wreckage. Despite assurances from Washington that the United States would not move on Iraq without United Nations backing, the ship was clearly preparing for action in the Gulf—as were the huge gray LMSR transports, which could each carry 950 Humvees, 65 Abrams tanks with full fuel and ammunition, and still have over 100,000 square feet of cargo space for sundry stores and supplies.

Access to these behemoths in 2002 (or by 2004, for that matter) was not restricted. Any pleasure craft could sail right up to them, blow a hole in the hull, mimicking the 2000 attack on the USS *Cole* in Yemen, and take out an entire tank battalion. Pleasure craft, in fact, could go anywhere in the harbor. America is remarkably accessible in that way. Seventy of the 103 nuclear power plants in the United States are on navigable waterways. One could kayak right up to the Indian Point Nuclear Power Station on the Hudson, just north of New York City. Sail next to aircraft carriers in San Diego. Drive into sensitive research centers. Even tour the White House, a security breach that struck me as an invitation for trouble. McClaskey readily agreed. "It's crazy," he acknowledged, though he was somewhat unsure as to what to do about space restrictions in the port. "We've set up a 1-800 number for people to report suspicious activity," he said, "and talked to all industry reps about beefing up their security guards and perimeter fences." But compliance with the requests was voluntary, and not all the plants were quick to take action, particularly as there was no point in building a seven-foot-tall fence when regulations might be soon passed stipulating nine- or ten-foot heights, with or without outriggers, sensors, razor wire, or lights spaced every so many yards. Until legislation was passed governing industrial security, the plants likely would remain poorly protected.

There was concrete evidence of new countermeasures in the Inner Harbor, however. Marine barriers had been installed at the foot of

Baltimore's twenty-seven-story World Trade Center, which stood on the seawall and by dint of its name and location was deemed an alluring target. The barriers rose out of the brackish water like stakes in a moat and were linked with thick steel cables suspended between reinforced pylons, stationary guillotines designed to slice into approaching high-speed craft and decapitate would-be suicide bombers before they reached their mark. It was an impressive sight. But the shoreline defense was only 50 yards long; that left another 94,999.9 miles of shoreline to go. The rest of the port was as vulnerable as it had ever been. And it was a maze of competing jurisdictions that jealously guarded their turf. The Fort McHenry Bridge alone was subject to six different state, local, and federal government bodies. Who would respond in the event that one of its trusses was struck? Which agency would take the lead? And which one was ultimately responsible for safeguarding it?

These issues of territoriality had yet to be resolved in 2002 and persist throughout most of the country, even after it became known that several of the 9/11 hijackers and thirty other known terrorists had slipped into the United States because the FBI, CIA, INS, State Department, and customs had had their wires crossed. The problem of interagency cooperation is compounded by the vastly different cultures of the various government bodies. In Baltimore the police, for instance, wanted cameras and more fast patrol boats to enforce restricted zones around key port installations—in other words, a beat cop's aquatic equivalent of greater street presence and visibility. Sergeants Coleman and McClaskey felt that terrorists would likely rent a waterfront property in the Chesapeake Bay from which to launch their assault, so reinforcements needed to be concentrated in the harbor. The Coast Guard, on the other hand, favored another, more liberal approach, influenced by the service's traditional humanitarian mission of rescuing people in distress rather than arresting them.

That do-gooder tradition had been most spectacularly on display during 9/11 when the Coast Guard orchestrated the waterborne escape of over half a million people from lower Manhattan. In an operation reminiscent of the World War II cross-channel evacuation of over 300,000 soldiers stranded on the French coast, Coast Guard captain Richard Bennis put together a volunteer flotilla of pleasure yachts to ferry people to safety and run supplies in to rescuers when all roads to Battery Park were blocked. For his quick thinking, he was promoted to admiral, because saving lives rather than policing was what the Coast Guard was all about.

"Ports have to be open," said Captain Robert G. Ross, who headed the Coast Guard's Office of Strategic Analysis in Washington. "You can't limit people's lawful right of movement by putting security zones around every ship or installation. It's a question of public tolerance."

The Coast Guard supported using the twelve-mile territorial water delineation as a goal-line defense against terrorist encroachment, screening foreign ships in the high seas before they near land. The Navy, which had lent its *Cyclone*-class cutters and P-3 surveillance aircraft to the homeland security effort, went further still. *"We choose not to defend the airport from the ticket counter,"* argued Rear Admiral Eric Olson. "We believe in taking the fight to where the enemy lives so that our shield is held at the farthest end of our reach."

All these diverging views made any kind of unified port protection policy virtually impossible. Each service brought its distinct corporate culture to the table and tried to tailor its strengths to counterterror rather than developing a whole new set of guidelines. The problem was by no means limited to Baltimore. Writ large, it would prove one of the greatest stumbling blocks to the creation of the Department of Homeland Security, as I would discover.

"So how would you defend against frogmen blowing up half the harbor?" I asked McClaskey. It was a valid question. The prospect of such a calamity had apparently so unnerved the Federal Bureau of Investigation that special agents had spent thousands of man-hours canvassing diving schools throughout the United States to compile dossiers on every scuba-diving student (including the actor Tom Cruise, who had taken lessons in L.A.). The Bureau also was tailoring its standard operating procedures to counterterror, regardless of whether laborious gumshoeing was the most efficient use of resources. Interrogating was what they knew. So they detained and interrogated indiscriminately, casting their nets so wide that many terrified Muslim immigrants preferred to hide and keep potentially useful tips to themselves rather than risk a run-in with federal authorities.

Back on the boat, the sergeants contemplated my question in silence. Coleman shrugged uneasily. "Honestly, I don't think it's possible," McClaskey finally confessed. At the very least, I admired his willingness to be frank. Like most law enforcement officials in the United States, he had been trained to catch crooks, not to stop submerged suicide bombers. Imagining terrorist doomsday scenarios was one thing; we'd all become good at it over the past thirteen months. Coming up with effective solutions was another story, often still beyond the scope of our imagination. But while that expertise did not yet widely exist in the United States, it was out there if you knew where to look.

"Sonar," said Rear Admiral Amiram Rafael, when I put the same question to him, some six thousand miles away in Israel, perhaps the one place in the world where terrorism is as much a part of daily life as commuter traffic. "It can distinguish between humans and large fish by mapping movement patterns and speed," explained Rafael, who had spent twenty-eight years protecting Israel's coastline from the likes of Hamas and Hezbollah. "If the alarm sounds, rapid response units in fast boats are dispatched. They're equipped with underwater concussion grenades."

"To stun the divers?" I asked. "No," said Rafael, flashing a fatherly smile at my naiveté. "To kill them."

2

THE MAXIMUM SECURITY STATE

I F THE UNITED STATES WAS STILL A NOVICE AT DEFENDING against terror in 2001/2002, Israel occupied the other extreme of the security spectrum: a nation under siege, where counterterrorist considerations factored into just about every corporate, civic, military, and even personal decision. The specter of a suicide bomber, a sniper, a stabber, or a chemical or biological attack by the likes of Hamas or Hezbollah hovered uncomfortably behind almost every facet of daily existence in Tel Aviv and Jerusalem. The warning sirens could go off at any minute in Israel. It was a fact of life. And people had grown accustomed to living with it. Alerts came and went almost on a daily basis, and the economy did not nosedive. First responders pulled mangled bodies out of restaurants and buses and did not gripe about crossed communications or inadequate equipment.

Since the answers to so many of my questions were still scarce in the United States, it made sense to go to Israel to see how they coped with terror, how it influenced daily life there, and what sacrifices they made to try to stay safe. There was only one minor problem with my plan; I didn't know a soul there, didn't have a single contact to call. My only lead was rumors in Washington that the United States had become "a giant piñata," to quote one official, for Israeli security consultants. So I logged on to Google, the Internet search engine, typed in "Israeli security consultants," and hit the "I'm feeling lucky" bar. Luck, as it turned out, had nothing to do with the hundreds of company listings that scrolled down my screen. I clicked on one at random, and that was how I came to know Offer Einav.

At the time, Einav was in the States meeting with clients. The Israeli company he worked for, GS-3, was formed in the weeks after 9/11 to fill the new—and growing—niche for counterterrorism expertise in the United States. Einav had just snagged several consulting gigs with airlines and nuclear power stations. I could fly back to Tel Aviv with him, he said. We agreed to meet at the El Al counter at John F. Kennedy Airport in New York City. "How will I recognize you?" I asked. "Don't worry," he said. "I'll find you."

El Al occupies a prime patch of real estate at JFK's new Terminal 4 building, albeit at a judicious distance from Saudi Arabian Airlines and Pakistan's main carrier. A long line had already formed in front of the check-in counter, although it was only nine-thirty and the flight didn't leave until midnight. This was not especially unusual. With El Al, one is always advised to budget an extra hour beyond the two now required for security procedures.

Four young El Al employees, all in their early twenties, sporting black casual wear and dead-serious expressions, scrutinized the travelers. Their unsmiling eyes scanned the crowd, looking for something suspicious: a nervous twitch in one of the passengers, a furtive glance, or perhaps one bead of perspiration too many. The passengers shuffled forward: yeshiva students and rabbis in Orthodox garb, youth groups with name tags identifying them as part of an organized tour, some college kids taking advantage of the Christmas break, a few middle-aged tourists, and the usual briefcase-toting business travelers.

There was an unquestionably military air about the El Al screeners, who, it was immediately apparent, were not your run-of-the-mill Delta or United employees politely inquiring if you packed your own bags. Nor were they the customary minimum-wage local hires U.S. airlines used to screen passengers at the ticket counter. These young men and women still carried the vigilant and authoritative swagger of the IDF—Israeli Defense Forces—from which El Al recruited its security personnel. Everyone in Israel, regardless of gender, served a stint in the armed forces, and the military did double duty as a talent pool for various intelligence, security, and secret services on the lookout for individuals with specific aptitudes.

The Israelis didn't trust foreigners to ensure their safety. El Al was too symbolic a target for terrorists. So wherever possible, they posted their own teams abroad to guard their planes on the tarmac, process luggage through pressure chambers to detect barometric bombs of the sort that brought down Pan Am flight 103 over Lockerbie in 1988, and make sure no one untoward got on board. The policy made flying El Al both inconvenient and expensive, but the Israelis had a perfect safety record that justified the security premium.

I was early for my appointed meeting with Einav, so I wandered over to the mezzanine for a quick coffee. On the way, a large clear tube with the rough dimensions of a walk-in shower caught my attention. Its prominent display was reminiscent of a museum exhibit, except that it was not a relic from the past but rather a harbinger of things to come. A small sign identified the futuristic booth as on loan from the Schiphol Airport authority in Amsterdam. The Dutch had won the concession to run JFK's Terminal 4 and were implementing many of the features that made Amsterdam one of the world's most advanced and efficient air hubs. I had already noted with keen interest the appearance of Schiphol's trademark horsefly on the urinals in the Terminal 4 men's rooms. This clever little sticker, when affixed to the center of the porcelain receptacle, keeps spillage to a minimum because, as a Dutch official explained to me, users subconsciously aim for it, resulting in cleaner, more hygienic washrooms.

The tube exhibit was decidedly more high tech, but no less ingenious, and was attracting a good number of curious onlookers. One traveler, however, seemed unimpressed. "Big deal," he said to no one in particular, slurring his words as if he had partaken of one too many cocktails. "They've had those in Europe for years."

Known as a circle lock, the contraption resembled a space age phone booth with crescent-shape Plexiglas doors on either side. Inside was a retina reader—manufactured, ironically, by Iridian Technologies of New Jersey—a built-in scale to weigh travelers to prevent anyone from trying to piggyback another person through the system, and an alarm that sounded if you tried to hang from the ceiling. "We use them in Holland," said Peter Boone of the Schiphol Group, when I later inquired about the machine. "They are for our trusted traveler program. You enroll. Your financial and criminal record is checked. You're then issued a smart card with an encoded digital image of your iris, and slide the card into a booth, which scans your eye to verify your identity. The whole process," he added, "takes twenty seconds. And that includes carry-on luggage screening."

Twenty seconds, as opposed to the twenty or more frustrating minutes it usually took to clear the chaotic new security procedures in the United States, was indeed a step forward. It was also another indication that while America led the planet in many a field, security was not one of them. I was contemplating this irony, when a voice interrupted my musings. "Mr. Matthew," it declared, without the questioning hesitancy that usually accompanies blind dates or first-time encounters. A meaty hand engulfed mine, squeezing the circulation from my fingers.

"Let's grab a beer," Einav said by way of introduction. He was short but powerfully built, like an Olympic wrestler. His face was broad, his nose looked broken, and his shaven head was scarred. Black jeans, paratrooper boots, and a leather jacket rounded out the intimidating look.

I glanced apprehensively at the long line forming in front of the El Al check-in counter. "Don't worry about it," said Einav. "We have time for a couple of rounds."

Moments later he was flirting with the waitress, bearhugging the El Al flight attendants who had repaired to the bar for a last smoke before going on duty, and exchanging pleasantries in Hebrew with female patrons, whom I couldn't decide if he knew. He certainly seemed to know a great many people in Terminal 4, waving, backslapping, and calling out greetings in a number of languages wherever he turned, which was everywhere, since it quickly became apparent that he rarely missed a beat.

Einav plucked an ashtray from a neighboring table. One could still smoke in those early days of Mayor Bloomberg's term. I lit up, but

noticed after some minutes that Einav wasn't reaching for his cigarettes. "Do you smoke?" I asked. "Used to," he said. "Two packs a day.
But I gave it up." How then did he know I was still puffing? Einav
smiled and shot me a mischievous look. "Hey"—he chuckled—"if I'm
going to spend ten hours on a plane with someone, I make it a point to
know something about them."

What else, I wondered, did he know about me? Einav, after all, was
a former senior officer of the Shin Bet, which he had joined after fifteen years as a commando in the IDF Special Ops forces (hence, I presumed, the scars). The Shin Bet, or Shabak, as it was also known, was
the Mossad's elite sister agency, responsible for all domestic intelligence and counterterrorism in Israel. Did that mean they had a file on
me? I was probably just flattering myself, being paranoid. But this was
the second time in as many months that I had been taken aback by the
familiarity of a stranger in such a way. The first time had occurred after
I made an appointment to visit Washington's main water treatment
plant. The FBI had issued one of its periodic terror alerts, this time
warning of unspecified al Qaeda plots to poison drinking water supplies, and I wanted to see what precautions were being taken. When I
showed up at the gate of the plant, an armed guard checked my social
security number and home address against a checklist on his clip-
board. Which would not have bothered me, only I had never given
out my address or SSN. How then did they have that information? I
asked the facility's security chief—a former military intelligence officer who had done stints on the East German and North Korean fronts,
and was absolutely adamant I not use his name. "I made a few calls,"
he had said with a laugh. "I can even tell you your bank balance."

"Not very impressive, is it?" I had also laughed, partly to conceal my
irritation at the intrusion. If the water authority could dig up my personal data with such ease, I could only imagine what the Shin Bet,
NSA, or FBI could unearth with a few keystrokes of their supercomputers. And yet, upon reflection, I didn't feel violated by the loss of privacy
so much as reassured that security was indeed a serious matter for the
people who supplied my two-year-old daughter's drinking water. After

all, I had voluntarily put myself on their radar screen, and it was only fair that they wanted to know whom they were dealing with. It was an invasive trade-off that, in this instance, I was willing to accept. Subsequent incidents, however, would leave me less sure of where the line between liberty and security should be drawn.

Our flight was called, and we made our way to the check-in counter. The Israeli screeners were still grilling passengers, but Einav went straight to the front desk. "He's with me," he said, handing my documents to the young woman processing the tickets. She smiled pertly and gave me my boarding pass. No questions. Not even if I had packed my own bags. Flying with Einav had its distinct advantages. He had served as El Al's security director, a job always held by an agent of the Shin Bet, which in addition to its counterterror responsibilities provided protection for the Israeli president, prime minister, defense minister, embassies, and the national airline.

"I promise you'll get a very different treatment when you'll be alone on the way back." Einav chuckled knowingly. "You'll see why the CIA uses El Al for training exercises." Apparently Langley held Israeli security procedures in such high regard that one of the final tests for prospective field agents was to fly to Tel Aviv on one set of false documents and get back out using another. Einav had nabbed a few of these trainees right here at JFK, discovering false-bottomed suitcases with forged passports and matching credit cards and driver's licenses. A couple of calls to Washington would usually clear up the situation, and Einav would send the flustered CIA rookies on their way with a tip or two on how to arouse less suspicion.

As we cleared the metal detectors at airport security, Einav grew uncharacteristically annoyed. He was one of those jovial people who tended to see the glass as half full—not the cynic one would expect, given his profession. But I could see his contempt rising, the color rushing to his features, his roguish charm leaving him. Finally he could no longer control himself. "Look at their fancy new badges," he said angrily within earshot of the TSA (Transportation Security Administration) screeners manning the equally new EDS machines that X-rayed carry-on luggage. Einav had pioneered the use of the gamma-ray and sniffer technology. A thousand of the machines, modeled after Israeli systems, had been bought and installed at every major airport in the United States, along with 54,800 hastily hired screeners at a total cost of $5.8 billion. The effort to meet the December 31, 2002, deadline for the nationwide airport security upgrade had been something of a Herculean effort, but Einav was not impressed. "What about baggage handlers and catering?" he asked, adopting the tone of a professional athlete commenting on an amateur exhibition match. "You still don't do proper background checks on people who work in those areas and allow those types of jobs to be filled by noncitizens. That's crazy," he added. "What's to stop a baggage handler from putting a bomb in the cargo hold or someone from crashing a fuel truck into a parked plane filled with passengers?"

As for the new screeners, he was just as critical. "Know what TSA stands for?" he winked. "Thousands standing around."

His scowl softened as he ran into an old acquaintance and heaved her off the ground in a hearty, flirtatious embrace. He was not exactly a looker, but clearly he had a way with the opposite sex. (My wife, who would later meet him in Washington, described the attraction as "alpha male.")

"Where were we?" he asked, after disengaging himself. His main beef with the new security procedure, as he explained it, was the wasteful emphasis on what he called political correctness. Individuals were chosen at random for searches, lest Muslim travelers feel singled out, and those taken aside for extra screening had included seventy-year-old blue-haired ladies, toddlers, United States senators, and, infamously, Al Gore. "Please explain to me," he asked, "under what criteria the former vice president poses a security risk? That's just a waste of time and resources, like pissing on the wall to see what sticks."

Random checks were democratic, Einav allowed, but also very inefficient. While Gore was being patted down, the bad guys could be getting through unchallenged. The Israelis, he said, preferred a different system: profiling. In Israel, it was done partly by computer programs that developed dossiers on passengers the moment they bought a ticket and assigned risk values to each one. Pay cash or trigger some other threshold, and you were guaranteed to be strip-searched. That was exactly what happened to shoe-bomber Richard Reid, who tried to probe El Al's security and found himself sitting in his underwear being questioned for over an hour. Eventually he settled on the softer target of American Airlines flight 63 from Paris to Miami. Only the quick thinking of several passengers prevented him from igniting his explosives and killing all 197 on board.

Israel's passenger profiling—referred to as positive profiling—differed fundamentally from the American version in that it was used not to roll the dice in the hope of ferreting out potential hijackers during a random check, but primarily to identify and eliminate honest travelers. These, like Holland's trusted travelers, whisked through automated formalities simply by placing a hand on a biometric palmprint reader, thus freeing up screeners to focus on the remaining passengers. "It's the Pareto principle," Einav explained; 80 percent of travelers are by definition good citizens who present no danger to security. Eighty percent of the bad guys, conversely, will be found in the remaining 20 percent of passengers. And that's where El Al devoted all its persistent energy, as I would discover, to my considerable discomfort, on my return flight solo.

"Your biggest problem in America is that you don't understand how terrorists operate," Einav lectured as we drove toward a checkpoint outside Tel Aviv's Ben-Gurion International Airport. The flight had been uneventful; El Al's flight attendants, though all trained in a martial arts form that prescribes kneeing troublemakers in the groin, had been at least as surly as their more peaceful American counterparts. Einav had slept the whole way, exhausted and uncommunicative—like some air marshal dozing on the job.

Now he was refreshed and expansive. "Do you know what the primary goal of people who carry out terrorist acts is?" he asked. To kill Americans, or Jews, I speculated. "Ha," he said, pleased that I had fallen into the trap. "Nope; that's planners. I'm talking about the pawns." He paused dramatically. "They want to become *shahid*—martyrs; to be remembered as somebody in their community." Mohammed Atta was Michael Jordan in many disaffected parts of the Middle East and South Asia, a hero who in death had climbed the peaks of celebrity and respect. In Israel, Einav said, there had been numerous cases when suicide bombers had for some reason or other missed the bus they had intended on blowing up. "Instead of waiting for the next bus," he said, "they just stood there grinning like idiots and blew themselves up without anyone around."

The first few times this had happened, Israeli investigators had been stumped. But eventually it led them to conclude that they were dealing with a *shahid*, or martyrdom, syndrome, what is known in Arabic as the *bassamat al-farah*, or the smile of death, which also means there is no point negotiating with most suicide bombers. The free pass to heaven, the seventy-two virgins that await the *shahid* in the afterlife gates, the honor and $6,000 payment that his murderous suicide would bring to his family, the thousands who would attend his funeral, his face added to the posters of the fallen heroes—these are powerful inducements to young Palestinians who feel they have no future.

"We build case files on every known terrorist and every terrorist incident," Einav added. "We study them until we know them by heart. And we make all the files available to everyone in law enforcement." I had heard this from Major Skinner of the Baltimore PD, who upon his return from Jerusalem had marveled at how freely information flowed in Israel. "Even the lowest beat cop over there," he had told me, "knows things that would be considered top secret in the States."

The study of terrorism was far from a precise science, Einav went on, but like any discipline, its purpose was to reveal patterns. One recent and worrisome trend had been the increasing use of women as suicide bombers, both in Israel and Chechnya. The women invariably tended to be single and past the traditional marrying age—or in

Chechnya, war widows. But they also tended to change their minds at the last minute more often than men, and terrorist organizers frequently sent a "minder" along with a remote-controlled detonation device in case the women had second thoughts.

Women thus far had not broken the glass ceiling in al Qaeda, but eventually that group, too, was likely to start conscripting females to foil profilers. Al Qaeda was already touting the joys of martyrdom in its recruiting videos, which listed the names of fallen heroes like Atta. "Terrorists usually stick to their game plan," Einav explained. "They only change methods when they see that we've caught on to them."

We slowed down at the roadblock. A pair of guards, sullen and stiff, scrutinized us from behind the stubby muzzles of their machine guns. It was dark and drizzly, and every few hundred yards military Jeeps with flashing blue lights whisked by. Doghouses and observation towers lined the airport perimeter, which was ringed with an electronic fence bristling with sensors. German shepherds prowled at the foot of the fence to discourage anyone contemplating a potshot at a passing plane.

In the gloom of the night, with the mist and the searchlights probing the slanting rain, the complex had the eerie feel of a Siberian labor camp. All that was missing was snow and Slavic accents. As first impressions went, the airport defenses made a definite statement. You were entering a militarized state, a country at war.

A jumbo jet roared overhead, coming in on its final approach. Pilots landed and took off at perilously steep angles at Ben-Gurion, not lingering in the kill zone of shoulder-fired missiles any longer than necessary. The pitched descent served as yet another reminder that it was civilians, not soldiers, who were the primary targets of this conflict.

"There hasn't been a single attempt on Ben-Gurion in over thirty years," said Einav, with evident pride. "You know why?" I could guess that the answer had something to do with the fact that it was protected like Fort Knox. "Because terrorists always search for the path of least resistance, and they know Ben-Gurion is too well guarded."

Terrorists aren't rocket scientists, Einav explained, despite the mythical proportions al Qaeda had achieved thanks to 9/11. "They're predictable," he said, not that different from thieves who search for targets of opportunity. If every house on the block has barred windows and alarm systems, burglars are most likely to break into the one un-protected home with the open screen door. Einav called it getting the monkey off your back and onto someone else's. So the Israelis made certain all their hard targets—symbols of the state, strategic infra-structure, and so on—had adequate bars on the windows. The de-fenses didn't necessarily have to be fancy, just thorough. "In America you are always dreaming up Hollywood scenarios to defend against," Einav continued. "Like training exercises with Navy SEALs rap-pelling from helicopters to simulate an attack on nuclear power plants. That's nonsense. Terrorists will just load up a truck with C4 [plastic explosive] and crash through the gate. Contrary to popular be-lief, they are not so sophisticated," he said. "They use the simplest, most logical plans. The genius of 9/11 was its simplicity."

We drove in silence for a few moments. Traffic was sparse, save for military patrols. "That's the Green Line," said Einav, pulling toward a ditch. An open field lay before us. It was clumpy, and strewn with boulders, broken glass, and chunks of concrete, as if it had been bull-dozed at some point. This was the 1967 border. Beyond it stretched the occupied territories. "Want to see why peace is so complicated?" asked Einav. "Look up at those hills."

A patchwork of lights winked on the scrubby foothills. Most were yellow in hue, dim and spread out. But others were bright white and tightly clustered. These were the Israeli settlements amid Palestinian villages. From our vantage point, the yellow and white lights were so closely knit that they formed a single exurban mosaic. Some 230,000 Israelis lived in the 150 settlements in the West Bank and Gaza. Un-der international law, they were illegally infringing on Palestinian territory, but Israel disputed this and continued to build more. The proliferation of those heavily guarded Israeli settlements and a huge network of military roads that connected them to Israel proper was the source of much of the Palestinian anger. In Gaza, an area about the size of Washington, D.C., 6,000 Israeli settlers occupied as much land as a million Palestinians, who were not allowed to leave what effectively was a giant outdoor prison. The impoverished Palestinian villages and refugee camps cut off by the new settlements supplied a steady stream of suicide bombers. To stem that flow, Israel was building military bases in the West Bank; one was to be built on the exact spot where we stood. It also conducted frequent and sometimes indiscriminately brutal reprisal raids, using heavy armor and combat helicopters, and was erecting a gigantic security barrier on the Green Line. More than half a football field wide, it included deep ditches and sand strips to preserve footprints, twenty-five-foot-tall cement walls and fences, rolls of razor wire stacked six feet high, sophisticated sensors to prevent tunneling, watchtower with spotlights and infrared night-vision surveillance equipment, and a paved road for military vehicles to speed along. Additional patrols were provided by unmanned aircraft similar to the Predator drones the United States was using in Afghanistan. A United Nations study estimated that, when completed, the wall would erode a further 15 percent of Palestinian territory and disrupt the lives and livelihood of some 600,000. Thus far, ninety miles of the $1.3 billion security cordon had been erected. But it hadn't put a big dent in terrorist traffic.

The day before my arrival, two Israelis had died in a bus bombing in Tel Aviv. The week before, a similar incident at a café in Jerusalem claimed three lives. During the week following my visit, twenty-three more would die in Tel Aviv, bringing the total to over seven hundred. By early 2003, physical barriers went only so far. They slowed down suicide bombers and made their task more difficult, but they did nothing to address the root causes of terror. In this regard Israel's approach was similar to the Bush administration's, which also favored fighting terror, preferably on the military front, rather than taking a cold hard look at policies that gave rise to it. No one in Washington seemed eager to examine the issue of why al Qaeda had targeted America in the first place. That Islamic extremists hated democracy and freedom, the simplistic answer put forth most frequently in political talk shows, couldn't be the whole story.

Just as Israelis probably were being overly optimistic in thinking that a wall was going to protect them from terror as long as they kept chipping away at Palestinian territory by building settlements in the West Bank, I wondered whether the impending U.S. invasion of Iraq would make the United States any safer in the end. Or could it have the opposite effect? After all, if we were to draw any historical lessons from Israel, fighting terror with conventional armed forces could be a battle of attrition more than anything else. That was the conclusion of four former Shin Bet directors—Yaakov Perry, Ami Ayalon, Avraham Shalom, and Carmi Gilon—who took the unprecedented step of going public with their misgivings about current Israeli policies. "If we go on living by the sword, we will continue to wallow in the mud and destroy ourselves," Perry warned. "The government is dealing solely with the question of how to prevent the next terrorist attack," said Gilon. "It ignores the question of how do we get out of the mess we find ourselves with."

Military options without a political process would ultimately backfire, added General Moshe Ya'lon, the IDF Army Chief of Staff, who also took the extraordinary step of publicly admonishing Prime Minister Ariel Sharon's heavy-handed and short-term solutions for strengthening the resolve of terrorist organizations. A group of Israeli pilots went further, refusing to fly missions that bombed civilians. By Israel's closed-rank security standards, this unprecedented series of establishment protests was almost mutinous. But it also sent a clear message that you couldn't defeat terrorism with the barrel of a gunship, or tank, no matter how good your military was. It was one of the principal Israeli lessons that America's policymakers would have benefited from.

For Israel, abandoning the ruinous settlements and returning the land to the Palestinians was not likely to end terror, but at least it could get the political process started once again and reclaim the high moral ground. Of course, that presumed that everyone in Israel actually wanted peace. The people certainly did. But I wondered about

some of the leaders. It almost seemed as if the hawkish Sharon, whose
C. V. was drenched in blood and involvement in atrocities that were a
stain on Israel's image, and Yasser Arafat needed each other to stay in
power, as if they were mirror reflections of all the political opportunities a perennial state of emergency created. After all, the people who
ran Israel, the military, and security establishments enjoyed vast powers justified by the terrorist siege. Under Sharon, the extreme right was
in charge. If normalcy ever returned, would they be forced to relinquish those privileges and adopt more moderate stands? This was an
important issue for America, because, like Sharon, Attorney General
Ashcroft and others in the administration frequently cited the specter
of terror to justify making the government bigger, more militaristic,
intrusive, and activist. "We need to use every tool at our disposal," he
told a gathering of U.S. Attorneys in Manhattan. A Pentecostal
preacher's son, John Ashcroft hails from the most conservative wing
of the Republican Party. He had fought desegregation so adamantly in
his home state of Missouri that, according to *Vanity Fair*, a federal
judge once threatened him with contempt. According to *Vanity Fair*'s
unflattering profile, throughout his political career Ashcroft has been
openly hostile to homosexuals, women in the workplace, and abortion, even for rape victims. Even voters in traditionally conservative
Missouri apparently found him so frightening that they elected a dead
man to replace him as a one-term senator, a historical first. Now 9/11
had Ashcroft in a position where he would be responsible for vastly increasing the powers of the government to intrude in people's lives and
homes in the name of terrorism prevention. It was an opportunity he
obviously relished. If the terrorist threat ever abated, how eager would
Ashcroft or other officials be to give up those powers? Might they suc-
cumb to the temptation of perpetuating the crisis, like Sharon, to retain their right to extraordinary measures?

"Invading Iraq is a good start," Einav said somewhat incongruously the
next day, in his office in downtown Tel Aviv. "But Syria and especially

Iran are the real problem. Jihad and suicide brigades are Iranian exports."

A growing number of Israelis are opposed to military solutions to their own terror problem, but just about everyone I spoke with relished the idea of U.S. Marines doing their dirty work for them in the region. The attacks on Washington and the World Trade Center had altered Middle Eastern politics like no other event in recent history. The televised shots of Palestinians in Gaza cheering as the twin towers fell had outraged the American public, undoing all the powerful imagery of intifada children being mowed down by IDF tanks. Arafat had rushed to donate his own blood to the 9/11 victims; but the damage was done. The spontaneous and rapturous joy in the occupied territories at America's tragedy tipped the scales once again in Israel's favor and wiped out any hope for serious political support for the Palestinians in Washington.

For Israel (although Israelis would never say so out loud), 9/11 was truly a boon. Not just for counterterrorist consultants like Einav, who on September 10 was newly retired from the Shin Bet and planning to coach soccer, but for politicians, military men, and hawks of all stripes. Israel's enemies were now America's enemies, and vice versa. Americans now had an inkling of how Israelis felt when a bomb ripped through a wedding reception or a crowded Sbarro's pizza outlet. "This is a clash of civilizations," I would hear over and over again, even from moderate Israelis; every Israeli I spoke to advocated that the United States "regime-change" the entire region. It was a convenient slogan that many in Washington also employed. But it isn't entirely accurate. Israel's conflict with the Arab world is not cultural, political, or theological. It is territorial and always has been. Even Einav—who was against the settlements and skeptical of the new wall—failed to make this important distinction.

Not wanting to offend my host, I steered the conversation toward the less controversial ground of how a remarkably large number of terrorist leaders began their careers as young idealists. "Yeah," Einav agreed. "At first they want to change the world, make it a better place, and fight injustice. But somewhere along the line, they get sucked in by the life: power, women, money, prestige. And in the end, they become nothing more than professional planners, hired hit men, who work for the highest bidder. Damascus and Beirut are full of them." There was another traditional route in the terrorist hierarchy Einav failed to mention, and it was exemplified by the career path of al Qaeda's number 2, Ayman al-Zawahiri. An idealist from an upper-middle-class family in Cairo, Zawahiri started as a student protester while at medical school, agitating against corruption and human-rights violations of the Egyptian government. Arrested and brutally tortured, he became a violent radical in prison, as have many others like him.

Einav's attractive receptionist poked her head in the door of his modern, minimalist office—lots of chrome and pale Scandinavian woods, all at harsh right angles. "Joel's here," she said. Joel Feldschuh was GS-3's chairman. He had served as a brigadier general in the air force and had been the president of El Al. In Israel, a disproportionate number of politicians and top business executives started their careers in the military or intelligence, giving new meaning to the term "military-industrial complex."

Einav had arranged for me to meet with many of his retired intelligence buddies (those still manning the barricades couldn't talk to the press), but they were all running late this morning. Heavy rains had brought traffic to a standstill in Tel Aviv, caused flash floods in the wadis, and made everyone as edgy as Einav's Swedish furniture. Funny, the Israelis could cope with bombs ripping through crowds, but a little rain had all of Tel Aviv frazzled. They were accustomed to bombs, I supposed. But rain was something out of the ordinary in the parched desert.

As if on cue, Einav's computer beeped with a terror alert. His screen saver was set to a local newspaper, which had just issued the warning. Intelligence had gotten word of an impending strike, and readers were asked to be on the lookout for a suicide bomber in the western Tel Aviv region near Jaffa. Astonishingly, Einav shrugged off the alert as if it were a mundane stock market update. He mentioned it only for my benefit, the way someone back home might say, "Oh, look, the NASDAQ closed up eight points."

How much blood had to be spilled before anyone became so inured to impending terrorist strikes? I recalled how anxiously everyone in Washington waited for updates during what was now being called the "23 days in October," when sniper John Muhammad and his teenage sidekick, John Lee Malvo, terrorized the capital region. I remember how our local playground was ordered closed after a message from the snipers warned that children would not be spared. School outings were canceled, and high school football games rescheduled and relocated. People had stopped shopping in suburbs, where most of the killings had taken place. Stores lost millions. Highways were closed. Fear reigned. Here it was business as usual—weather permitting.

"We think of it as a war," explained Einav. "In America, it's become a cliché. But here we really are in a war on terror. And that means we have to be prepared to accept casualties. Look," he added. "Life has to go on, otherwise they win."

The price, however, seemed high. The specter of terrorism permeated the culture in Israel in ways that would be hard for most Americans to grasp. Radio and television commercials regularly ran public service announcements advising viewers to be on the lookout for signs of suspicious activity. Volunteer police militias with arrest powers were formed to patrol neighborhoods. Counterterror tactics were even taught to schoolchildren. "I was out with my seven-year-old granddaughter the other day," recalled General Feldschuh. "And she sees a bag on the street and starts shouting 'Granddaddy, Granddaddy, look. Quickly, call a policeman. It could be left by terrorists.'"

Kids not only learned how to spot suspicious packages, but also how to prepare and don gas masks. Every elementary school in the country practiced changing gas mask filters and ran evacuation drills. At home, Israelis were supposed to seal off a safe room with tape and cellophane, and every household was responsible for laying in emergency supplies. One of the questions I often heard on the eve of the

Iraqi conflict was whether residents had "refreshed" their gas masks—
that is, replaced their gas mask filters.

Not surprisingly, growing up with such a siege mentality did not
make Israelis the most trusting of people. With friends they were warm
and embracing. But with outsiders they could be positively paranoid. I
found that out at my hotel bar my first night in town. I had struck up a
conversation with a young salesman from Eilat and asked if he knew
anyone in the volunteer police force there. The smile faded from his
face. Why did I want to know? Just curious, I said. What was I doing in
Israel? he suddenly demanded. I was a journalist. Did I have identification? I handed him a business card. He shot me a look that could chill
vodka. "Anyone," he said, "can print one of those up."

Terrorism was not only embedded in the psyche of Israelis; it
greeted you at every door. Entry to my beachfront hotel involved security checks. Sophisticated radar masts on its roof were capable of detecting any small craft that approached the beach. These advanced
radar stations (radar typically used in the United States can only spot
larger vessels) had been designed specifically after terrorists had come
ashore in rubber boats and attacked hotels with grenade launchers and
AK-47s.

A visit to virtually any mall or restaurant in Tel Aviv, in fact,
started with a search outside the main entrance, where uniformed
guards behind steel barriers patted down would-be customers, rum-
maged through handbags, and ran metal detectors over every entrant.
It took me seven minutes to clear security at the swanky Dizengoff
Center downtown, and that was before the food court and Cineplex
had opened for business. There was even a five-shekel—roughly one-
dollar—security surcharge per person on itemized restaurant and hotel
bills.

Remarkably, few people complained. Israelis had learned to shrug
off the added expense and inconvenience as a fact of life, a by-product
of living in the epicenter of global terrorism. Some, in fact, found it reassuring. "I was shocked when I first came to the States and could go
into any shopping plaza without going through security," said Aviv

Tene, a thirty-three-year-old Haifa attorney whom Einav had hired to open GS-3's Washington office. "It seemed so strange, and risky."

I understood what he meant. During the 1990s I had lived in Moscow, where the mob ruled, car bombs and contract killings numbered in the thousands, and everyone with money had their own bodyguards. At first, it was a shock to see men with machine guns posted outside a restaurant. But I got used to it pretty quickly, to the point that it did indeed seem risky and strange when venturing into an eatery without security.

In Israel's environment of total terrorist preparedness, security was simply factored into one's daily equation, just as the threat of organized crime was for the new rich in Russia. You simply adapted. "For instance, say you're planning a wedding," Tene elaborated. "You go through the to-do checklist. Did I hire the DJ, the caterer, the florist, two guards for the reception?"

Israel, Russia, Colombia, or the Philippines—another hotbed of terrorism—were one thing. The United States was quite another. It was hard to imagine Americans taking to this vigilant lifestyle. I couldn't quite picture customers stamping their feet to ward away the cold in Maine or Minnesota as they waited amid the dirty slush and snowdrifts outside a mall security checkpoint, I told Tene. I didn't think they would stand for being searched before going to the movies, or having the valet-parking attendant make them pop open the trunk of their cars to check for explosives.

"Really?" said Tene, arching an eyebrow. "What if al Qaeda hit a dozen shopping centers in different U.S. cities? I bet you Americans would demand security then."

Later I put the question to Ralph Morten. He was a detective with the LAPD bomb squad who had been to Tel Aviv and Jerusalem twice to prepare for just such a contingency, and had taught Israeli tactics to more than five thousand law enforcement officers across the United States. "If we are ever hit by a wave of suicide bombers," he predicted, "things will change as quickly and dramatically for the retail sector as they did for commercial aviation after 9/11."

That seemed to be the general consensus among those who followed homeland security in Washington. "From what we have seen over the past year, it's now al Qaeda policy to go after soft economic targets that are less defended than symbols of U.S. power," said CNN terrorist expert Peter Bergen in 2002. Bergen is one of only a handful of westerners to have actually met Osama bin Laden. "For the life of me, I can't understand why bin Laden hasn't sent a half dozen suicide bombers to U.S. shopping centers, especially during the Christmas shopping season. The result would absolutely cripple the retail sector."

Ironically, it would not be such a big leap to Israeli-style security. American shopping centers, department stores, and many fast-food outlets already have guards. Their job is to make sure you don't walk out with anything not paid for, rather than carry in anything you aren't supposed to. All it would take would be to turn security priorities inside out. "Your approach to security in the United States has been dictated mostly by crime and the Cold War," explained one of Einav's colleagues, Hezy Ribak. "Stopping crooks from breaking in, or vandalizing the premises, or spies from stealing industrial secrets. But suicide bombers have entirely different agendas, and you are going to have to change your whole philosophy to fight terrorism."

Ribak, like Einav, had been in the secret services and now ran a consulting company that provided protection services for a host of international clients, ranging from Chevron's Nigerian affiliate, to maximum security prisons in Virginia, to a country club in Singapore. He just returned from conducting a security survey of nuclear power stations for a major American energy conglomerate, and his findings apparently had so unnerved Washington that officials had asked him to delete all e-mails and shred all hard copies of his report.

Security at malls wasn't the big issue for him. Industry was. "I'm always amazed at how lightly defended your industry is compared to most other countries," he said. "In Israel we treat security at our industrial facilities the way we do borders. The stakes," he adds, "are just as high, higher if you consider the damage terrorists can do if they infiltrate a nuclear power plant or blow up a gas reservoir."

Israel took industrial security so seriously that during the 1991 Gulf War, it began deploying Patriot missile batteries near sensitive industrial facilities that could be targeted by Saddam's Scuds. "I live close to a power station," Ribak recalled. "And I remember watching three Patriots blast off after a Scud and fly right over the roof of my building. They all missed their target, but fortunately so did the Scud, which splashed into the sea next to the electricity plant."

I wanted a sense of how the Israelis went about protecting their infrastructure and asked Tene to drive me around Tel Aviv. It was Friday, so all the stores and offices were closed. (Sunday is a workday—another thing that takes some getting used to.) We drove out to the north end of town, along the fancy new condominiums that lined the road to Haifa, when a cluster of reservoirs caught my eye. The sign on the highway indicated that this was the P-Glilot turnoff. From a distance, the P-Glilot gas reservoirs didn't seem all that different from similar installations in New Jersey, Ohio, or Texas. The massive storage tanks were even painted with quaint butterflies and birds. But just as we turned off the highway, watchtowers appeared. As we drove closer the complex took on the feel of a military garrison, with high walls and electric fences bristling with sensors and cameras, and notices posted in Hebrew, English, and Arabic warning: "No Photography." I asked Tene to pull over and park by the perimeter fence. We had not idled for more than fifteen seconds when a metallic voice sounded from an unseen loudspeaker. "Peugeot 206," it barked. "Move on."

In the United States, even nuclear silos were not this well guarded. Security precautions back home typically concentrated around the core of the targets—whether they were reactors, pumping stations, or chemical plants. "Security at the main buildings might stop environmental protesters or the lone crazy, but it doesn't help in the case of a truck loaded with explosives because the terrorists have already reached their objective," said Ribak. "Why give yourself so little room? There should be as big a buffer as possible between the first line of defense—the perimeter of the property—and the target, to give yourself early warning." Perimeters, added Ribak, needed to be equipped with vibration sensors; thermal and infrared cameras; buried magnetic detection devices that can distinguish between humans, animals, and vehicles; and several rows of old-fashioned razor coil to delay intruders, giving guards time to respond to alarms.

Of course, all this security costs a small fortune. One reason Israel could afford such precautions was that the country had less than half a dozen such gas reservoirs to protect, as opposed to the two thousand petroleum depots alone in the United States. This was also a good example of why Israel had its limitations as a role model for the States. It's a matter of scale. New York's subway system carries almost as many daily riders as Israel's entire population. El Al has a fleet of twenty-seven planes, against the nearly seven thousand commercial craft that fly America's considerably busier skies. Borders in Israel are measured in hundreds of miles, not tens of thousands. Everything in Israel is miniaturized when stacked up against the United States, making even the costs of trying to replicate the Israeli model stateside incalculable.

Later that evening, over a vodka dinner at a Tex-Mex restaurant, it dawned on me that I had completely forgotten about the terror alert the day before. There had been no news of a bombing. Perhaps it had been a false alarm of the sort the FBI issued in Washington in the hope of not being caught accused of sleeping on the job again. "Terror alert?" Einav scratched his head. Yesterday morning, I reminded him. "Oh, yeah," he finally said. "They caught the guy."

Strangely, that hadn't made the news. Back home, the Justice Department trumpeted its every arrest, although precious few ever resulted in indictments. Here there was only modest silence. Apparently such captures were almost daily occurrences. "We catch 90 percent of suicide bombers before they reach their target," Einav said. This translated into thousands of arrests. How did they do it? "Intelligence," said my host. A less delicate way of putting it, though, was interrogation. Every time a suspect was apprehended, interrogators went to work on him, or her, literally.

"I remember one guy," one of Einav's colleagues recalled, "who said he would never talk. No matter what we did. Well, within half an hour he was singing like a bird." How did you persuade him? I inquired. The colleague smiled malevolently. "Let's just say we scared him a little."

Fear, I was told repeatedly, not pain, was the most potent weapon in the interrogator's arsenal. But for fear to be effective, the threat of pain had to be real, and this was one of the more controversial aspects of Israel's war on terror. The Shin Bet was given wide leeway to conduct its interrogations and was legally permitted to employ methods that won't fly in U.S. courts. One of these powers was what investigators here called the 1987 "ticking time bomb law," which allowed them to use "moderate physical pressure" in order to save lives in scenarios where time was of the essence and suspects might have vital information on impending attacks. "Sometimes you just don't have the luxury to read people their rights, because while you are waiting around for their attorney to show up, innocent people are about to die," explained Nery Yarkoni, a former Israeli district attorney.

An even more sensitive subject was the precise nature of the moderate physical pressure that could be exerted by Shin Bet interrogators. On this prickly topic, I heard different and often contradictory stories from the Israelis as to what precisely "moderate" meant. It was also a serious legal issue. Following the brief détente period after the Oslo Peace Accords, the Israeli Supreme Court had struck down the ticking time bomb law in 1999. But the suicide bombing campaign that began the following year had put renewed onus on interrogators to pry information from suspects. There was talk of reversing the ban on coercion and persistent rumors that many interrogators ignored the court's ruling anyway.

What are some of these methods? Sleep and sensory deprivation are widely acknowledged, even by the CIA, which also uses drugs, hunger, cold, and cramped confinement to disorient suspects. Langley often remands its most pressing al Qaeda cases, however, to Egypt, Syria, or Pakistan, where suspects have allegedly been strung up, been beaten on the soles of their feet, and have received electric shock through their scrotum or anus. U.S. diplomats even have a sanitized term for the prisoner handovers: rendering. In Uzbekistan, another brutal regime and a key U.S. ally during the October 2001 invasion of neighboring Afghanistan, I met several torture victims, and their stories are truly harrowing.

The French admit to playing rough; a retired general bragged on 60 *Minutes* that Parisian interrogators in the 1960s and '70s induced the drowning sensation by throwing towels over the faces of Algerian terrorists and pouring water on them. Britain's MI5 is said to use special chambers where the oxygen flow is gradually shut off, but since MI5 has a policy of never speaking to the press, I have no way of confirming this.

Whether it is ever justifiable, torture occasionally can be effective. Ramzi Youssef, for instance, the mastermind of the 1993 WTC attempt and 9/11's blueprint, Bojinka, was apprehended thanks to Filipino "tactical interrogation" of accomplice Murad. In a Manhattan court Murad later accused the Filipinos of beating him to within an inch of his life. But apparently even that had not made him spill all the beans. He had finally broken only when interrogators in Manila threatened to hand him over to the Mossad. What additional inducements the Israelis could offer after Filipino interrogators had worked him over for sixty-seven days I can only shudder to think.

Many of the big breaks in the worldwide hunt for al Qaeda leaders, including the capture of 9/11 organizer Khalid Sheik Mohammed, had come from interrogations by America's less squeamish allies. Mohammed himself had become very cooperative after being informed that the Pakistanis held his two sons. And there are many nonviolent ways to break a man, as I would discover when I later met a terror suspect in Arkansas who had spent months in U.S. captivity.

All of this raised a whole host of uncomfortable questions. Like so many of the thorny trade-offs in the war on terror, I tended to flip-flop back and forth on the issue of whether torture was ever justifiable. It was undeniably a slippery slope. Alan Dershowitz, the respected Harvard law professor, has proposed that U.S. courts issue special "torture warrants" in ticking time bomb cases. If my daughter's life was at stake, I wouldn't hesitate for a moment to issue such a warrant. But what if it was my neighbor's child? Or someone's in Seattle? Would I then be so quick to advocate Israeli tactics? Many in the U.S. law enforcement community have warned against it. "Look, they have no choice but to use aggressive methods," said Detective Morten, the LAPD explosives expert, who was dead against the notion. "They're in survival mode over there. At this stage in our history," he added, "we are nowhere near that point."

He was right, although we were undeniably inching closer to the Israeli position—playing rougher and looser with the Geneva Convention, as would become clear with the April 2004 publication of photos depicting the abuse of Iraqi prisoners by GIs.

Of course, there has always been a double standard for what the United States condones abroad and what is acceptable at home. Only now the home front has become the central battlefield in the war on terror. Virtually everyone I spoke with predicted that suicide bombers will eventually reach our shores. When that happens, they said, proposals like Dershowitz's torture warrants might get more serious consideration. Einav, for his part, didn't think there was much to debate. "If you could have put the screws to Mohammed Atta on September 10, 2001, and prevented 9/11," he asked. "would you really lose any sleep over his constitutional rights?"

On my last night in Israel, I got a small taste of what it might be like to be on the receiving end of an Israeli interrogation. True to his word,

Einav did not escort me through airport security at Ben-Gurion International so that I would get a firsthand sense of how the Israeli system worked.

Einav had already warned me that with my travel history, I would almost certainly fall under some scrutiny. For one thing, I held a Canadian passport, a favorite of forgers—including, ironically, the Mossad, whose agents had once embarrassingly been caught in Jordan with false Canadian papers during a botched assassination attempt. For another, my passport contained visas indicating that I had lived in the former Soviet Union, a traditional recruiting and training ground for PLO operatives, and I had all sorts of stamps showing recent travels to countries ending in -stan. "You can be sure they'll want to take a closer look at you," Einav had predicted.

I expected some attention from screeners, but I wasn't prepared for the grilling I eventually got. The first check was perfunctory, about a mile from the terminal itself, where guards stopped all traffic. This was the buffer that Ribak had spoken of, meant to alert officials at the terminal itself in the event a truck filled with explosives was on the way. At the main terminal entrance, uniformed and plainclothes officers stopped passengers getting out of cars and cabs. One such officer—jeans and a corduroy jacket—approached me. "Where are you flying?" he asked. "Can I see your documents?" He flipped through my passport, all the while shooting me appraising glances. "How long were you in Israel?" he demanded. "Okay," he said after I told him, and returned my ticket.

This, too, was standard operating procedure. Einav called it layering. "You confront people at every opportunity, and eventually they will slip up or crack under the pressure of repeated inquiry."

More questions followed minutes later, when I presented myself at the check-in line. A young screener addressed me in Hebrew. My blank expression must have been sign enough that I didn't speak the language, for she directed me to another line. This obviously was the higher security section for foreigners. After some minutes of waiting another screener asked for my documents, this time in English.

"How was your trip?" she asked politely. Einav had told me that screeners often tried to throw terrorists off track with such seemingly innocuous queries. "The bad guys will have rehearsed their bios or prepared answers to standard security questions," he said. "But you can sometimes trip them up with a very simple question they didn't expect."

The screener sent me to yet another line, which hardly moved at all. I had been funneled into the maximum security section, the 20 percent of travelers that under the Pareto principle concealed 80 percent of the bad guys.

I felt myself starting to sweat, even though I knew I had nothing to hide. A young woman started the examination. What was the purpose of my trip to Israel? Counterterrorism was probably the wrong answer. "Follow me, please," she said. My bags were placed on a stainless steel side table, and the questions continued while their contents were examined. *Who did you meet? Where did you meet? What was the address? Do you have the business cards of the people you met? May I see them? What did you discuss? Can we see your notes? Do you have any maps with you? Did you take any photographs while you were in Israel? Are you sure? Did you rent a car? Where did you drive to?*

P-Glilot was probably also the wrong answer. "Why P-Glilot?" she wanted to know, and not at all in a friendly, conversational way. "Did you know there was an attempt on it a few months ago?" Actually I hadn't, but I was beginning to wish that Einav had taken me through security. Twenty minutes had passed, and the woman seemed to grow more suspicious with every passing moment.

She started the same line of questioning again. "You've already asked me that," I protested. "Are you always this nervous?" she shot back. A few minutes later: "Okay, wait here."

She scooped up my documents and walked over to a thin, hawk-ish man in plain clothes. As they conferred, he kept flipping through my passport and looking my way. The woman returned. *Do you have a copy of your hotel bill? Why do you have a visa to Pakistan? Why do you live in Washington? Can we see your D.C. driver's license? Where did you live before Washington? Why did you live in Moscow?*

"Follow that gentleman," she said at last. Taken to a separate room, I was asked to remove my shirt, and my clothes and belongings were swabbed for explosives residue. By the time I was finally cleared, forty anxious minutes had passed and I was in real danger of missing my flight. A young security officer handed me a boarding pass. "Sorry for the delay," he apologized. "Don't take it personally."

A month or so after my return from Tel Aviv, the new Department of Homeland Security (still largely a cyberentity with only a permanent URL address and no full-time staff or budget yet) issued a code orange alert. In the five-tier terror warning system, this was the second highest rung, although the first two levels—green and blue—were pretty much wishful thinking, since it was unlikely that the United States would in the foreseeable future ever consider itself completely or even reasonably safe from terrorist attack. The reason for the heightened alert was the gathering storm in the Gulf. The second major offensive in the war on terror was now imminent. Although the Bush administration had failed to make its case with the international community that invading Iraq was necessary to prevent the spread of Saddam's weapons of mass destruction—or to even prove to the UN's satisfaction that he actually possessed any—President Bush had steadfastly vowed to go it alone.

In case Saddam harbored any ideas of retaliating on U.S. soil, preparations were in full swing to shore up our defenses at home with Operation Liberty Shield, which greatly reassured the populace since it contained a synonym for freedom. The National Guard took to the streets. Blackhawk UH-60A helicopters and F-15 Strike fighters buzzed around the Statue of Liberty, even though it was a gift from the vile French. Patriot missile batteries were deployed on Capitol Hill. Police went on twelve-hour shifts and drove with their siren lights permanently flashing, stopping random trucks to check for explosives.

Bomb-sniffing dogs prowled subway stations, while Israeli-style notices were posted in buses warning passengers to be on the lookout for
suicide bombers with bulky clothing or bags that emitted strange
smells. And children practiced evacuation drills at high schools in
suburban Virginia.

At Superbowl XXXVII, which was held that January in San Diego,
military aircraft also flew overhead, enforcing a seven-mile no-fly zone
around Qualcomm Stadium. The 67,000 fans in attendance had to
park at least five miles from the venue and board shuttle buses to the
stadium gates, lest anyone ruin the festivities with a truck bomb. No
one could bring bags or cushions to games, or anything else that could
conceal a weapon. And to ensure that no explosives or nasty chemicals were snuck past security, crowds were funneled through airport-
style metal detectors and monitored by a network of fifty cameras
installed throughout the stadium.

In New York City, National Guardsmen with M16 rifles slung over
their shoulders positioned themselves in hubs like Penn Station,
where a large, Orwellian banner ominously reminded commuters that
"Freedom Has a Price." (For football fans at the Superbowl, it was $9
million, an additional $134 per ticket.) Outside Manhattan hotels,
the trunks of cars were being searched, while music lovers attending
the opera were being scanned with metal detectors. Police officers
armed with 250 portable radiation detectors fanned out in the streets
and subways; checkpoints on Broadway and in the Holland Tunnel
also screened trucks.

In San Francisco, military Humvees were stationed at either end of
the Golden Gate Bridge, while at water level the Coast Guard in-
spected the trusses and columns for signs of C4 explosive. Throughout
the country, police departments racked up $2 billion in overtime.
Frightened citizens from Des Moines to Miami, responding to an
overly zealous warning by newly appointed security czar Tom Ridge,
cleaned out the country's supply of duct tape, which could be used to
seal Israeli-style safe rooms in the event of chemical attack, even as
Ridge was inadvertently scaring little old ladies in Peoria into stock-
piling bottled water and emergency supplies of nonperishable foods.

Whether all this was simply a temporary overreaction of the sort that periodically grips the stock market following some scandal or economic crisis, one thing was clear: Waving the banner of freedom, we had just taken a giant step closer to the Israeli end of the security spectrum.

3

THE SURVEILLANCE STATE

WHILE THE UNITED STATES IN EARLY 2003 WAS STILL A long, long way from becoming a maximum security state, the gap between America and Israel was undoubtedly narrowing. The key question now was, how far would it shrink in the years to come? How far would we—could we, or even should we—go with security measures? On that point, I recalled something that Einav had told me during one of our more animated discussions in Tel Aviv. "If you put your mind to it," he had said, "the United States can be a world leader in security within five years."

Already, as Einav liked to point out, Americans went to far greater lengths to secure their homes than did Israelis. It had become an accepted part of American culture over the past twenty years to live in gated communities, hire private guards to patrol our neighborhoods, wire our homes with sophisticated alarm systems, and arm ourselves with deadly weapons. What if this kind of intensity was turned outward into the public sphere over the next few decades? What if we started treating our public spaces the way we protected our own private property? All we needed was to become as frightened of terrorism as we had become of crime.

Einav wasn't the only one making this supposition. Another catastrophic attack on the scale of 9/11, and America would be a vastly different place, warned Ambassador L. Paul Bremer, when I spoke to him shortly before his appointment as Iraq's first civilian overseer. "The public outcry for added security measures would be unstoppable," he said.

What might it be like living in Einav's America five years from now, a place obsessed with security and bristling with futuristic technology? Perhaps something like this:

2008: The camera on the north entrance to the Reuther Liberal Arts Building has registered a hit. In the bowels of the Learning Technology Center, a computer beeps.

The campus security guard monitoring the video screens peers over his copy of the *Detroit Free Press* with mild irritation. Probably another sniffer acting up, he thinks. The Henry Ford Community College just put in the pathogen sensors, which monitor the air for the presence of chemical agents phosgene, tabun, sarin, and mustard gas. First installed in Washington subway stations after the 1995 Tokyo sarin gas attack and in New York following 9/11, by 2008 safety codes require them in all large public buildings, much like smoke detectors. But the contractors that installed the air and water quality warning systems did a lousy job, and they are prone to false alarms: A spike in chlorine levels in the city water mains or the wind abruptly shifting over the smokestacks of the nearby pickup-truck assembly plant sometimes sets them off.

The guard's expression of bored annoyance suddenly changes to intense interest when he sees the cause of the alert. It is the college's face recognition system, a software program that scans facial features, breaks them down into three-dimensional plots, and compares them to a vast data bank of student IDs. The program is an advanced version of technology originally developed at MIT. Used in the 1990s mainly by casinos to ferret out known card sharks, the system gained wider favor after 9/11, when airports like Boston's Logan and counties like Pinellas in Florida began experimenting with it. The first school in the United States to install it was Royal Palm Middle School of Phoenix, Arizona, in December 2003, and it was programmed with a national database of sex offenders, pedophiles, missing children, and alleged abductors. In January 2004 the INS started using a low-tech form of facial recognition technology at border

crossings as part of the new Visitor and Immigrant Status and Indication Technology system, which electronically verifies the biometric
identity of foreign nationals from all but twenty-seven countries as
they enter and leave the United States.

Face recognition, by 2008, has multiple applications, not all re-
lated to homeland security. "It can be used at ATMs to cut down on
fraud, [as well as at] car-rental agencies and DMV offices," prophesies
Cameron Queeno, a vice president of marketing for Viisage Technologies Inc., maker of the Face-Finder recognition system. Campus
security uses it primarily to cut down on vandalism and petty theft.
But it is also linked to a vast federal database of criminal mug shots,
INS and DMV files, government-issue IDs, and watch lists. Initially,
college administrators flatly rejected the Dearborn Police Department's request to link with their systems, but after terrorist strikes in
Chicago and Minneapolis, they decided to grant permission.

The guard punches in a few strokes on the keyboard, and the
photo of the subject that tripped the facial recognition program pops
up on his screen. It is a picture of a scruffy young man in his early
twenties, of Middle Eastern origin. None of that is unusual. Students
are notorious slobs and a third of Dearborn's population, according to
2002 census figures, is of Middle Eastern ancestry. Dearborn, in fact,
boasts the largest Arabic concentration in the western hemisphere.
What is unusual is the tag line on the bottom of the computer screen.
"Notify JOCC," it says in bold, flashing print.

JOCC stands for Joint Operations Command Center, and every
major metropolitan area in the United States has one by 2008. At
the Command Centers, police technicians perform much the same
tasks as campus security, only on a citywide scale, with over a thousand cameras. "We got a hit," says one of the technicians. "We'll take
it from here," he e-mails the campus security guard, plugging in to
the school's CCTV system.

JOCC technicians watch as the subject stubs out a cigarette outside the Reuther Building. He throws his empty pack into the trash
can. It is one of the new bombproof bins that were first developed in

London during the IRA terror spree. Manufactured by Mistral Security, these garbage cans have a special lining made of a composite with pockets of water and air that absorb the force of any blast. Washington's transit authority was the first to deploy them in the United States, allocating $1 million dollars in its 2003 budget to purchase the high-tech trash receptacles, according to *Popular Science* magazine. Now they are commonly used in public spaces throughout the country.

The surveillance subject is a graduate of the community college, now majoring in chemistry at Michigan State. Or so says the brief bio on the watch list. Such watch lists have proliferated since 9/11, with the State Department, customs and Immigration, the FBI, CIA, the TSA, state and local authorities, and the Department of Homeland Security each compiling its own. The widest-ranging list, however, might be provided by the Total Information Awareness program. A controversial arm of the Pentagon's Defense Advanced Research Projects Agency, the TIA was launched in 2002, and subsequently scrapped by Congress in 2003. Lawmakers, however, left the door open to revive the project. In 2008, it is back in business.

The logo of the TIA is the all-seeing eye and the Latin motto *scientia est potential,* "information is power." It is perhaps the most powerful twenty-first-century cyberweapon in the war on terror. Since its inception following 9/11, it has grown from a modest Pentagon pet project of Rear Admiral John Poindexter of Iran-contra fame into a sprawling data-mining operation whose electronic tentacles reach into every crevasse of American daily life. It is capable of sifting through billions of gigabytes of electronic information in real time, tracking the everyday personal and commercial transactions of virtually every man, woman, and child in America.

Few outsiders know how the TIA works, partly because of its complexity and partly because of the military secrecy that shrouds it. What little has been disclosed is that the TIA employs a network of powerful computer-generated algorithms to uncover hidden patterns in mundane life that could give early warnings of possible terrorist activity. It hunts through private and public sector databases, online ticket reservations, telephone and credit card bills, medical records, or just about anywhere we leave an electronic trail, including website visits.

It is unclear how the chemistry student landed in the TIA's sights. Perhaps his credit cards were maxed out, so he had to use cash to buy an airline ticket, and had left the return date open, because he wasn't sure when he wanted to return. Maybe he had gone to the emergency room at Kindred Hospital in nearby Lincoln Park with skin irritation or burns on his hands, or he took out a book on water parameters from the Dearborn public library, or bought it on Amazon.com. Under the 2001 USA Patriot Act, the Justice Department has the right to subpoena library records without warrants and demand that the FBI be informed if certain books are checked out. The same provision of the Patriot Act obligates Internet service providers to turn over individuals' web browsing records, including terms entered into search engines, pages surfed, session durations and times, and all web purchases or financial transactions conducted.

None of this means that the student intends to poison Detroit's water supply. It could all be the product of an innocent hobby, starting a saltwater coral reef tank for instance, where he'd have to fuss over strontium, nitrate, and phosphate levels and regulate ammonia, boron, and iodine doses.

Or maybe he was indiscreet in an e-mail, making a crude joke about a recent airline crash or the rumors of a new terrorist threat. Something as innocuous as that could have been loaded with enough key words to trip the TIA's security wires or the FBI's Internet filter screening system called Carnivore.

Software programs that scan for suspect words are nothing new. Corporations have long used software like IBM Auditor 2.0 to automatically block employee e-mails containing, for instance, multiple references to sex or to notify management if an employee is communicating with a competitor, sending proprietary information, or simply having an online romance on company time. The National Security Agency's Echelon global spy satellite constellation combined with its Cray X-MP supercomputers take the search capability to the next level, listening in on up to two million calls and e-mail messages per hour from around the world (including those of Osama bin Laden, whose satellite phone number until September 11, 2001, was 00-873-68-250-5331).

Or the student may have said something indiscreet during an overseas call. Like a quarter of Dearborn's residents, he was born abroad, say in Iraq. Perhaps an aunt in Baghdad complained about the continued American occupation, and Echelon picked it up. After 9/11 the NSA embarked on an ambitious program with researchers from the University of Maryland to teach its computer the nuances of Arabic, Farsi, and Urdu. The agency did this by offering to pick up the tab for calls from immigrants in the United States to their families in the Middle East and South Asia on the condition that it could record them to teach the computer to recognize voices, text, and dialects, thus diminishing the need for human translators.

Whatever has drawn the TIA's attention to this man, once he is on its computer radar screen, it will be hard for him to get off—as anyone who has ever found themselves on a mailing or telemarketer's list can attest. Refinance a mortgage, and suddenly every financial institution in America wants to send you a preapproved platinum card. Order a couch for your den, and you can expect Crate and Barrel and Pottery Barn catalogs to come streaming through your mail slot for months to come. Once a computer detects a pattern, hidden or overt, your identity in the digital world is fixed.

Technicians manning the Command Center probably don't know why their subject is on a surveillance list, or whether he should even be on it in the first place. That is classified, as are most aspects of the TIA's counterterrorist calculations. Nonetheless, they begin to monitor his movements.

Cameras inside the Reuther Liberal Arts Building pick him up as he enters a third-floor office. A check of the college's registry reveals that it is the office of a history professor by the name of John Smith. The technicians punch Smith's name into the computer and get another pop. Smith also is on a watch list, this one issued by the Secret Service. Again, the techies have no idea why Smith has been flagged. Maybe it dates all the way back to spring 2003, when he organized an antiwar faculty protest of President Bush's speech at the Dearborn Performing Arts Center. As part of Attorney General Ashcroft's counterterror initiatives, restrictions placed on the FBI's investigations of political gatherings and activities following abuses of the J. Edgar Hoover and Vietnam eras were loosened. According to a report by Eric Lichtblau of the *New York Times*, the Bureau was once again given the green light to scrutinize anti-Iraq war rallies and "collect . . . extensive information" on demonstrators and organizers. But perhaps the rallies had not gotten Smith watch-listed. Maybe it was his indignant commentaries about civil liberties violations on WHFR-FM, the college radio station. Whichever the case, the JOCC spotter calls his supervisor. Two watch-list subjects are meeting. It could be a coincidence—a former student visiting his old teacher to get a letter of reference for his graduate school scholarship application. Then again it could be something much more nefarious. What the JOCC watch commander sees could be the beginning of a terrorist conspiracy—one slightly suspicious character has just crossed paths with another slightly suspicious character, and that makes them seriously suspicious. Innocence or guilt no longer matter at this stage. By then subjects are presumed guilty and must be proved innocent.

That is exactly what happened to Maher Arar, a thirty-three-year-old telecommunications engineer from Ottawa, Canada. During a layover at JFK Airport, Arar was arrested by U.S. officials in 2002 for alleged al Qaeda ties. Questioned by the FBI for two weeks at a detention center in Brooklyn, he was put on a U.S. government plane in the dead of night and "rendered" to Syria. There Syrian military and intelligence interrogators threw him in a tiny, unlit underground cell where they beat his feet with rods, shoved his head under water, and tortured him for ten months before clearing and releasing him. How had the unfortunate Arar found himself in such a tragic mess? Canadian authorities had mistakenly put his name on a terror watch list submitted to Washington. How could that happen? A series of coincidences and guilt by association, according to the *Toronto Globe and Mail*. Arar first came to the attention of the Royal Canadian Mounted Police in January 2002, during a routine investigation into Arab immigrants in the Ottawa region. The Mounties called and asked Arar if they could interview him. He agreed on condition that he have a lawyer present. Apparently he had heard what was happening to Muslim immigrants south of the border and wanted to protect himself from unlawful detention. Unbeknownst to him, by "lawyering up" he had raised the RCMP's hackles. The Mounties started keeping tabs on him, ramping up surveillance when they noticed one day that he had a casual encounter with another member of the local Muslim community who was "a subject of interest," according to the *Globe*. Alarm bells rang at RCMP headquarters when Arar suddenly moved out of his apartment in the city's Bayshore neighborhood. The Mounties tailing him somehow missed the fact that he had rented a larger pad only a few blocks away. When, a short time later, Arar purchased a ticket to Tunisia for himself, his wife, Monia Mazigh, and their two small children, the RCMP didn't make the connection that Ms. Mazigh's parents lived in Tunis and the trip was simply a visit to the in-laws. The Mounties feared Arar was getting ready to bolt. His status on the watch list was upgraded, and the list was circulated to American authorities. And that was how the INS official at JFK flagged Arar during a stopover on his flight back to Canada from Tunisia. A chance encounter, a family vacation, and a move to a bigger apartment cost Arar a year of his life, and, as the *Globe* reproachfully noted, "a terrible physical and psychological ordeal because our national police force made a mistake."

Watch lists aren't perfect, but that's not the JOCC's concern. They have two watch-list subjects making contact, and that's evidence enough of potential mischief. It's time to call in the cavalry. Rather

than alerting the FBI, the case is forwarded to the new domestic
intelligence agency. "Call it the NCS," says General William Odom,
who in the real world was a former head of the National Security
Agency.

The National Counterintelligence Service does not exist as of this
writing, but its creation—with the brief of taking over counterterrorism duties from the FBI—is advocated by the likes of Ambassador
Paul Bremer, former CIA directors John Deutsch and James Woolsey,
and General Odom. The idea of breaking up the FBI and creating a
new domestic intelligence agency began gaining momentum in
Washington in late 2002, when President Bush first floated the con-
cept for a new Terrorist Threat Integration Center, a separate body
manned by FBI personnel under CIA command. Supporters of the
plan note that cultural and structural problems prevent the FBI from
being an effective force in the war on terror. "The Bureau is probably
the best law enforcement agency on the planet, but it is just that: a
policing body," argues Bremer. Counterterrorism requires a different
set of skills and priorities. "Spies or terrorists will always beat cops,"
adds Odom, "because they have very different motivations than
criminals, and standard law enforcement techniques like wiretaps or
informants don't usually work on them."

Whether modeled after Britain's MI5 (an organization without
arrest powers but so secretive that until recently the real names of its
heads were never disclosed) or Israel's much more proactive Shin
Bet, the NCS would likely require a budget similar to the FBI's $5 bil-
lion and nearly as many personnel as the Bureau's 11,400-strong special agent force. Most of the staff would be used for surveillance
duties. "The core, though, would be five hundred highly trained and
specialized counterintelligence officers," says Odom.

A good number of those agents would likely be posted to Detroit
because the city sits right on the porous Canadian border and has
such a significant Muslim population for terrorists to blend into. Al

Qaeda operatives are far more likely to attract unwanted attention in more homogeneous towns like Boise, Salt Lake City, or Memphis.

By the time an NCS surveillance unit is mobilized, the student and professor have gone their separate ways. What they discussed during the twenty minutes they spent together in Smith's cluttered office is not known. Smith, however, seems an odd candidate for any watch list. A registered Republican with acknowledged libertarian leanings, he is active in his community. He sits on the PTA board of Maples Elementary School over on Meade Street, where his daughter Emily is in fifth grade, and he is an active member of the Citizen Corps. Created in January 2002 by President Bush, the corps is a community counterterror program designed, according to its website, to provide "opportunities for citizens to become an integral part of protecting the homeland." By early 2004 forty communities, including Laredo, Texas; Chattanooga, Tennessee; Santa Fe, New Mexico; and Charlotte, North Carolina, have Citizen Corps preparedness programs with Neighborhood Terror Watch patrols and emergency food and water stockpiles. By 2008 Citizen Corps has spread to every state, including Michigan, where twice a month Smith takes his turn patrolling Salina Street.

All this is known to the NCS teams dispatched to follow Smith and his student contact. The agents momentarily lose their trail, but no one is worried. The JOCC's cameras will pick up their scent soon enough. Indeed, Smith's Ford (Dearborn, after all, is a company town) is quickly spotted getting on an access ramp to the I-75.

As a matter of routine procedure, the tags of all vehicles entering the ramp are filmed and read by a special software program that runs the plate numbers against DMV vehicle registration data. So even though every third car could be a blue Ford Escort like the one Smith drives, the computer will instantly know which car he is driving. The software was first developed in Israel in the 1990s to detect stolen vehicles and cars registered to suspected terrorist sympathizers. In 2003

it was introduced in the financial district of London to identify motorists who have not paid peak-hour traffic tariffs; by 2008, it has
been adopted in the United States.

The NCS teams would have many ways of following Smith from a
safe distance so as not to tip him off that he is under surveillance.
One tool at their disposal could be a nationwide vehicle tracking system, inspired by Singapore's Land Transport Authority, which in the
1990s turned to radio-frequency identification to regulate traffic and
parking. The system works on the same principle as the EZ-Pass toll-
road technology, in which scanners at toll booths read bar codes or
microchips installed on the windshields of passing vehicles to automatically debit tolls. In Singapore, where the number of registered
vehicles is closely controlled by the authorities and permits can cost
almost as much as a car, every automobile is fitted with a microchip
encoded with registration data. Scanners deduct user fares, which go
up at peak traffic hours in the city center. In 2003 police in Baltimore
used EZ-Pass records to retrace the steps of a missing prosecutor, who
was later found in a Pennsylvania creek, murdered.

In the future, electronic readers installed throughout major
American metropolitan centers could pinpoint the location of just
about any vehicle equipped with mandatory microchip windshield
stickers. Every vehicle might also come with a GPS-enabled Auto-
matic Vehicle Locator, allowing satellites to track it instantly. High-
end Jaguars, Mercedes, and BMWs already come with a standard
ATX telematics system that combines GPS transmitters and built-in
cellular phones to allow drivers to push one button to call for roadside assistance in case they get lost or have mechanical failures. General Motors installs another version of this safety system, known as
OnStar, as standard issue in many of its models. Using telematics,
OnStar and ATX can locate stolen vehicles, and even operate some
vehicle features remotely, such as the power locks or the telephone.
In a landmark 2003 case, the FBI used the system's remote capabilities to surreptitiously turn on the speaker phone and eavesdrop on

occupants of a car under surveillance. According to the *New York Times*, the Court of Appeals in San Francisco, which heard the case, left the door open for such safety system wiretaps.

By 2003, in fact, about a quarter of all vehicles at U.S. car rental agencies used some form of GPS technology, such as the Hertz Never Lost system. The technology allows drivers to find their way to exact locations, but also permits rental agencies to keep tabs on drivers. Acme Rent-A-Car, for instance, has a GPS-enabled software program called AirlQ to monitor remotely the location, speed, and direction of their vehicles. In 2000, according to *Popular Science* magazine, a James Turner of New Haven, Connecticut, successfully sued Acme Rent-A-Car for debiting his bank account $450 as a penalty for speeding, based on information the company obtained from its AirlQ system. The judge ruled that Acme had not informed Turner that his movements could be remotely monitored. In a similar 2003 case, a Canadian tourist was shocked to find his expected $259 car rental bill from Payless Car Rental in San Francisco swell to over $3,000 when the company presented him with a detailed route map based on its GPS locator system showing he had violated terms of his rental contract by driving the car out of state to Las Vegas and then to the Grand Canyon in Arizona.

Let's say Smith's Escort is an old model without an ATX system. Smith could still make life easy for the agents trying to tail him if he has a cell phone. By the late 1990s, the cell phone could be used to trace people. By 2006 a new regulation mandated by the Federal Communications Commission will go into effect requiring mobile phone providers to be able to pinpoint the exact location of all customers who call 911. Known as E911, the service is intended to help rescuers quickly find victims of an accident or crime, in the same way that calling 911 on a land line automatically flashes your address on the dispatcher's computer screen. If a commuter is using the Verizon network, the three closest microwave towers will triangulate the driver's position to within a dozen yards. If she's on Nextel or Sprint-

PCS, a GPS chip that the companies plan to embed in all new phones starting in late 2004 will be able to interact with satellites to compute her exact longitude and latitude. Say she borrowed her teenage son's cell phone. That phone may have a specific tracking chip. As of 2003, telecoms such as AT&T's FindAFriend and Nextel's uLocate offered services that allow worried parents to know where their offspring are. By 2005 an estimated 42 million Americans will be using some form of location-enabled technology, according to a 2002 telecom industry survey.

Smith turns off the I-75 exit to the Ambassador Bridge. This worries his watchers, since the other side of the bridge is Windsor, Ontario, no longer their jurisdiction. Smith's Ford gets stuck in traffic on the busy border crossing. A quarter of all merchandise traded between the United States and Canada crosses the 9,200-foot bridge: some twelve thousand tractor trailers daily laden with automotive parts, pulp and paper products, and all manner of goods. All the trucks are equipped with transponders read by scanners on the bridge to facilitate the speedy flow of goods. The prototype for the program, which uses radio-frequency identification technology to rapidly tell customs what truck is carrying what goods, was first tested in 2003 at border crossings in Detroit, Buffalo, El Paso, and Laredo. It is now standard at all ports of entry into the United States.

The Ambassador Bridge, in fact, was a testing ground for many homeland security innovations. The first radiation portal monitor used in the United States was deployed there in November 2002, at a cost of $222,660 (and 21 cents, but who's counting). Resembling the black monolith in 2001: A Space Odyssey, the sensor monitors all vehicles that pass beside it for the presence of hidden radioactive materials that could be used in a dirty bomb. In 2003 such portals were also installed at key access tunnels and bridges to New York City and in a cargo container port. By 2008 they are everywhere.

Sophisticated sensors also protect the underside of the bridge from a terrorist attack, which could disrupt commerce by cutting off Detroit's car plants from their Canadian spare parts suppliers.

Acoustic sensors and underwater sonar devices anchored to the base of the bridge's huge cement columns check for the presence of divers, to prevent anyone from placing explosives on the riverbed. Above the waterline, cameras belonging to the new USHomeGuard network pan over the trusses along the bridge's underside. USHome-Guard is the brainchild of Internet entrepreneur Jay Walker, the founder of Priceline.com. It uses over a million webcams to watch over 47,000 pieces of critical infrastructure across the United States: pipelines, chemical plants, bridges, dams, and the like. Tens of thousands of so-called spotters sit at their home computers like cyber–security guards watching for any suspicious signs of activity on the web feeds, for which they are paid $10 an hour and tested periodically with dummy photos to make sure they are not sloughing off on the job. Companies pay USHomeGuard $5,000 a month for the surveillance, which is still considerably cheaper than hiring security guards to physically patrol perimeter fences. As of 2004, USHomeGuard is still largely an idea waiting for the Department of Homeland Security to test a prototype, but by 2008 the network is to be fully operational.

Even with all the technology, old-fashioned bottlenecks still frequently choke the bridge, and Smith's Ford inches forward at a painfully slow pace. While he languishes in traffic, another NCS unit is hastily arranging to put his house under surveillance. The 2001 Patriot Act permits law enforcement agencies to secretly break into homes to search for incriminating evidence without tipping off suspects with search warrants. This is known as sneak and peek, a temporary provision of the Patriot Act expiring in 2005, which President Bush in his 2004 State of the Union address pleaded with Congress to extend through 2008.

A search of his home might provide clues as to what he is doing in Canada. He might simply be shopping for cheaper prescription drugs, as thousands of Americans do, or just taking advantage of the relative purchasing power of the U.S. dollar, worth $1.65 Canadian. Then again he might be meeting terrorists. Canada has much laxer immigration and asylum policies than the United States, a source of contention between the two countries, and officials in Washington constantly worry that al Qaeda uses border towns like Windsor to stage their U.S. operations.

Smith, it turns out, is a frequent visitor to Canada. The NCS knows this because each trip is encoded in his national ID, which is now required to cross the border. Before 9/11, one did not even need to produce ID on either side of the border. But following 9/11, computer database industry leaders like Oracle CEO Larry Ellison started advocating new national identity cards for all U.S. citizens. Such forms of identification have long been used in western Europe, the former Soviet bloc, and some Southeast Asian countries. "You can barely sneeze in Singapore without having to produce a national identity card," says Kenneth Katz, a fund manager from Los Angeles who has lived there since 2000.

The new IDs could be modeled after digital smart cards that Chinese authorities introduced in Hong Kong in 2003. These contain computer chips with stored biographical, financial, and medical histories and tamper-proof algorithms of the cardholder's thumbprint that can be verified instantly by handheld optical readers. Based on the $394 million Hong Kong has budgeted for smart cards for its 6.8 million residents, a similar program in the United States could run as high as $16 billion. But it would certainly help prevent members of sleeper cells from slipping through dragnets, as occurred in Baltimore on the eve of the first anniversary of 9/11.

"We got a tip on some suspicious individuals," recalls Major John Skinner, head of Baltimore's Criminal Intelligence division. "We found eight guys from Pakistan, Afghanistan, Somalia, and Egypt together in a flophouse without any furniture." The only furnishings were a couple of computers with downloaded materials from websites on small local airports, some fake IDs, and jihadist pamphlets belonging to the group's spiritual leader, an imam. Skinner could not hold the men on any charges, so they were turned over to the Immigration and Naturalization Service, which detained all but the imam, whose papers appeared in order. "Turns out he had assumed someone else's identity, and last I heard he fled across the border to Canada."

Identity theft almost doubled in the United States in 2002, according to a report by the Federal Trade Commission. With new biometric smart cards mandatory for all citizens by 2008, identity theft and fraud could be sharply cut, and police officers would have the right to stop anyone at any time for document spot checks, as in many other parts of the world.

By the time Smith returns from his day trip in Windsor, his home has been placed under twenty-four-hour aerial surveillance. The technology, discreet and effective, was first deployed in Washington, when the Pentagon used RC-7 reconnaissance planes during the sniper siege in fall 2002. The surveillance craft, which have proven their worth along the demilitarized zone in North Korea and against drug barons in Colombia, come loaded with long-range night-vision and heat-seeking infrared equipment that permits operators to snap photos of virtually anyone's backyard from as far as twenty miles away. Fully automated surveillance drones of the sort used by the Israelis to search for militants in the West Bank or by the U.S. military in Afghanistan and Iraq could also be called on to snoop from the American skies. Undersecretary of Homeland Security Asa Hutchinson told me in 2003 of his intention to test such drones along the Mexican border by 2005. Within five years drones could be commonplace along the northern frontier, as well. Compact miniature models weighing 160 pounds that can hover in place for four hours are being tested by a Virginia company called Aurora. Known as the Golden Eye, the prototype of the five-foot-tall drone is so silent that it cannot be heard beyond a 150-yard radius and is ideally suited for urban environments. A half-scale $50,000 version of the stealthy Golden Eye priced for crimped police department budgets is on the drawing board, according to the *Economist*. By 2008 Golden Eyes would give the authorities the ability to keep a discreet, watchful eye over neighborhoods across the country.

The surveillance of Smith's home would be completely lawful. The USA Patriot Act has given government agencies wide latitude to invoke the Foreign Intelligence Surveillance Act to get around judicial restraints on search, seizure, and surveillance of U.S. citizens.

FISA, originally intended to hunt down Soviet spies during the Cold War, permits the authorities to wiretap virtually at will and break into people's homes and plant bugs or copy documents. In 2002 surveillance requests by the federal government under FISA outnumbered all requests of previous years combined.

Unlike the FBI, the new NCS domestic intelligence agency might not have the patience or mandate to painstakingly gather evidence on Smith or his young chemist friend over many months. They might just opt to round everyone up. "The goal of counterterrorism is to disrupt cells, to prevent terrorist acts," as Einav reminded me. "The FBI is obsessed with gathering enough evidence for prosecution. That's their law enforcement mentality. But by then it's too late. The damage has already been done, blood has been shed."

By 2008—if Attorney General Ashcroft's proposed sequel to the Patriot Act, the Domestic Security Enhancement Act, or Patriot Act II, as it is more commonly known around Washington, has gone into effect—the NCS could detain anyone in the country in a preemptive strike. Under section 201 of the Patriot II bill, the government would not even be required to disclose the identity of anyone detained in a terror investigation. Section 501 of Patriot II goes even further: The Justice Department could revoke the citizenship of those suspected of "providing material support" to terrorists. They also could be held without access to counsel, just as anyone declared an "enemy combatant" under the 2001 Patriot Act can be. And the names of those arrested, whether American or foreign nationals, would be exempt from the Freedom of Information Act, according to the Center for Public Integrity, a Washington rights group, which obtained a copy of Ashcroft's proposed bill in early 2003. So even though Smith is an American citizen, he could be held by investigators without anyone being notified. In fact, if the authorities are convinced that he is at the heart of a nefarious terrorist plot, he could simply disappear without a trace.

———

The decisions to fully implement these measures won't, of course, come all at once. Much would depend on the severity of the threat we face, how we fare in the war on terror abroad, and how well al Qaeda manages to regroup and adapt to the heightened global security environment. It is also quite likely that we will change our minds in the coming years about what we will accept as a reasonable trade-off in the balancing act between public safety and private freedoms, although the farther the calendar moves from 9/11 without major terrorist incident, the less tolerant we may become of intrusive measures that impinge significantly on our privacy. The Pentagon's Total Information Awareness program was among the first victims of this swinging pendulum. Congress, voting on the 2004 military budget, found that the danger of having the government look over our credit card statements and phone bills outweighed its promised benefits, and ordered the TIA program shut down. Its author, Rear Admiral Poindexter, was asked to resign after word leaked out that he was planning a futures market that would allow investors to hedge against terrorist strikes.

Similarly, Attorney General Ashcroft had to postpone submitting his proposed sequel to the Patriot Act to Congress, when a copy of the secret draft was leaked to the press. In reality, Ashcroft's bark was often louder than his bite, though he was clearly trying to fashion himself a sharp set of legal teeth. When it came to public relations he was his own worst enemy, distrusting the media with almost Nixonian antipathy, insisting on secrecy when a little openness could have served him better, and mocking critics as "unpatriotic" and spreaders of "baseless hysteria" instead of directly addressing their concerns. Truth was, there had been only 113 cases of FISA surveillance warrants, not the tens of thousands the media sometimes made them out to be. The Enemy Combatant clause, which effectively stripped U.S. citizens and foreign nationals of all constitutional rights, had also been used extremely sparingly. In fact, by 2004, only two U.S. citizens had been classified enemy combatants: Yasser Essam Hamdi and José Padilla. Hamdi was a U.S. citizen caught fighting alongside the

Taliban. Padilla was apprehended in Chicago as a material witness to a dirty bomb plot.

While FBI agents were widely presumed to be poring over all our reading records at public libraries, the so-called anti-library law subpoenaing records had in fact rarely been used. "The Department of Justice has neither the staffing, the time, nor the inclination to monitor the reading habits of Americans," Ashcroft tried to explain in a September 2003 speech. The ten thousand members of the American Library Association were not mollified, however. The Patriot Act represented "a present danger to the constitutional rights and privacy rights of library users," they declared at their 2004 annual meeting. "A textbook case of liberal paranoia," commented columnist Joseph Button in the *New York Post*. If the liberals didn't have Ashcroft, they'd have to invent him, he wrote.

Ashcroft, of course, didn't help his public relations case. His daily prayer meetings at the Justice Department were widely reported by the media, as were allegations (exaggerations, Ashcroft said) that his aides scurried about draping veils on nude statues that offended his piety. There was the infamous incident reported by *Vanity Fair* where his advance teams cleared an ambassador's residence he visited of calico cats, which Ashcroft was said to consider instruments of the devil. (A charge he denied, as well.) Not surprisingly, his devotion did not sit well with many Americans or career people at Justice, where turnover has been high. One state attorney I spoke to called him "Mullah Ashcroft."

Public anxiety was also hampering the TSA's controversial CAPPS II passenger profiling plan. The system, the acronym of which stands for second-generation computer-assisted passenger prescreening, was among the largest surveillance efforts ever undertaken by the government on U.S. citizens, according to the *Washington Post*. It was designed to screen the 612 million people who flew annually by examining commercially available data for evidence that people "are rooted in the community"—in other words, that they go to the dentist, shop at the supermarket, have good credit, or belong to the PTA or the Lions Club. What made CAPPS II odious to civil liberties groups, which claimed it was just a milder version of the TIA, was that it broke down the Chinese wall that had previously existed in exchanging information between the public and private sectors. The concern was that once the government knew our taste in clothing or wine, whether we were behind on our car payments or mortgage, if we recently had orthopedic surgery or a venereal disease treated, all this sensitive data could be abused or fall into the wrong hands. Still, CAPPS II was going ahead, as were other data-driven surveillance schemes, like MATRIX.

Short for Multistate Anti-Terrorism Information Exchange, MATRIX was a federally backed Florida initiative that combined police records and commercially available data on ordinary citizens so that law enforcement officials could, for instance, find every owner of a hang glider, saltwater aquarium, or other recently purchased consumer goods within a ten-mile radius of Tampa or Tallahassee with the click of a mouse. By mid-2003 over 150 police departments in the Sunshine State had signed up for the service, which combines government records with twelve billion pieces of commercial information on ordinary citizens. Pennsylvania, New York, and Michigan have announced their intentions to share records with MATRIX.

In many other respects, the future was now. An aerial photo of my backyard, for instance, was on file at the Joint Operations Command Center in Washington, which, unlike the NCS, already existed prior to 9/11. (It looked like something straight out of some sci-fi thriller, starting with the biometric palm print scanners that control access to its reinforced steel doors.)

Of course, I had not been singled out for any special surveillance. My neighbors' houses were all pictured, too, as were still shots and even three-dimensional images of just about every building, landmark, and lot in central D.C. The technology wasn't even revolutionary. Europe had a long tradition of monitoring public spaces with closed-circuit TV. At last count, over three million CCTVs were deployed in England alone, where police could track the progress of, say, a shoplifter from store to sidewalk to street. In central London alone there were 150,000 cameras, and according to the *Guardian*, a British newspaper, the average Londoner appeared on camera at least three hundred times a day.

Face recognition programs had a distinguished tradition in Europe and had gone a long way toward cutting down on violence at soccer games by comparing shots of fans to archives of known hooligans. A Siemens computer program similar to the one being developed by the Department of Homeland Security analyzed live CCTV images for "video motion anomalies"—in other words, anything from British drivers making U-turns on busy streets to Dutch kids climbing security fences, according to the *Economist*.

Europeans accepted the video monitoring with little grumbling about expectations of privacy or Big Brother. What made us so different? After all, how many times a day was the average American already on camera? In Manhattan in 1998, according to a study by the American Civil Liberties Union, there were 2,397 surveillance cameras. In Washington, there was one in the corner deli where I got my morning coffee and bagel. There was another one at the ATM outside. (It was courtesy of two ATMs in Portland, Maine, that photos of hijackers Mohammed Atta and Abdulaziz Alomari taken on the eve of September 11 were made public so quickly.) Yet another one filmed traffic on Connecticut Avenue when I drove my wife to work. The lobby of her office building on Eye Street had several. So that was at least four photos before 9:00 A.M.

Of course, all these cameras were owned by separate entities, mostly in the private sector. They were not interconnected in any way. It was when the monitors were linked to a central hub like the Joint Operations Command Center that things got more interesting.

The street cameras on Connecticut or Wisconsin formed part of a network of several hundred CCTVs positioned throughout the capital that could feed into the Command Center, which had been operational since 9/11. Most belonged to a half dozen federal agencies, which shared the experimental facility with the Metropolitan Police Department, the FBI, the Secret Service, the State Department, and the Defense Intelligence Agency, to name a few. Agents from different law enforcement bodies manned the JOCC's thirty-four computer terminals, which were arrayed in long rows beneath wall-size plasma screens, like those of the Houston Space Center. The wall screens simultaneously displayed live feeds, digital simulations, city maps with the locations of recently released felons, and gory crime scene footage.

"From here we can tap into schools, subways, landmarks, and main streets," said D.C. Police Chief Charles Ramsey with evident pride. With a few clicks of the mouse (and prior permission), the system could also link up with closed-circuit cameras in shopping malls, department stores, and office buildings, and was programmed to handle live feeds from up to six helicopters simultaneously. Ramsey was careful to add that, for now, the majority of the cameras remained off-line most of the time, and that the police weren't using them to look into elevators or spy on individuals.

But they could if they wanted to. I asked for a demonstration of the system's capabilities. A technician punched in a few keystrokes. An aerial photo of the city shot earlier from a surveillance plane flashed on one of the big screens. "Can you zoom in on Dupont Circle?" The screen flickered, and the thoroughfare's round fountain came into view. "Go up Connecticut Avenue." The outline of the Hilton Hotel where President Reagan was shot materialized. "Up a few more blocks, and toward Rock Creek Park," I instructed. "There, can you get any closer?" The image blurred and focused, and I could suddenly see the air-conditioning unit on my roof, my garden furniture, even the cypress hedge I had recently planted in my yard.

The fact that the government could, from a remote location, snoop into the backyards of most Washingtonians opened up a whole new level of easily accessible information. They could keep track of when you came and left your house, discovering in the process that you worked a second job or that you were carrying on an extramarital affair. Under normal circumstances, there's not much the government could do with this information. But given the increasing frequency with which we'll interact with security forces, it might just give domestic intelligence agents a critical piece of information they could use to get you to cooperate with an investigation you might otherwise feel uncomfortable about. For example, if they needed to know more about someone you work with. Or your next-door neighbor.

Chief Ramsey acknowledged the Orwellian implications. "We've offered to show the ACLU around to put invasion of privacy concerns at rest. Look," he added, turning to a live feed from the exterior of Union Station. "You can't see people's faces, but that white truck there is a good illustration of how this is a useful counterterrorist tool. It's not parked in a loading or passenger pickup zone. So we'll keep an eye on it, and if it stays there too long, we'll send out a patrolman to check it out."

There were other ways in which the new system had already helped fight the war on terror. A three-dimensional spatial visualization map of all downtown buildings allowed technicians to simulate bomb blasts and debris projections. They could also tap into the weather bureau for real-time data on wind speeds and directions to determine which parts of the city would have to be evacuated first in the event of a radioactive or biochemical plume. Programmers were working on an underground map of the capital that would show water and gas distribution and power grids.

And then there was the data bank of known criminals and terrorists, and a map that showed the exact location of recently released convicts and what they served time for. Pull a terrorist file up at random, and a life-size bearded image of one Ayman al-Zawahiri filled the plasma screen, along with a résumé that included his aliases, date of birth, medical school degree, and affiliation with the Egyptian Islamic Jihad. (Al-Zawahiri, Osama bin Laden's personal physician and right-hand man, was among the twenty-five senior al Qaeda leaders on a CIA hit list authorized by President Bush.)

The Command Center was sufficiently cutting edge by U.S. standards that the president himself had accompanied Tom Ridge on a tour of the site in the fall of 2002. Among the topics discussed during the visit was the possibility of expanding the camera network to over a thousand units and establishing similar facilities in big urban centers like Los Angeles, Chicago, Atlanta, and New York. (As of 2004, only New York City had a JOCC comparable to Washington's; L.A. was still upgrading its preexisting command central.) One of the chief benefits of the JOCCs was that they were relatively cheap to set up, particularly since most major cities already had surveillance equipment in tunnels and bridges. There was also talk of connecting all the facilities together so that officials in different parts of the country could coordinate response efforts to terrorism, although by 2003 that had been done only in test runs of terrorist attack simulations in Chicago and Seattle. "Attacks will likely occur in different cities simultaneously," said Chief Ramsey. And as for those civil libertarians uneasy with the notion of blanket national surveillance, Ramsey just shrugged. "We can't pretend we live in the nineteenth century. We have to take advantage of technology."

Four hundred twenty-three miles above Chief Ramsey, the IKONOS remote sensing satellite was traveling at a speed of 17,000 miles an hour, its powerful high-resolution lens panning the Eastern Seaboard. Technicians monitored its progress on a large digital map at flight control, a dim windowless room in Thorton, Colorado. Outside, a colony of gophers frolicked in the grass at the foot of giant white antenna dishes that controlled the craft, specifying the telemetry of footage to be shot and retrieving the digital images.

Gene Colabatistto, a former Marine, military intelligence officer, and Gulf War I veteran, watched IKONOS circumnavigate the globe. It did this every ninety-eight minutes, traveling in a polar orbit so that after dipping into South America, it emerged in the

Indian Ocean, traveled up the Gulf into Saudi Arabia, Kuwait, and then Iraq, where its close-ups of Saddam's smoldering palaces during the siege of Baghdad International Airport had aired on the cable news networks when the second Iraqi war, to no one's surprise, had finally started.

"We took the first aerial photographs of the World Trade Center on September 11," said Colabatistto, who in a previous career had worked on modeling the dispersal of chemical agents and how they could be carried by air currents in the D.C. Metro, "when all planes and helicopters were grounded." A large color photo of the devastation hung in the hall outside mission control, not too far from a notice board spelling out the fine print of the Employee Polygraph Protection Act. This was not a secret installation, however, but rather a for-profit corporation whose single largest client was the U.S. government.

Owned by a consortium of defense contractors led by Lockheed Martin and Raytheon, Space Imaging Inc. boasted the world's first constellation of commercial reconnaissance craft, including the IRS (infrared) satellite, Landsats 1, 5, and 7, DAIS (Digital Airborne Imaging System), and RADARSAT. RADARSAT utilized synthetic aperture radar to see through clouds, smoke, or dust, prompting one Space Imaging promotional brochure touting homeland security applications to declare that there is "Nowhere to Hide." But IKONOS was the pride of the fleet, because it could see from 423 miles out in space to within a three-foot resolution anywhere on earth. That made it the biggest zoom lens in the world outside of the military. And unlike the CIA or NSA's billion-dollar-each KEYHOLE-11 satellites (which reportedly had a 10-inch resolution, meaning that spooks at NSA headquarters in Crypto City in Fort Meade, Maryland, could make out the headlines of a newspaper being read on a park bench in North Korea), IKONOS could be used legally to photograph subjects in America.

Space Imaging owed its market niche to the Posse Comitatus Act of 1878 which, following the carnage of the Civil War, prohibited the U.S. military from ever again being sent into action on U.S. soil. (Hence the creation of the National Guard as an alternative militia.) Because virtually all spy satellites are military, the NSA was barred from using its vast surveillance capability at home. The CIA was in the same boat; its charter was to gather foreign intelligence, and it was expressly forbidden to operate domestically. That left a giant blind spot on the world map for U.S. surveillance capability. Until 9/11, that had not been seen as a dramatic vulnerability. The terror attacks on New York and Washington changed that perception. We needed better eyes and ears at home, it was reasoned, and a way had to be found around the Posse Comitatus restrictions. That was where outfits like Space Imaging entered into the picture. Nothing prohibited the government from awarding private satellite providers contracts, which was exactly what CIA director George Tenet recommended, shortly before Space Imaging won a $120 million deal to help update U.S. maps. In fall 2003 Tenet was pushing for that contract to be increased to nearly $500 million and recommending that such companies be permitted to upgrade to even higher-resolution satellites, such as those used by spy agencies.

For me, there is only one logical explanation for the CIA's or NSA's sudden enthusiasm for commercial satellite providers: to upgrade the government's domestic surveillance capabilities. Nonsense, laughed Colabatistto, I've seen too many movies. Space Imaging's contract, he said, had nothing to do with snooping. Rather, it was intended to help monitor borders and critical infrastructure; update U.S. maps, which on average were twenty-two years old; and locate areas where urban sprawl butted residential neighborhoods against toxic industrial facilities, so that emergency evacuation routes could be planned.

"This isn't *Enemy of the State*," Colabatistto said, referring to the high-tech thriller in which actor Will Smith plays a Washington attorney who finds himself the target of a rogue government agency able to track his every move using super-sophisticated spy satellites. "That's just not very realistic."

About an hour's drive north of Space Imaging's headquarters, near
Colorado's border with Wyoming, I went to see another technology
that had potential homeland security applications.

Granted, it was an odd place to preview the cutting edge. Farms
sprawled on both sides of the highway, which ran unimpeded over
the flat green plains, with little other than the occasional silo and
the smokestacks of a brewery to distract the eye. When I pulled
off the gravel road past a tractor shed, Cleon Kimberling was waiting for me by the sheep pens. Kimberling was a veterinarian with
Colorado State University, and the green and gold coveralls he
and his two graduate student assistants wore matched the school's
colors. While we made our introductions, his assistants cajoled a
squirming lamb into a narrow enclosure. Dr. Kimberling then inserted a large syringe into its rump, just beneath the tail. The animal
bleated in protest and bolted the moment it was released. One of
Kimberling's assistants then retrieved a white handheld device that
resembled a speed gun. She pointed it at the retreating lamb, the
machine beeped, and a number flashed on the LED readout:
AVID*059*558**073.

This was the bar code of the transponder Kimberling had injected
into the animal and my introduction to the brave new world of radio
frequency identification, or RFID, the wave of the future. About the
size of a grain of wild rice, it was a tiny microchip plus relay antenna
sealed in a glass capsule coated with Parylene C, a compound compatible with living cells that promotes tissue growth around the device. It can be injected anywhere and transmit information about its
host, such as body temperature fluctuations. It can also contain a
complete medical history and can be used to track an animal's
progress in the commercial food chain, from pen to slaughterhouse to
meat processing facility, in the event a meat contamination occurred
and the source needed to be identified.

Automated readers are installed at choke points throughout
the pens so that the animals can be remotely monitored. I asked Dr.

Kimberling about other applications. "I know where you're headed with this." He smiled. "Alzheimer's patients are an obvious example. They often wander out without ID and get lost. Sex offenders," he added, "are another candidate. I think they should lose certain basic rights to privacy the moment they are convicted."

Elsie McCoy listened to Kimberling in silence, shifting uncomfortably from foot to foot. She sold the transponders for a California-based company called EZID. "I don't know," she finally said. "There's a lot of potential for abuse. That's putting an awful lot of trust in the government."

She was not the only one uneasy about the technology's far-reaching potential, in the hands of both the government and the private sector. "It's paving the way for a police state," said Katherine Albrecht, head of Consumers Against Supermarket Privacy Invasion and Numbering (CASPIAN), a grassroots consumer group fighting retail surveillance since 1999. "Brace yourself for major surveillance."

Nonetheless, RFID was generating intense interest on the part of the military, businesses, and governments. Many corporations were using the technology to better track inventory. "It's basically bar codes on steroids," explained Glover Ferguson, chief scientist at financial services giant Accenture. "It can tell me what it is. It can tell me where it is. It can tell me how it got there, or even how it feels, if it has sensor capability." The technology had many applications. Some UPS trucks, said Ferguson, can start only if the driver wears an RFID bracelet. "They don't even use keys." UPS's competitor, FedEx, uses RFID to track shipments so efficiently that customers can query the precise status and location of their delivery at any given time. Michelin is testing smart tires embedded with chips that warn the car's onboard computer if the air pressure is low or if the tread is worn. Ferguson's laboratory in Chicago is taking RFID technology to the next level: crates that can warn truckers if they are being off-loaded in the wrong place; medicine cabinets that warn you if you are taking the wrong prescription pill; clothes that beep if they don't match—even marketing tools that scan the sidewalk outside stores and automatically dial the cell phone of passersby to let them know about a sale or offer a discount to come in and buy something. "I know, I know," said Ferguson. "It can be annoying."

Here's how the technology works: A basic RFID system consists of three components: an antenna or coil, a transceiver (with decoder), and a transponder (RF tag) electronically programmed with unique information. The antenna emits radio signals to activate the tag and read and send data to it. Antennae are the conduits between the tag and the transceiver, which controls the system's data acquisition and communication. Transceivers are available in a variety of shapes and sizes; they can be built into a door frame to receive tag data from persons or things passing through the door, or mounted on an interstate toll booth to monitor passing traffic.

Not surprisingly, the military was an early pioneer of RFID. After a multitude of lost shipments during Desert Storm, the Department of Defense placed RFID tags on 270,000 cargo containers. Special Ops forces reportedly had tiny chips injected in their hips on sensitive missions where they could not wear dog tags, but the Pentagon will not comment. The Army also issued to some soldiers fighting in Iraq RFID wristbands that contain pertinent medical information about who they are and their medical histories, said Mike Cossolotto, who handled public relations for Applied Digital Solutions, a Florida-based company that had started experimenting with RFID tags designed for humans.

Cossolotto has a microchip implanted in the triceps of his right arm. Applied Digital Solutions developed the chip for use in humans after its founder, Dr. Richard Seelig, watched firefighters before they entered the World Trade Center on September 11, 2001. "He saw a lot of firefighters writing their names on their arms," said Cossolotto. "They wanted to be identified before going in.

"In a number of years, this will become pretty common, once people get a sense of how convenient it is. There are many valuable uses for the chip. It's more secure than the information in my wallet," Cossolotto continued.

Along with the potential medical uses, he says he likes the notion of one day not having to carry a wallet full of cash or credit cards, or being able to withdraw money from an ATM with a wave of his hand. It's also a great tool to prove one's identity, he says.

Watchdogs like Katherine Albrecht, however, warned in congressional testimony of mounting evidence that the technology is poised to be used in more sinister ways. The Chinese government wants to use chips to monitor the whereabouts of political prisoners, said Albrecht, who, as a lifelong member of the National Rifle Association, doesn't fit the profile of your typical bleeding-heart liberal. She said she had been contacted by an employee of a high-tech company "in the western hemisphere," though she refused to be more specific, whose firm was working with the Chinese government to "iron out the kinks for a full-based government surveillance system" that would allow it to monitor the whereabouts of political dissenters, among other uses. The Chinese apparently made first steps in the monitoring of humans when, according to Albrecht, delegates to the Chinese Communist Party Congress in May 2003 were required to wear RFID-equipped badges at all times so their movements could be tracked and recorded.

Hearing all this, Elsie McCoy suddenly seemed less certain about the RFID implants she sold for livestock. "I'll tell you," she said, handing me one of the rice-size transponders as a souvenir. "This stuff is OK for farm animals. But the moment they start putting it in people, well, it's time for me to find another job."

The technological and legal foundations for blanket surveillance had already been laid in 2003. All that was lacking was the political and social will to bring all this technical wizardry to bear in the war on terror. It wouldn't happen overnight or without another catastrophic incident, something that upped the ante and put America in survival

mode on a par with Israel's: a nuclear detonation, a biological outbreak, a mass casualty event. But if the stakes were high enough,
would we be more willing to accept life in a maximum security surveillance state?

I was once invited to discuss that prospect on a National Public
Radio program produced out of Boston. A woman called in. She was
a widow, she said. Her husband had been a pilot, one of the victims
of 9/11 in New York. "I would accept all those measures, regardless
of the costs," she said, "if it meant that my children were guaranteed to be spared from the same fate as my husband."

How many other relatives of 9/11 victims felt the same way? A
good number, I imagined. To the larger audience, however, selling
the surveillance state would undoubtedly be harder—maybe only
somewhat more palatable if it was made clear that the targets of the
watchers would not be third-generation Caucasians like Professor
Smith, but immigrants from Muslim nations like the unfortunate
Canadian telecommunications engineer or the thousands of other
foreigners detained after 9/11. These sorts of people "should not
have the same rights as the rest of us," anyway, one caller from
California with a very heavy Eastern European accent declared during another call-in show I participated in on C-SPAN's *Washington
Journal*.

My own status as a transplanted Canadian immigrant—my application for U.S. citizenship was in the INS logjam somewhere—
and my brief encounter with Israeli airport screeners made me
more sympathetic. It wasn't privacy issues that troubled me. I had
had my phone tapped while working in the former Soviet Union
and stayed in hotel rooms which U.S. diplomats warned me contained both audio and video surveillance. What worried me about
blanket surveillance was how easily a few innocent coincidences
could land you on a watch list that could forever alter your life. And
what, I wondered, would it be like to run afoul of the surveillance
state; to be designated an enemy of a paranoid, unsympathetic nation that believes it's fighting for its very survival? To find that out I

didn't have to travel to Israel again or engage in more hypothetical future scenarios. All I had to do was fly to Tulsa, Oklahoma, rent a car (with a tracking device?) to drive across the dusty Indian reservations into the lush backwoods of Arkansas, and ask a young man from Egypt to take me back in time to the weeks and months that followed his arrest on September 12, 2001.

4

ENEMY OF THE STATE

I T BEGAN INNOCENTLY ENOUGH, WITH A KNOCK AT THE door. The visitor was a big man. He wore jeans and a white polo shirt. A service revolver hung from his belt, along with a gold shield identifying him as a deputy from the nearby sheriff's office in Fort Smith, Arkansas.

Two other strangers were waiting outside, next to an unmarked SUV parked in the driveway where Candrice Omar's husband had been playing with their nine-month-old infant, Jasmine. The men also sported sidearms and denim, and one carried a badge from the Federal Bureau of Investigation.

"Ma'am, could you come outside please," asked the deputy. Candrice's first thought was of her nineteen-year-old niece, Angela. She was the wild one in the family, always piling up unpaid tickets and ignoring court summonses. But that wasn't why the law was at her door. "They just want to ask me a few questions," Hady Hassan Omar told his wife, as an officer handed Jasmine over to Candrice. Omar didn't look especially worried or frightened—maybe just a little tired from the fourteen hours he'd spent at the Houston airport the day before, after his flight from Florida got grounded, along with all air traffic in the country following the catastrophic events in New York and Washington. Candrice—Candy, as everyone called her—was tired, too. Her blond hair was unruly, and her clothes had that rumpled, slept-in look. She had driven all night to pick Omar up at the airport in Houston, where his Continental Airlines flight from Fort Lauderdale to Little

Rock had been rerouted. She was so exhausted, in fact, that she had not noticed that a red Camaro with black-tinted windows had followed her for a good part of the journey on Highway 71.

"I'll be home soon," Omar promised, with a reassuring smile and only a hint of the Egyptian accent that Candy had found exotic when he had first pestered her for her phone number at the Electric Cowboy club some sixteen months back. It hadn't been love at first sight, but Omar had been persistent, "romantic and goofy," as she put it, and by their third date he had won her heart.

"We just have some routine questions about a gun permit your husband applied for," the deputy, who introduced himself as Billy, reassured Candy. She didn't see Billy's fellow deputy, Bob, handcuff her young husband, or she might have been more concerned. Nor did she see the FBI agent in the white Dodge SUV place a call on his cell phone and tell his superior: "Yeah. We got him. . . . Okay, we'll bring her in, too."

While Billy and Bob sat in the front of the Dodge, the FBI man rode in silence in the back with Omar. "Do you know why we really want to talk to you?" the agent finally asked. "I guess it's because I'm Egyptian," Omar answered. Lead hijacker Mohammed Atta was Egyptian; that much was already known. "Yes," conceded the agent, "that's one of the reasons."

Omar wasn't taking any of this too seriously. The feds probably were canvassing all Muslim immigrants in the area, he figured, looking for tips. Even when summoned that afternoon to the small FBI office in Fort Smith, a few rooms in a medical building next to a pediatrician's office, the gravity of the situation had not yet dawned on Candy, either. The FBI agents, after all, were relaxed and friendly and had assured her they simply needed to ask routine questions about the local gun club Omar had recently joined. Still, the line of questioning seemed somewhat incongruous. "One kept asking if Hady was a good Muslim," she recalled. "I said not really." It was true that Omar didn't eat pork. But he didn't pray five times a day, go to mosque, or deny himself the occasional vodka or Marlboro Ultra Light. An affable federal agent named Ed sat next to Candy in the waiting room, passing the time watching the television news. Periodically he pointed at the photos of the nineteen hijackers that the networks showed and asked Candy if she'd ever seen any of them before. Had Omar ever gone to flight school? Who were his friends? Why was he in Florida on September 11? Agent Ed seemed especially interested in the grainy picture of Mohammed Atta. "You know what this is really about, don't you?" he kept asking. Candy didn't have a clue what possible connection her husband could have with the lead hijacker. But she would find out soon enough.

Little more than twenty-four hours had passed since American Airlines flight 11 struck the south tower of the World Trade Center, and the war on terror had begun. Hady Hassan Omar wasn't the only Middle Eastern immigrant the authorities wanted to interview. All across the country, young Muslim men were being hauled in for questioning as the intelligence community and law enforcement agencies worked feverishly to track down the hijackers' possible accomplices and flush out al Qaeda sleeper cells before they struck again. No one knew just how many people were snared in the raids, since the government imposed a gag order on the dragnet after the toll reached 1,200 detainees. Even the names of those arrested in the aftermath of 9/11 were secret, and would to continue to be classified as of January 2004, when courts struck down Freedom of Information petitions by newspapers to compel the Justice Department to disclose their identities. The sweep, although it would draw heavy criticism in time, was a natural reaction to the deep uncertainties of the moment. America had just been dealt its biggest blow since Pearl Harbor. Half of lower Manhattan was buried in rubble, dust, and smoke. The Pentagon, the symbol of U.S. invincibility, was smoldering. Citizens were terrified; the country was clearly under attack. And enemy agents could still be somewhere within its borders. The only thing known about them was that they were likely to be young Muslim immigrant men, because that was the profile of the nineteen hijackers. The authorities had little else to go on. But they needed to defend the nation, to use every resource at their disposal to prevent another attack. Immigrants from the Middle East and South Asia were a natural place to start. That federal agencies had cast their net so wide, said David Cole, a prominent Georgetown law professor, was one indication of how stunned the FBI had been on September 11. "Their intelligence was so poor that they had to sweep broadly, using ethnic or religious criteria. Essentially, they were stabbing in the dark."

Regardless of criteria, the FBI had, for the first time since its inception, the primary responsibility of stopping any secondary strikes al Qaeda might have planned rather than bringing those responsible for the initial attack to justice. It was uncharted territory for the Bureau. For the first time in its history, it was primarily focused on prevention, not prosecution. In other words, in the days and weeks following September 11, 2001, the FBI acted more like Israel's Shin Bet than the law enforcement agency it had always been.

"Am I here because I'm Egyptian?" Omar asked again once he had been brought into the FBI interrogation room and joined by another agent who introduced himself as Jim. Omar didn't buy the concealed-weapons permit excuse any longer and had already guessed that the questioning had something to do with the attacks on America. The FBI had taken his weapons permit, along with his driver's license, social security card, work permit, and the thirteen credit cards he'd accumulated during his two years in the country. "I'll need those back," Omar requested. He had an interview in a few days with the Immigration and Naturalization Service to get the coveted green card and was going off on vacation with Candy to celebrate their one-year anniversary. Don't worry, he was assured. Now tell us about your friends. The FBI wanted names and numbers—whom Omar had dated, roomed with, worked for, and so on—and whenever Omar gave them one, an agent would scribble it down on a piece of paper and leave the room.

(The Fort Smith FBI branch office declined to comment, when I called about Omar's case, as did Brian Marshall, a spokesman for the Bureau's Arkansas headquarters in Little Rock.) They asked many questions about religion. "Why do you believe killing people is right?"

A short, bald agent named Mike did most of the talking. "What do you think about the attacks?" Omar said they were a tragedy. He was asked to provide a handwriting sample in Arabic. The questions continued for several hours. Why did you fly on September 11? Why did you make your ticket reservation online? Omar hadn't the slightest clue why that might interest the authorities.

Candy, meanwhile, had signed a consent form allowing the search of their apartment. Half a dozen agents followed her home. They were polite and professional, and very thorough. Omar caught a glimpse of the agents returning with his home computer, documents, credit card statements, and correspondence, his collection of Arabic-language videos, and even a copy of *Scarface*, the Al Pacino gangster classic.

At that point, what still worried Omar the most was how all this would affect his credit rating. He'd signed up for all those credit cards and even taken a few small bank loans just to repay them because he had been told that was how one built a credit history in America, and he dreamed of owning his own business someday. That's what he had been doing in Florida on September 11, getting ready to open an Egyptian antiques store with a friend who worked for Lucent Technologies in Cairo.

Pizza was brought in to the FBI office around nine, and Candy ate a slice with the agents. They pressed her about Omar's religious beliefs. Would their daughter Jasmine be raised Muslim or Baptist? they wanted to know. Candy was still sure her husband was coming home that night. But it was getting late. "Can Hady go now?" she asked. Not just yet, she was told. A little after 11:00 P.M. she was informed she could leave. Omar, meanwhile, had been left alone to stew. Then a senior agent walked into the interrogation room angrily waving a fax from Washington. "This comes from the very top," he shouted, and instantly Omar knew he was not going home that night.

Candrice Omar woke the next morning to find the banner head-line "TERROR STRIKES HOME" blazing across the front page of the Fort Smith *Times-Record*, over a four-column photograph of her handcuffed husband being led away to the county jail.

His arrest was on all the local stations, as well; their lead story be-gan, "Local man arrested in connection to 9/11." There were the ubiq-uitous interviews with neighbors and former coworkers at the restaurant where Omar worked as a waiter, all expressing varying de-grees of shock, disbelief, and outrage. Omar's wife from a brief first marriage was also interviewed—the shot only showing the back of her bleached-blond head, since she didn't want her face on camera—and she complained that Omar had always been "secretive," adding that she was not at all surprised to find him mixed up in something nefari-ous, though she thought it would have been drugs.

None of the media accounts dwelled on the fact that Omar had not yet been charged with any crime. At central booking at the Sebas-tian County Detention Center in Fort Smith where Omar was taken, strip-searched, and given orange prison fatigues, the line reserved for charges read vaguely: "Hold for INS." But the contents of that fax sent from Washington were damning. Omar had bought his September 11 plane ticket online at the very same computer terminal in the same Boca Raton Kinko's outlet around the same time as his fellow country-man Mohammed Atta. And he fit the hijackers' profile to a T: young, from a well-to-do background—his father was an engineer working in Qatar—computer-literate, with a taste for vodka and nightclubs and working out at the gym, just like Atta.

It was certainly not surprising the FBI wanted to talk to him. But was his plane ticket purchase merely a coincidence in a time of para-noia? Or was Hady Hassan Omar trying to get away with conspiracy to mass murder?

Similar questions were being posed with respect to the hundreds of other young Muslim men the FBI was interviewing that day. But the

Bureau faced a serious problem, as was exemplified by the mysterious "Hold for INS" that had been scribbled in Omar's arrest sheet. On September 12, 2001, no laws dealt with extraordinary situations such as the one now facing the United States. The FBI was racing against time to stop more potential terrorist acts, but it did not have the legal means to do the job. Omar, and all the others like him, could not be held under criminal statutes because buying an airline ticket at the same place, around the same time, as Atta was not even enough circumstantial evidence for a search warrant, much less an arrest warrant. But these people couldn't simply be let go to possibly continue their murderous missions, either. It wasn't a matter of whether Omar was guilty or not, it was a question of whether the government could afford to take the chance that he was. The pre-9/11 laws didn't address this now-critical issue. In Europe and Israel, where antiterror legislation has been on the books for years, grounds can always be found to hold such suspects. But not in the United States. Some legal basis needed to be found to justify the preventive detentions. But what?

At Candy's apartment, the phone rang incessantly. A friend of Omar's called to say she should forget about her husband and move on with her life. Omar called, too, from jail. He sounded hysterical, and tearfully begged Candy to believe that he was "not a murderer, or involved in any way."

The FBI agents returned to Omar's holding cell in the county jail around noon, this time in suits and ties. They brought with them another agent flown up from Little Rock in a special government plane. "Is there anything you didn't tell us last night?" asked Jim. Omar said no. But he was dazed; he hadn't slept a wink, because one of the guards kept slamming on his cell door whenever he nodded off. The special agent from Little Rock asked Omar if he knew what a lie detector test was. "Oh," Omar said. "Like in *Meet the Parents*"—the comedy where Robert De Niro plays a retired CIA officer who subjects future sons-in-law to polygraphs. "Do you mind taking one?" Omar said he had no objection. But his hands were shaking and he was visibly distraught, so the agent arranged for some Coke, sandwiches, and cigarettes to be brought in to calm his nerves.

After the electrodes had been strapped to his chest and index and ring fingers, and a blood pressure gauge was wrapped around his biceps, a series of seven questions began, repeated three times in different order. Some were innocuous: "Is your date of birth January 19, 1979?" Others less so: "Were you planning on hitting U.S. targets or hurting Americans?" or "Are you lying to us right now or have you lied to us in the past?" Omar was again asked if he recognized or knew any of the nineteen hijackers.

The test lasted ninety minutes, and the results were faxed to Washington. While they waited for word from headquarters, Omar turned to the agent he knew as Jim. "Do you really think I had something to do with the hijackings?"

"I don't know, Hady," said Jim. "Ted Bundy seemed like a nice guy, too." Omar was left to contemplate this. Good news, said the agent from Little Rock, when he finally returned, all smiles now and patting Omar on the back. Omar was told he had passed.

Relief swept over the frightened young immigrant. He would make his green card hearing after all, and in a few days he'd be celebrating his wedding anniversary with Candy at a spa in Hot Springs, all this a bad memory. "I can go now, right?" he asked eagerly. "We're done with you," said Jim, also smiling. "We don't want anything else from you."

What Omar did not know was that in Washington officials at the Justice Department were working around the clock to come up with emergency legal guidelines to fight the war on terror. Extraordinary times called for extraordinary measures, and the government was in a race against time. Anthrax scares were occurring from Florida to New York, ordinary citizens were afraid to pick up the mail, and no one knew where or when al Qaeda would strike next. Intelligence and law enforcement agencies needed expanded powers of surveillance, interrogation, and especially detention to combat the terrorist threat and prevent the next catastrophe. Washington simply couldn't afford to take chances with people like Omar. Too much was at stake.

It would take six weeks for the USA Patriot Act to be rushed through a bipartisan Congress and signed into law by President Bush. But in the meantime, the dangers facing America were very real, and the Immigration and Naturalization Service was enlisted to help buy the FBI time. Leads had to be followed up, stories checked out, bank records and phone logs verified. All this was painstakingly slow work, and suspects could not be detained by law for more than twenty-four hours without being charged with a crime. The INS, however, had always had the power to hold immigrants for overstaying tourist or student visas, taking too few college credits, or any number of other minor or major immigration violations. They could launch deportation proceedings against illegal aliens and keep them locked up if they were deemed a flight risk. It was, to be sure, a technicality, one of those lawyerly tricks defense attorneys are famous for exploiting to get their guilty clients off. Except the government would be using it to keep people locked up. But it was perfectly legal, as long as the detainees were charged under immigration statutes within twenty-four hours. After 9/11, that time frame was extended to forty-eight hours by the Justice Department, then seven days. In special "emergency" cases, said William Strassberger, a spokesman for the INS in Washington, detainees could be held without charges for a "reasonable" though unspecified period. That also would later apply to U.S. citizens designated as "enemy combatants," who could be held without charges, bail, or access to counsel.

In the days and weeks that followed 9/11, INS officials across the country rounded up suspects on what Georgetown law professor David Cole called "pretextual charges." Initially, no one even knew how many individuals had been detained in the nationwide raids. There was, however, a good reason for the secrecy, although the public was kept in the dark about that, as well. "It's standard procedure," explained a Washington insider with intimate knowledge of intelligence practices who spoke on condition of anonymity. "You round up a bunch of people and then listen to traffic." The hope was that the National Security Agency's satellites and supercomputers would intercept telephone conversations between al Qaeda members in Pakistan or Afghanistan asking if their U.S. operatives had been picked up. (The insider did not know—or would not say—if the ruse was successful.)

The other unspoken rationale behind the detentions reflected Israeli-style reasoning. If only one out of every hundred, or even thousand, immigrants detained had an al Qaeda connection, the entire effort was worth it because another 9/11 might have been prevented. This I heard from several senior officials, although naturally it would never be the government's official line since preventive detention is unconstitutional. It was also a good illustration of the difficult position the FBI found itself in. The Bureau was under tremendous political pressure to be more proactive. The intelligence failure of 9/11 had been a stinging blow to the agency's prestige: It was said to be too bureaucratic, risk averse, and reactive to combat terror. If it waited around for terrorists to strike again, it probably would not survive another blow and would be broken up. But if it tried to stay ahead of the bad guys by rounding up hundreds of people—many if not most of whom were bound to be innocent—it would face charges of trampling on civil liberties and be accused of unconstitutional, heavy-handed ways. In short, it was damned if it did and damned if it didn't.

The Justice Department eventually did release a partial list of the results of the dragnet. As of November 2001—when, according to the ACLU executive director Anthony Romero, the government stopped issuing any information on the detainees—a total of 1,147 individuals were being held: 725 under immigration-status violations and about 120 for federal crimes ranging from tax evasion to perjury and credit card fraud. It was not disclosed why the remaining detainees were in captivity, or when and where any of them would be given the public hearings to which nonnationals, like U.S. citizens, are entitled. On September 21, 2001, the Justice Department issued a memorandum reversing that right to open hearings. In "special inter-est cases," according to the memorandum, hearings would be held be-hind closed doors. The INS would not be required to confirm whether such cases were on the docket, and not even the relatives of detainees would be allowed to attend the secret trials. "Opening sen-sitive immigration hearings could compromise the security of our nation and our ongoing investigations," Justice Department spokes-woman Barbara Comstock elaborated. "We are at war, facing a ter-rorist threat from unidentified foes who operate in covert ways and unknown places. This makes it essential that the United States take every legal step possible to protect the American people from acts of terrorism." Attorney General John Ashcroft himself defended the decision to beef up security measures at the expense of individuals' rights. "History instructs us," he said during a 2002 speech to U.S. at-torneys in New York, "that caution and complacency are not de-fenses of freedom. Caution and complacency are a capitulation before freedom's enemies—the terrorists." For the attorney general, it was a delicate balancing act. The interests of national security had to be weighed against constitutional guarantees, the safety of 280 mil-lion citizens squared against the rights of a few, or a few thousand, in-dividuals—mostly foreign nationals. The United States had not faced such a quandary since the attack on Pearl Harbor, when it was deemed necessary to intern 110,000 Japanese and people of Japanese descent, 70,000 of whom were U.S. citizens, to stop possible sabotage or espionage. Many prominent legal scholars supported the attorney general, arguing that the necessity of preventing future terrorist at-tacks superseded the rights of any individual and that standards of due process needed to be amended to suit extreme circumstances. "Human rights norms recognize that in times of grave emergency, governments can take steps that are different from peacetime so long as they are strictly necessary and proportional," said Ruth Wedg-wood, a professor of international law at Yale and a former federal prosecutor. "On September 12 no one knew the extent of the threat, whether al Qaeda succeeded in finding fissile materials, so there was great concern that the other shoe might drop, that next time it could be 30,000 casualties."

None of this boded well for Omar and the other September 11 detainees. Although he had been told he'd passed his lie detector test, he was far from being in the clear. Polygraphs are not foolproof, and people can be trained to beat them. That is one reason they are not admissible in court. Late in the afternoon of September 13, after Omar had been in custody for less than twenty-four hours, an armed INS agent in a cowboy hat named Vince served him with a document known as "a notice to appear." Omar had no idea what that meant. It was not a criminal charge, he assumed, yet he was being taken for mug shots and fingerprinting. "We're sending you back to Egypt," he was finally informed. Stunned, Omar demanded to know on what grounds. "You overstayed your tourist visa," the INS agent with the cowboy hat declared. "B-but I'm legal," Omar stammered; his marriage to an American citizen entitled him to permanent residency. "I've got a work permit and everything."

By now Omar was bitterly regretting that he'd signed a form for the FBI waiving his right to an attorney. ("It's not necessary," he recalled being told. "They just cost a lot of money.") He was still cursing that decision when his cell door was flung open sometime after midnight and several INS agents in bulletproof vests slapped leg irons on him and cuffed him to a thick chain that was wrapped around his waist. "What's happening?" he demanded. "Let's go," they said, fingering their shotguns.

A tan Chevy Lumina idled in the basement. Omar was put in the back, and the sedan sped off. "Where are we going? What's happening?" But no one said anything. They drove through the night, listening to country music, Omar dozing against the broad shoulder of an INS guard.

"I kept asking for an attorney," Omar recalled. Finally one of the agents in the car lost his temper and yelled, "Listen, let me explain this to you. We're not going to baby-sit you like the FBI." The FBI back in Fort Smith had sent out for sandwiches at Subway, allowed Omar to smoke and call whomever he wanted—perhaps out of kindness, perhaps so that they could keep tabs on whom he talked to. But the stern-faced men who were now holding him seemed to be far less accommodating. During the eleven hours they drove, they stopped to eat, but would let Omar have neither food nor drink. He still had no idea where they were taking him, though he could tell by the license plates and road signs that they had crossed over to Louisiana. The sun was already up when they pulled into a gas station, where an unmarked Ford Explorer, a police cruiser, and half a dozen men brandishing shotguns were waiting for them.

Their destination was an INS office in Oakdale, Louisiana. Omar, still in shackles, was brought into a room with a large glass partition. "Everyone in the office was staring at me as if I was something nasty or dirty," he remembers. Still handcuffed, he was given a form to sign, and did so without even reading it. The cuffs had been on for twelve hours and were chafing his skin. He was dizzy with hunger. "Can you take these off?" he pleaded. "Hell, no," he was told.

Several hours later Omar was moved again, this time to the Orleans Parish Prison in New Orleans. "Strip and spread your legs," he was ordered on arrival, before being searched, issued a jumpsuit, and placed in an isolation cell where a camera filmed his every move, including his bowel movements. Once in the corridor, he was accosted by another prisoner. "We're going to get you, you terrorist fuck," promised the convict.

Omar was near panic. "I want to call the Egyptian embassy," he demanded, but was reminded that it was already the weekend and the consulate was closed. He could phone Candy, however, to let her know where he was.

She had been frantic, afraid to leave her apartment because of the battalion of reporters camped outside her door. But the call from her husband galvanized her into action. She arranged to drop off Jasmine with her mother, emptied their $700 bank account at an ATM, and started driving to Louisiana. The trip took more than twelve hours, and she was exhausted by the time she finally arrived at the prison. But Omar was already gone. Sometime after 2:00 A.M. on September 16, he had been woken up, placed in leg irons, and transferred, though no one would tell her where he had been sent. Despondent, Candy checked into a motel. Almost immediately two FBI agents knocked at the door. They had brought photographs of Middle Eastern men and a list of names for her to look at. Recognize anyone? asked one of the agents. "That one," she said, pointing to a shot of Mohammed Atta. "From the news." Again, the agents wanted to know about flight schools and what Omar had been doing in Florida on September 11. "I already told you," she said. "Tell us again," she was told. Finally she lost patience. "I'm calling a lawyer."

The next morning she hired Louisiana attorney Lawrence Fabacher. Fabacher found out that Omar had been moved to the federal maximum security penitentiary at Pollock, but had been unable to reach him or get any more information. Candy called Pollock, but officials refused to confirm whether Omar was being held there. "He is my husband, I need to find him!" she pleaded with a prison administrator. "I think national security is more important right now," the administrator replied.

All over the country, Muslim men were literally disappearing into the prison system. On September 20, Shakir Baloch, a Canadian citizen of Pakistani origin, was arrested in New York by the INS and FBI. Despite official inquiries from Ottawa, his detention was not disclosed for over three months. He was held for half a year before being sent back to Canada. In California, an Egyptian-born dentist was taken into custody at a Los Angeles area gas station and, while his friends searched for him in local jails, was flown to a detention center in Brooklyn. In Kentucky, Ali Maqtari, a Yemeni citizen, was dropping off his American wife at Fort Campbell, where she was reporting for Army basic training, when the FBI arrested him. Although he passed a lie detector test, the INS detained him on the grounds that he had been in the country for two days illegally while changing his status from tourist to permanent resident. In New Jersey, Anser Mehmood's wife spent six weeks searching for her husband, who was arrested in late September, not formally charged with visa violations until March 2002, and held in an isolation cell with twenty-four-hour lighting for almost seven months. The wife of an Egyptian national arrested in early September did not see her husband until December 19. She passed on a letter he eventually wrote to Amnesty International. "I have now been in solitary confinement for three-and-a-half months.... Why am I imprisoned? And why under maximum security measures? I have many questions and no answers. What are they accusing me of?"

It was only when he got to the maximum security federal penitentiary in Pollock that Omar realized how deep his troubles were. Initially no one even knew he was there, and he was not permitted to make any calls. "Strip," he was told once again. A dozen prison officials in blue and gray uniforms, including two women, he recalls, looked on. Someone produced a camcorder and began filming as Omar undressed. "Your underwear, too," a guard motioned. Omar stood naked while his bodily cavities were examined for contraband for the second time in less than twenty-four hours, in spite of the fact that he had been in the custody of agents without a break. Cavity searches are standard practice in the penal system (Bureau of Prisons policy no. 5521.05), designed to prevent inmates from smuggling narcotics or knives into the cell blocks. But they are usually limited to visual examinations, said Bureau of Prisons spokesperson Tracy Billingsley, and only in "extremely rare cases" go beyond that.

"Lift your testicles." Omar blushed but did as he was told, while the camera zoomed in for a close-up. "You sure you're not hiding anything in there," the guard said, prodding Omar's buttocks. "I think he's got something in there," he announced to the others. One of the correctional officers placed a call, and a man in white medical scrubs entered the room. He wore a thick latex glove. "Bend over," he said. Squinting from the pain, Omar looked up at the two female prison officials. They were laughing.

Isolation cell number I measured ten feet by ten feet. At its center was a concrete bunk. The only other furnishing was a stainless steel toilet. Now dressed in a prison-issue orange jumpsuit, Omar desperately needed to use the bathroom, but was still shackled. "Can you take these off?" he asked. The answer was no. "But how am I going to—" The question was cut off by a corrections officer who motioned for another guard to join him. Each grabbed one of Omar's elbows and steered him to the bowl. But with the handcuffs still on, he could barely manage his zipper, much less aim. Urine began running down his pant leg as the guards laughed.

Warden Carl Casterline came to visit him the next morning. "I have orders from Washington to keep you here until further notice," Omar recalled him saying. Omar again asked to telephone an attorney, but says his request was denied. The warden was polite but firm on the matter. Unbeknownst to Hady, Candy had already hired one. He had instructions from D.C., he said. "I don't eat pork," Omar told the warden as the interview wound down and he was asked if he had any special dietary needs. Lunch was brought to him soon after: bologna and ham.

Warden Casterline's office declined to comment on any aspect of Omar's case, referring queries to the Bureau of Prisons in Washington. Tracy Billingsley, the BOP spokesperson, said she could not speak to Omar's case specifically, but explained that federal policy allows inmates access to telephones for up to 300 minutes a month, guarantees alternative religious diets, and mandates that prisoners be given daily exercise periods outside of their cells.

The lights were on twenty-four hours a day in Omar's cell. Three cameras filmed everything, and a corrections officer sat at a desk positioned just outside his glass partition. "I thought I was dreaming, that

I'd gone to hell," Omar said. He had to get out of there. He decided to go on a hunger strike until he was allowed to call counsel. The guards were unmoved. "The attorney general just signed a new law today," one told him. "We can keep you here as long as we like."

"I demand to know why I am here," he shouted. "You should know," the corrections officer shot back.

For the next ten days, Omar was not allowed out of his cell. His attorney, Fabacher, was being told that Pollock had no record of a Hady Hassan Omar. "I felt as though life stopped," said Omar. He kept having a recurring dream that his mother and little brother in Egypt were dead and that he was holding his daughter, Jasmine. He would wake crying and hide under his blanket so that the guards did not see.

The FBI returned a few days later with a consent form they wanted him to sign allowing the search of a crate of sample antiques he had received from Cairo and other effects in the apartment he had been staying at in Orlando. He signed the papers and again asked for a lawyer. A week later his request was granted—but only under the condition that his meetings with the attorney be monitored, another of the new antiterror regulations intended to prevent attorneys from passing on information from detainees to terror networks under the guise of attorney-client privilege. By the time Fabacher reached his client, it was too late to prepare for Omar's immigration hearing, which had been scheduled for October 2. The hearing was pushed back two weeks, which meant Omar would have to languish in jail. He made a crude calendar, as they do in prison movies, and started counting the days to freedom.

"I tried to sleep as much as possible to make the time go faster," Omar recalls. He did push-ups and sit-ups to try to keep fit, but his air-conditioned cell was so cold that he got the chills whenever he broke a sweat. They had turned off the hot water to his shower, so he had stopped bathing. He was not allowed to smoke in his cell. Pork was served at least twice a day. Still, his spirits were high. Fabacher was going to request a bond hearing to get him out on bail, and Omar had faith in the American system. "That's why I came to this country," he told me. Soon the judge at his hearing would realize that this was all a big mistake and he would be out of there.

He had a newfound desire to practice his religion, something that also seems to happen in the movies quite often. In reality, many terrorists were radicalized by stints in Saudi, Pakistani, or Egyptian jails. Just as some convicts go into prison as minor crooks and emerge as hard-core criminals, many dissidents in the more repressive Arab nations only gravitated to the more firebrand form of Wahabi or Deobandi Islam after the beatings and torture they endured at the hands of their captors. Omar was never physically tormented, but religion, he felt, was the reason he was being held, so naturally he turned to it. He tried to guess the correct hours for prayers by following the changing of the guards. They would congregate outside his cell and make faces whenever he tried to pray. So he prayed under his blanket.

On October 16, two days before his INS hearing, two FBI agents appeared. Omar recognized one as the polygraph technician from Little Rock. They wanted to know about his financial affairs; around that time, the hunt for al Qaeda had shifted to tracing the money trail. For over four hours, they pored over his banking and credit card statements. Omar was questioned about every deposit, withdrawal, and major purchase he'd made since coming to America and asked about the nature of the antiques business he wanted to start.

Again he was shown photographs of the hijackers and Osama bin Laden, and asked if he recognized any of them. "Sure," Omar said, pointing to bin Laden. The agents pounced. "Where do you know him from?" "Television," Omar answered.

He would have to submit to another lie detector test, he was informed. It was similar to the one he'd taken in Fort Smith, but now included questions about whether he had ever lied on INS application forms or was currently married to Candy.

The results of the test were faxed to Washington. "D.C.'s not happy," the technician said when he returned. "The results are not conclusive." The exam was readministered, with the same result. "We have to send for a specialist," the technician said.

The specialist arrived from Houston the following day, lugging a latest-generation digital polygraph machine that was hooked up to a laptop computer that could send data directly to Washington.

By this time, Omar could recite the questions by rote. But Washington still was not satisfied. "You didn't fail, but you didn't pass," he was told. One answer in particular kept coming up as inconclusive. And it happened to be the most important one: "Do you know anyone in the picture [of the hijackers] shown to you?"

The specialist from Houston blew up. He leaned in so close that his nose was almost touching Omar's. "You know somebody," he shouted. "No," protested Omar. "Yes," the specialist yelled back. "I can see your mind on my [computer] screen."

Just as suddenly as he had flared up, the specialist adopted a softer tone. "We can help you," Omar remembered him saying, "if you help us. We can get you a new identity. We can get you money. You know there's a $25 million reward for Osama's capture. We can move you anyplace and protect Jasmine and Candy."

"I don't know anything," said Omar. The specialist abruptly got up. "Thank you for being honest with us," he said, though Omar could not tell if he was being facetious.

The next morning Omar's immigration hearing in Oakdale went surprisingly well. The judge seemed sympathetic, and ordered him released on the relatively low bond of $5,000. "I was so excited," Omar recalls. He ate his first complete meal in days, and cleaned his cell. He could barely sleep that night and woke early. Candy would be coming to collect him at the opening of business hours. He sat expectantly on his bunk, his few belongings in a neat pile. The hours passed: nine, noon, three in the afternoon, then four, and finally five. At six he finally called a prison administrator. The prosecutor had appealed his bond. Under the new antiterror measures, the Justice Department could overturn judges' decisions in "special interest cases."

Even a year later, Omar choked up when describing how he felt when he heard the news. He stopped eating. For sixty-eight hours he didn't touch food or drink. He was too weak to get out of bed, and determined to continue his hunger strike. The captain of the watch was finally summoned. He threatened to strap Omar to a gurney, put tubes up his nose, and force-feed him if necessary. Omar relented and ate some soup.

As the days passed, his mental and physical condition worsened. He was in a near-catatonic state. He couldn't tell the difference between day and night, weekdays and weekends. As the weeks passed, his depression grew deeper. He'd lost twenty pounds and developed bedsores. His limbs were swollen from inactivity. A second closed immigration hearing in mid-November had not gone well. The judge had been apologetic, but had said there was nothing he could do; the government had made the call.

Omar now hardly moved from his concrete bunk. His hair was greasy and he had stopped shaving. He was starting to look like those Taliban prisoners in Guantánamo, restricted to a prone position nearly twenty-four hours a day. "I thought I would have to stay in that room forever," he recalled.

Hope and dignity carry people through crises, and Omar was running out of both. His only solace now was prayer, always under his blanket so that he did not have to face the guards' ridicule. Of one thing he was certain: He would never leave this place or see his beautiful American wife again. His daughter would take her first steps, utter her first words, and grow up without him. No, he decided. If he could not be with her on her first birthday in December, life was not worth living. He couldn't take it any longer. He had decided to kill himself.

Suddenly everyone seemed very concerned. The warden visited and sent a psychiatrist. The FBI man came and kept asking if he was serious about suicide. They could probably tell he had reached the end of his rope. And maybe, in the end, that was what saved him.

There are many ways to break a man, to make sure he is not holding anything back. Violence may be the quickest method, but it is not necessarily the most effective. To be absolutely certain that someone is telling the truth, you have to crush his spirit. It's impossible to say precisely why the authorities finally decided that Omar had been telling the truth. One senior law enforcement official in Washington did, however, agree to share a theory on the condition that neither his name nor the agency he worked for be revealed.

"If your subject has a complete breakdown," he said, "the barriers to resistance are lessened. Once a person is at that point, he's lost the will to deceive, and you can be pretty certain that he's not lying."

Omar had passed his final test. On November 20 he was told to get his stuff together. "Do you want to go home?" a cheerful INS official asked. Three days later he was with Candy on the freeway, driving to Arkansas to see his daughter. He had been in captivity for seventy-three days. No charges were ever filed against him.

Of the 762 people like Omar detained during the 9/11 investigation on immigration violations, not a single one turned out to have any links to terrorism. A June 2003 report by the Justice Department's own inspector general, Glenn A. Fine, found Ashcroft's enforcement of immigration laws "indiscriminate, and haphazard." The report noted "significant problems" in the way the INS and FBI arrested and treated the detainees, a number of whom, it said, were physically and verbally abused. The report also criticized the Justice Department for making no effort to distinguish between legitimate terrorist suspects and innocent individuals who simply got caught up in the sweep.

"Essentially," said Robert Rubin, an attorney for the Lawyers Committee for Civil Liberties, a nonprofit San Francisco rights group that has taken over Omar's case, "the Justice Department operated under the premise that everyone was guilty until proven innocent. And that's fundamentally un-American."

For Hady Hassan Omar, the ordeal did not end with his release. He and Candy were broke; they had been forced to sell their car and furniture and move in with Candy's father, a postal worker. Many of their friends had deserted them. Employment prospects for Omar were bleak: He was fired by his pre-9/11 employer, and the only work he could find was volunteering for a charity for disadvantaged children. And worst of all, as of January 2004, the government was continuing deportation proceedings against him. "After putting Hady and his family through hell," said Rubin, "instead of apologizing, it's as if the government is now spitefully trying to punish him by breaking up his family. That, too," he added, "is not the American way."

As Omar's case graphically showed, there would be human costs to the new counterterror effort. Freedom had a price, and some people were going to have to pay for the rest of us. Much as I grew to like Omar as a person—he was bright, good-natured, and not bitter—and much as I sympathized with him as a victim, I didn't necessarily blame the Justice Department for its actions. At the time, given the context of what was at stake in September 2001, the steps taken by the FBI and attorney general appeared reasonable. Tens of thousands of people were not arrested, as I'm sure would have been the case in European countries such as France, had al Qaeda aimed passenger planes at Paris rather than Manhattan. None of the detainees had been tortured, although some documented cases of mild physical and verbal abuse would be uncovered by the inspector general at the Brooklyn detention center. But given the anguish and anger that gripped the nation, the guards generally showed restraint. The scope of the entire detention operation was also relatively restrained for a nation with nearly 300 million inhabitants. It was not a repeat of the Japanese internments. All in all, it could have been much worse.

But a dangerous legal precedent had been set. The state, during times of emergency, could henceforth lock people up at will, deny due process, and throw a sanctioned veil of secrecy over the entire process. What implications would this have if there was another 9/11, an attack that resulted in even greater casualties? Next time would the numbers of those detained swell proportionally? Could, in the name of national security, a hundred thousand immigrants be locked up? What if some of the terrorists were recruited from the African American Muslim community? According to *Foreign Affairs* magazine, al Qaeda has identified African American Muslims, particularly those in prisons, where the teachings of Islam are mixed with violent gang culture, as a potential talent pool. Majid Khan, the al Qaeda operative who had intended to blow up dozens of gas stations in Baltimore, had sought to find disaffected African Americans to do the deed. Had he been successful, the profile of potential terrorists could span millions of people. Once the cat was out of the bag, where did one draw the line? "History has shown," warned Cole, the Georgetown law professor, "that many repressive regimes begin by targeting immigrant outsiders, then minorities, and in time the general population."

There was one other dangerous precedent of the 9/11 roundup: secrecy. It was understandable that the dragnet was conducted quietly. But now, almost three years later, the Justice Department was still refusing to disclose the names of those involved. National security could reasonably be invoked during the operation. But two and a half years later, the detainees were all free. The overwhelming majority were no longer in the country; the Justice Department had chartered commercial jets to deport them together in large groups as soon as they were released. What was the harm in disclosing their identities now? If any had been sleepers, al Qaeda long knew their cover had been blown. But in 2004 the attorney general's office was fighting court orders to release the names of 9/11 detainees. And why was the government persisting in its efforts to expel the handful of ex-detainees like Omar still in the country? Was it because they were an embarrassment that needed to be silenced? Were the authorities invoking secrecy to cover up cases of incompetence or clear violations of the law? Would secrecy and national security henceforth become a counterargument to accountability?

These were indeed serious issues that ran against the grain of how

America defined itself. Fortunately, they seemed more of an aberration caused by anxiety and overreaction than the new norm. And they had some traditional remedies. Omar and the unfortunate Canadian apprehended in transit at JFK and sent by mistake to Syria's torture chambers for ten months were both suing the federal government for damages. Now that, at least, was very American.

TERRORIST GAMES

Don't be afraid . . . BE READY.

—*Department of Homeland Security website*

challenges and fresh dilemmas for our leaders that cannot wait until the Supreme Court justices lay down the law. As new terrorist scenarios arise, as new extremists crawl out of some cave brandishing new vehicles for mass murder, the government will have to react—and possibly overreact—quickly. On a moment's notice Washington may be compelled to quarantine millions of people, deny basic freedom of movement, ground all aviation again, seal borders, close interstate traffic, shut down privately owned power or chemical plants, surround and detain everyone on a city block or in an entire neighborhood. On what legal grounds might the federal government justify any of these emergency measures?

These are questions that preoccupy leaders to a surprising degree. Every time the government raises the five-tier terror alert level, the lives of tens of millions of ordinary Americans are temporarily disrupted. Travel plans are altered and daily commutes disturbed. Hundreds of millions of tax dollars in extra security costs are racked up. And the financial markets jitter anxiously from the added stress of terrorist uncertainty.

The decision to raise the alert level is not one to be taken lightly, given the far-ranging implications of putting the entire nation on guard. And yet the administration has done so five times in the two years following the March 2002 introduction of the color-coded warning system, at a direct cost of over $5 billion (far more if macroeconomic implications of the added insecurity for the delicate recovery from recession are factored in). With each successive false alarm, criticism of the alert system mounted. Overreaction, panic, poor intelligence, and fear-mongering have all been blamed for the decisions to ratchet up security. How the government judges when a threat justifies going to code orange has become one of Washington's great mysteries, much debated by dubiously informed pundits and self-styled security experts on cable news networks. The process has been couched in the utmost secrecy, for obvious reasons, but that does not mean that there are no clues as to how the alert system works. A simulation of an emergency session of the National Secu-

5

THE THREAT MATRIX: EXECUTIVE DECISION

O MAR'S LAWSUIT AGAINST THE UNITED STATES GOVERN-
ment was just one of literally hundreds of legal assaults on the
counterterror measures implemented after 9/11. The suits ranged
widely from individual and class actions by 9/11 detainees, to petitions
under the Freedom of Information Act brought by media giants, to
constitutional challenges by civil liberties advocate groups such as the
American Civil Liberties Union or Omar's pro bono counsel, the San
Francisco–based Lawyers Committee for Civil Liberties. The cases all
had one common thread, however: They each sought to set legal limits on how far the government could take antiterror measures. For victims like Omar, there was also a cathartic element to having their day
in court. "You know," he said, "after we filed suit, and the local press
wrote about it, people came up to me on the street, saying 'I heard
what they did to you, it's terrible.' For the first time in months I was
able to hold my head up high. Friends who had refused to talk to me
since my arrest called to say they were sorry, that they had jumped to
the wrong conclusion. It's really given me hope again."

The larger issue, of course, is that the United States should not
erode basic freedoms in the name of defending freedom from terrorism. Ultimately it will be for the courts to decide how to strike a balance between security and liberty. Case by case the Supreme Court
will rule on the limits of the government's counterterror powers. This,
however, will take time—years in some cases, as the wheels of justice
grind slowly. Meanwhile the threat of terror will continue to pose new

rity Council offered one behind-the-scenes glimpse at the mysterious inner workings of the process that went into terror alert hikes. The drill, organized by the Center for Strategic and International Studies at a secure facility just outside the capital, provided a rare chance to answer some of the questions plaguing the color-coded system: what criteria trigger the heightened alerts or determine when it is safe once again to stand down; how much the reliability of intelligence plays into the final decision-making process; how closely economic impacts factor into the equation; and how widely information needs to be shared. The exercise was meticulously planned and at times chillingly realistic. It has never been made public before, and CSIS allowed me to reproduce it only on the condition that the names of participants be kept secret and that the text be vetted for security reasons. With the exception of CSIS employees, participants are identified only by their cabinet position titles, and some details of the game, such as the real names of targets and sites, are deleted. The simulation paints an unusually candid picture of just how dauntingly difficult the president's job can be.

"Mr. President." The deputy director of the Central Intelligence Agency stood up. "Our review of all source intelligence reporting over the past few days leads us to conclude that elements of al Qaeda are planning to carry out a major terrorist attack in the United States."

A hush fell over the dimly lit conference room at Andrews Air Force Base. Outside, Secret Service details secured the president's plane, while F-15s took off noisily to patrol the twenty-three-mile no-fly zone around the White House. But inside the soundproof chamber there was only an expectant silence as the CIA man continued his emergency briefing.

"Three days ago a walk-in to the embassy in Kuala Lumpur, who claims to be a member of a local Jemaah Islamiyah cell tied to al Qaeda, said that a Saudi who had fought in Afghanistan left Malaysia for the U.S. in early January. The Saudi told his fellow militants that he would be avenging the deaths of his brothers in Afghanistan and that February 4, 2003, would be a date that will be remembered."

He paused to survey the nineteen senior officials seated around the octagonal conference room table. They wore dark suits and dead-serious expressions. He had their attention. The walk-in, he elaborated, had failed a polygraph test, but his information jibed with a recent report by the Russian Federal Security Service that Chechen al Qaeda fighters departed the Pankisi Gorge in Georgia in early January on their way to the United States to "conduct martyrdom operations." Pakistan's Directorate for Inter-services Intelligence had provided the CIA with similar information from interrogations of recently captured al Qaeda operatives in Karachi that pointed to plans for an attack at unspecified economic targets in the eastern United States on that day.

"The day before yesterday," the deputy director continued, "a CIA clandestine source in Indonesia with access to a participant in a meeting of elements of Jemaah Islamiyah in central Java reported that an associate of Jemaah Islamiyah's leader Abu Bakar Basir said that an event would soon occur that will 'turn out the lights in the land of the infidel.' All this leads us to conclude," he summarized, "that (1) al Qaeda is planning a large-scale and coordinated attack in the eastern U.S., very likely targeted at multiple energy-related targets, and (2) the date of the attack would appear to be February 4, 2003."

Once again the room fell silent. The chairman of the Joint Chiefs of Staff and the FBI director exchanged an anxious glance. In the exercise, February 4 was two days away. They had less than forty-eight hours to prevent the next 9/11.

Thus was the die cast for an ambitious terrorist drill simulating an emergency session at the White House war room. Over two days, a group of seventeen men and two women—all current and former senior national officials—would test their decision-making skills in an exercise of what was called "prevention response consequence management." The clock would be ticking in real time, and they would be fed information sparingly. Tempers would flare, and factions would form. Interagency rivalries would surface and boil over. The game, in short, provided about as close a vantage point as an outside observer could get to actually sitting in on an emergency meeting of the National Security Council with the president and his key advisors. In the game, which was staged in October 2002, over a dozen prominent officials, many of them household names, role-played the membership and staff of the National Security Council. Also present was a former state governor as well as experts from the uppermost ranks of the military, intelligence, and law enforcement communities.

The floor was turned over to Phil Anderson, a retired Marine with a Ph.D. who had devised the exercise. It was his job to feed the assembled politicians with just enough information to narrow the search and force the president to make executive decisions.

"Good evening, ladies and gentlemen," he began. "I'm deputy director of critical infrastructure protection at the Department of Homeland Security. The brief you are about to receive comes as a result of thirty-six hours of research and analysis conducted by the counterterrorism working group. Based on available intelligence from all sources, and the best available information on relevant infrastructure, we've developed a threat vulnerability integration matrix that I will walk you through."

For the next hour Anderson went through the types of weapons terrorists could use, possible modes of delivering the weapons, and the exhaustingly long list of potential targets. Using a complex matrix that assigned numerical values to the destructive capabilities of various weapons and the relative vulnerability of different targets, the list was slowly whittled down to hijacked trucks and charter aircraft and chemical and energy facilities on the East Coast: 43 nuclear power plants, 7 refineries, 50 liquid natural gas/liquid petroleum gas storage facilities, 110 pipelines and petroleum terminals, 1,400 chemical operations, and 25 dams—some 2,000 potential targets.

"Aviation," Anderson concluded, "thus represents the highest risk among the attack means, while chemical operations, and in some specific cases, liquid petroleum gas, liquid natural gas storage operations, and nuclear power plants are the highest-risk targets. Ladies and gentlemen, that concludes my brief."

There was a slight pause while everyone digested this. Were they even on the right track? "What gives you confidence that it is the energy sector that is being targeted?" asked the president, turning to his CIA director. "If we're shaky on the intelligence to begin with, how do we rope off one area and say it's likely to be energy?"

The official playing the director of intelligence had actually served as an associate director at the Agency. "Well, I think that this is a good starting place," he said. "But I would point out that walk-ins come and go every day with varying amounts of credibility. This person may have been run as a blind. This could be an effort at denial, disruption, and deception. That has to be factored in. Mr. President, walk-ins can sometimes bring in gold and often bring in sand. In this case the walk-in failed. But there's other intelligence. Some of it that is corroborated with SIGINT and HUMINT says that something is going on right now, and rather than focus on a particular date, I think we have to understand that we're entering a period of greater tension. We know from their statements, we know from their interviews of captured al Qaeda that they have an interest in damaging the economic sector, but it is by no means limited to that. So it is that combination of things that raises our concern."

"What's been the state of public knowledge on this?" the president, played by a seasoned politician, wanted to know. "Has there been any news articles, any leaks?"

"So far on specific intelligence there have been no leaks," the director of intelligence assured him. But they would not be able to keep it secret long. "If we're talking of having to protect more than two thousand potential targets in the next forty-eight hours," someone said, "we're going to have to bring in a lot more help than this."

"Are you recommending to me that we protect two thousand targets and ignore everything else?" the president demanded of his national security advisor.

"Mr. President, we're still in the situation of saying do we have enough confidence in what we know to order protective action? And if we do think we have to order protective action, what is it we're gonna try to protect? And do we have enough of a consensus on at least a strategy about protection? I must say I'm getting worried. I'm not sure how we proceed."

"So what do we do?" the president asked the FBI director, role-played by a former top FBI official. "I think we take the matrices they've given us," said the head of the FBI, "and begin to work on that as rapidly as we can within the next twelve hours or fifteen hours and then make our best guess as to where it's going."

"That means the energy sector then?"

"I would think so," answered the FBI man. "Yeah, that's where it's pointing."

"What do we do to our economy if we notify and nothing happens?" the president persisted. "Four days from now we get another threat, we notify, nothing happens. Ten days, two weeks, we notify, nothing happens. What do we do to our economy?"

Someone suggested declaring the alert as a training exercise to prevent panic. "I like that idea," said the president. The chairman of the Joint Chiefs, played by a well-known retired four-star general, agreed. "Well, first of all, I think the exercise idea is a great idea and this could be the first in a series of exercises to answer your question, Mr. President, about what happens if they do this again to us two weeks from now or four weeks from now."

But the one state governor present didn't seem to be on board. "Mr. President," he said, "I was a little startled a few moments ago about how casually the idea was dismissed of the notification of the proper authorities."

"Governor," snapped the president, "can you assure me that if we decide for this evening that we do not want this to go out, the whole information to be leaked out, that if we notify the governors it will not leak out? I seem to recall there was a major hemorrhage in California." Everyone laughed at the reference to Gray Davis's holding a hysterical press conference about California's bridges coming under attack.

"You would tell them everything we know about the threat even though it's vague, even though we're not sure of it?" the president pressed on. "Well, of course," replied the governor. "I can think of no other responsible course."

"Mr. President," interjected the attorney general (a former senior Justice Department official), visibly aghast, "I think that if we do that on every threat we have for the next twenty years, I think we're going to have our economy so shot we will neither have security nor an economy."

"Good point," said the president, looking grave. "When do we let the general public know? Do we go to a higher state of alert? Do we announce that? What is my public communication advice?"

"I believe that it is appropriate for us to be considering a higher overall alert situation with respect to the five-color tier system run by the secretary of homeland security," said the CIA director.

"What level do you recommend?" asked the president, turning to the homeland security secretary. "I am recommending that we take the energy sector to a severe risk," said the secretary, who in fact was one of the top people at the Department of Homeland Security. "And leave the aviation sector where it is, at code orange."

"Is there any disagreement with that recommendation?" asked the president, glancing around the table. A suggestion was made to put an air cap around all nuclear facilities, creating no-fly zones. "Tell me," asked the president, "what is this going to do to civil aviation?"

"Well," said the homeland security czar, whose day job made him something of an expert on the subject, "civil aviation would simply not be allowed to enter that temporary flight-restricted space."

"What do we have in place right now," asked the president, "if you go out and get on a private aircraft at a terminal, to make sure you're not a terrorist and taking over that plane? What kind of procedures do we have right now?"

"We have a set of voluntary controls on the part of the pilot and the owner to make sure his aircraft is controlled not only when it's on the ground, but as it relates to the passengers and cargo—" the DHS official began, only to be interrupted by an incredulous commander in chief. "No detection device . . . no detection device at all," the president said, clearly shocked.

"Only—only a very minimal set of inspectors are going around and checking on that," the secretary of homeland security answered somewhat sheepishly.

"No guards out there to protect against somebody coming in with machine guns?" the president repeated, stunned.

"Only when the owner has stood up for that locally," said the homeland security official.

"I find this absolutely unacceptable," said the president, his voice rising. "I don't see how you can basically say you are gonna have these things people go through when they get on Delta Airlines, and United, but they don't do any of that if they are wealthy enough to fly on a general aviation aircraft."

"It's all about resources, Mr. President."

The president shook his head in disbelief. There was some murmuring around the table. "What if an aircraft strayed into the protected air space?" someone asked. Would it be shot down? The chairman of the Joint Chiefs fielded that question. "It depends on how far away you can get the aircraft, what the flight time is, how quickly you can get it up there."

One airport was in the flight path of a certain nuclear power station, the man playing the energy secretary remarked. (He had high-level Energy Department experience.) Would the home of all East Coast shuttles need to be closed too? "Absolutely," he was told. At this stage, the president, who had been shaking his head morosely, began to lose patience. "Gentlemen," he interrupted loudly. "I say to all here, we cannot slam down our economy every time we have an alert. These things could go on and on and on and on. We may be in this for twenty or thirty years. We've got to lay down ground rules here that make sense for security but also balance security and the economy. I'm not hearing that kind of balance."

The outburst did not intimidate his national security advisor, an old hand at many real-life emergency NSC meetings. "May I ask," he demanded, "what is it that we tell governors to do on the ground? I mean, stop all oil tankers that are coming within three miles of a nuclear power plant? What do we tell them to do? That's what I'm trying, I'm trying to operationalize this exercise that we say we want to have. We've never done anything of this scale before. We've got two thousand things we're going to try to protect in the next forty-eight hours. So what are we telling them to do? I'm very concerned we're issuing a directive that's not executed."

"You mean nobody in our government has ever even put on a piece of paper a plan for an exercise of protecting a sector of critical infrastructure?" asked the president, his anger mounting. "My national security advisor is telling me there's nothing in writing. No plan, nothing to talk about. Is that what I'm hearing?"

Tension rose in the room, as many of the president's advisors shifted uncomfortably in their seats. A lengthy discussion followed, with the president and his national security advisor hammering at each other.

"I want a plan on this by tomorrow morning," the president finally snapped. "I want to see a plan as to what impact it would have if you restrict airspace over every power plant. What is that going to do to commercial aviation, to civil aviation? I have to have a way to balance the economic and the security aspects. And that's what I'm frustrated about tonight because we all are talking about security. And that's *fine*. But this may be one of many alerts and we have to balance the economic part of it. And I'd like to have a better communication plan, including whether the president goes on television, or the director of homeland security, and notifies people. And what's going to be said about it? Who's going to be the spokesman?"

Now the debate really heated up. No one favored telling all fifty governors of the threat warning that night because, as one official put it, "It would be in the papers tomorrow morning." The FBI director was ordered to put all his agents out in the field, canvassing all night if necessary for leads of the impending plot. But that raised another problem. How could the FBI do this without tipping off local law enforcement that something major was afoot? It was decided that some public announcement needed to be made at 10:00 A.M. the next morning, because the story would not hold. But no one at the White House wanted to go out on a limb with the general public and be made to look foolish if the alert was a false alarm. The issue of whether to call the alert an exercise was revisited. If the ruse was exposed, warned the FBI deputy director, "your credibility with the American people, Mr. President, is shot. And besides," he added, with agents rousting people out of bed all over the country, "how long do you think that exercise scam would work? About twenty minutes."

At this point the FBI director leaned over to whisper something in his deputy's ear. "He just told me I was transferred to Alaska," said the deputy to general guffaws. When the laughter subsided, he continued. "Go out front, Mr. President, go out front with the information you have. Treat it as routine. This is one of many threats, we've handled these in the past. It's important, though, that your best assessment is we have a threat here. Or we sit on our hands and we react. And then people, the intelligence community and the American public, will say, 'You had this information, why didn't you do something? What did you do? You ran an exercise as a scam to try to jack up the energy people. Why didn't you tell them?'"

The president mulled this over. "We're not going to call it an exercise," he finally said. "We're going to go straightforward and do all the things we would do in the energy sector at this alert level. And yet it could just as easily be the banking sector, it could be Wall Street, it could be telecom, it could be transportation, it could be anything. I'd like to have better intelligence."

"Absolutely," said the CIA director. "Mr. President, you're right. There is a bit of purporting toward the energy sector, but there is again [intelligence], back to the strategic threat that points to symbolic targets, to transportation targets, energy targets which have been on the list for a long time and take new importance in the face of the events in Iraq and the threat of public venues that we've been worrying about."

"Would you bet your job that if we were going to have an attack in the next forty-eight hours, it is going to be on the energy sector?" snapped the president. "No, sir," said the CIA man, looking abashed.

"Mr. President," the national security advisor interjected, "this economy is right on the edge of tipping back into a recession. And we're talking about taking us to a level that's going to be very disquieting. I just have to say, I think we have to be much more careful about giving a very broad and general warning that's going to be misunderstood if we can't get a better focus on what we're trying to warn people about. If it isn't the energy sector, then maybe we're forced to that. But I—just to go out and tip five or six sectors into a high state of frenzy is going to be a real problem."

The meeting broke up for the evening with strict admonitions from the president for the FBI and CIA to put their differences aside and work together through the night to shore up intelligence on the veracity of the threat. When the meeting was reconvened the next morning, the FBI director had news: "Mr. President, we received specific information this morning at five o'clock from a twenty-three-year-old Somali student being interviewed down in southern Virginia that there is an intent to attack a chemical company in Virginia on February 4, employing a petroleum tanker truck. He has not been polygraphed as of this time, but it's very specific target news and information."

"What's our confidence level in the source?" asked the president.

"That again is a result of an interview," said the head of the FBI. "He also admitted, by the way, admitted general knowledge of other attacks against other energy or energy-related facilities in Virginia."

"Do you have a high confidence that the source is reliable?" the president repeated. "Let me put it this way," his FBI director responded. "We went out to get this last night and we got it this morning. It is not complete. The CIA may have other information. We're just trying to evaluate in light of what we know is an imminent fourth of February attack. We'll continue to develop information with that informant, Mr. President. The deputy director of the FBI will brief you on the potential impact of the attack."

The deputy director had to shout to be heard over the commotion in the hall. Everyone was speaking at once, as a large map of Virginia was projected on the wall, showing the military installations nearby. "Mr. President, as the director has advised you, let me show you a graph of the location and the potential damage of a chemical release over this area. This is a graph of the prevailing wind from the southwest from a chlorine chemical plant in this area. The bulk of the military installations are approximately in this area, and this is a likely area of contamination from one breach of a chemical rail tanker." He pointed at the ominous plume that had been superimposed on the map.

"What's the lethal rate radius out there?" asked the chairman of the Joint Chiefs. "Is that a lethal contamination? Everybody in that zone is killed?"

"General," said the FBI deputy director, "we think that based on the wind model we have absolutely validated two miles, which would be about here. We have 26.3 parts per million at ten kilometers, which is probably lethal and potential lethality here, out to twenty kilometers based on the model we have on chlorine."

The national security advisor's hand shot up. "I have a question about the modus operandi," he said. "It was to be a petroleum tanker truck. What was the target of the truck? Was it another tank truck or railroad car filled with chlorine, or was it some fixed facility?"

"I have no information on that, sir," said the FBI briefer. "Okay, fine," said the national security advisor, turning to the governor of Virginia. "Governor, what can we do to prevent the attack?"

"The best move," replied the man (played by a former governor), "would be to alert the Guard and place the Guard in a perimeter around the facility, with state police and shooters inside, and then to notify local law enforcement so they can begin to watch the adjoining transportation networks. I don't think we need any federal intervention."

"Let's hear from the secretary of defense," said the national security advisor. "We can't have all this military equipment and the people sitting there and have them subjected to this plume."

"Can you move them out without causing panic in the whole area?" asked the president.

"We can't move them out without everyone knowing that we're doing it," the secretary of defense conceded. "We could do it secretly in the sense of what the reasoning is. We have a war we're worrying about in Iraq. So we've got pretext."

"I agree," said the president. "But do it in a way that relates to the overall, so that unless we're planning to evacuate everyone in the area, we gotta be careful how we move them."

"I have a really serious concern about this," said the FEMA director (played by a man with high-level FEMA experience), speaking up for the first time. "If this is that much of a credible threat, and we've already got the plume model, what's the populace in that plume that should be notified to be evacuated, then, because somebody in the media is going to pick this up. And I think what you're talking about, you've got to evacuate them. You're going to have panicked folks around there."

The governor agreed. "We have to think very seriously about notifying people in that area."

"I think, Governor," said the president, "we need to be thinking about all this, but I want to get back to what the national security advisor said. I think we need to work on prevention as much as we possibly can. That ought to be our first focus. And in the meantime we will. I'd like to have questions like, What gives you the confidence that you can have a big wind shift. This plume could change dramatically. It seems to me you have to wait until a little bit more timely information comes in to even determine where you would evacuate."

At that moment, an aide rushed in to brief the assemblage on another troubling development. A second suspected terrorist had been apprehended that morning, this time in New Jersey. He was a Pakistani chemical engineer. So far he had not confessed to anything other than being "a candidate for martyrdom." Given recent developments and specific new information that multiple chemical facilities were going to be hit in less than thirty-five hours, the decision needed to be made whether to ground all aircraft.

"Well, General," said the president, addressing his chairman of the Joint Chiefs. "You've heard everything I've heard here. You've heard the intelligence. You've heard the update on intelligence. What do you recommend? What are you recommending?"

"Shut down general [private] aviation along the East Coast and in the area along the Gulf Coast, in the areas where we think the highest concentration of targets is. Shut it down for a period of three to five days. If we look at the air cargo flights, and if we put the air marshals on, we can prioritize this so some critical air cargo flights in these eight, nine states can continue. If we increase the air marshal program on the commercial flights on the East Coast and we shut off the air cargo coming from abroad, our flights can still exit. We don't want foreign carriers bringing their cargo."

"What's the economic effect of that?" the president wanted to know. There was a long pause. "Come on," he demanded. "Who knows?"

"I don't think we're capable of quantifying the degree of granularity you'd like, Mr. President," said the director of the National Economic Council, played by one of President Bush's senior advisors.

"So I'm being asked to take an action here to shut down all general aviation and I have no idea what the economic effect is?"

One of the NEC aides stood up to give a lengthy analysis of the economic impact. "The airline industry spends around $340 million a day. The direct cost of the four-day halt in operations after 9/11 was $1.36 billion," he explained. "If you add on the cargo, that gets up to about $5 billion for a four-day shutdown."

He went on to provide a detailed overview of the contribution of energy on the East Coast economy. "Our analysis encompasses seventeen states from Maine to Florida, plus the District of Columbia. The total population of this region is 101 million, and 37 percent of the United States. Four-fifths of the population lives in urban areas. The total gross state product in 2000 was $3.9 trillion. This represents 39 percent of total U.S. output. The region is a net consumer of energy, consuming and importing approximately 30 percent more energy than it produces. Over half of the energy use is for industry and transportation," he said. New Jersey, New York Harbor, the Delaware River, and Philadelphia regions were target-rich environments, containing eleven of the sixteen refineries on the Eastern Seaboard and processing 10 percent of U.S. distillate daily. One refinery in the New York–New Jersey area had among the largest fluid catalytic cracking (processing) units in the world and processed close to 50 percent of the area's distillation capacity. It also had a huge storage tank of anhydrous ammonium. The facility was strategically near a New York–New Jersey international airport and within close proximity of major New York–New Jersey road arteries.

The president interrupted him. "That's not what I asked. Do we have no economic analysis at all about the effect of shutting down [general] aviation? Because I haven't heard any response to that one."

The aide stammered. "If the answer is no," snapped the national security advisor, "somebody say so, and we'll move on."

"I think the answer is no," conceded the aide in a defeated tone.

"I'd like to hear from the secretary of homeland security and what his recommendation is," said the president. "Do you agree with the chairman of the Joint Chiefs?"

The secretary pondered for a moment. "My counsel is this, sir. Everything the chairman talked about is a normal part of the step from yellow to orange, with the exception of shutting down all of general aviation. That's normally something that we would consider at the red condition alert level. In this instance, given the threat, I agree with the chairman that we should. My counsel to you is to shut down general aviation."

"Okay," said the president. "I'm going to make this decision based on the recommendation of the secretary of homeland security and the chairman of the Joint Chiefs. But I want it to be noted in the future that I've got no economic impact whatsoever. I have no earthly idea of what I'm doing in terms of what its effect is on the economy. My press secretary is going out in fifty-eight minutes and that will be the first question asked if we make this announcement. Let's tentatively plan to shut it down at noon and that will give us two, three hours," he added. "And we will not announce it at the ten o'clock press conference because we may want to alter the plan."

A second decision now needed to be made. The National Guard was to be deployed around the chemical plant in Virginia. But should governors all along the East Coast be notified to take similar steps, and should the road and rail shipment of all chemicals be halted?

"Mr. President," said the national security advisor, "if I may say, I don't think we need to stop the chemical industry in its tracks. The salient threat is railroad cars or tank trucks filled with hazardous chemicals at *fixed* locations. When they're moving, they're a lot harder to hit, whether you're trying to run a business jet into them or shoot them with an RPG [rocket-propelled grenade]. And where they're at the facilities themselves, it's my understanding that the chemicals are largely stored underground. It's these tank trucks and railroad cars where they are standing still for a substantial period of time that, experts tell me, is the major problem. And protecting those areas from anybody getting close to them with RPGs or truck bombs or anything else. It seems to me, that is the issue."

"It seems to me," said the president, "that you're assuming the people driving those trucks are good guys. How do we know that a bad guy hasn't already gotten into possession of a truck?"

"Sir," said the FBI deputy director, "we need to stay focused on what the facts are. The facts are that we have a potential threat down in one chemical plant. We need to work to find out if this plot is true and whatever other plans were in the works."

"Mr. President," interjected the national security advisor. "Based on some earlier experience, I would just caution everyone not to expect too much from intelligence in this area. I would suggest that as we get a report from the Department of Homeland Security on the precise types of steps we would recommend to the governors, that we be alert to particularly the possibility of needing to go out to a number of other governors on the East Coast."

The president agreed, and the homeland security secretary was told to prepare the report ASAP. "Mr. President." The national security advisor looked uncharacteristically uncertain. "Ah. Um, there's an added point which I think is a little sensitive but, given the emergency that we are in, I feel obligated to bring it up. When I travel these days, I feel that the one threat that is clearly under scrutiny by airport employees is grandmothers with nail files. Ah, we've got that threat knocked. But with respect to young men, who are after all highly likely to be the instruments of terror here, particularly young men from the Middle East, um, there has been a certain understandable political correctness that has crept into our behavior over the course of a year and a half now since 9/11. I would suggest that in an appropriate way, this political correctness be *suspended* and that the National Guard and the police who are looking for infiltrators, car bomb drivers and the like, at these facilities over the course of the next several days be told to focus specifically, as much as possible, on young men, particularly any that may be from the Middle East. I think it is time, given that kind of plume of chlorine gas, I think it is time to suspend political correctness."

There was a murmur in the room, people whispering to one another. "Mr. President," the attorney general jumped in. "Let me underscore the value of that advice and the legal appropriateness of it. Ah, the terms 'discrimination' and 'profile' have become dirty words in our popular lexicon. The fact of the matter is that the way a law enforcement officer or other person exercising your national security authority discriminates between those persons who represent danger and those who don't is based in part on profile. We ought to recognize that fact and have the political will to act on it."

"Is this a permanent recommendation, or are you saying for the next three days?" asked the president. "Well, let's worry about the next three days now, would be my suggestion, sir," answered the attorney general. "Then we'll see how, if that pushes the ball toward where we need it to be on a permanent basis."

Now it was the national security advisor's turn to interrupt. "It seems to me that we are in a *desperate* situation here and in a war to try to save hundreds of thousands of lives from an event such as this, and it is time to do what is effective."

"That goes to my point, if I may finish, Mr. President," said the attorney general. The room was dead quiet, everyone intently listening. "Ah, we need the Bureau [FBI] and the Agency [CIA] to give us that profile so that we can make the maximum use of the Guardsmen that the governor is willing to deploy and frankly put in harm's way so that they know what they are being asked to do and what they're being asked to look for."

The president soaked this in. "Are there any other views on this subject specifically?"

"A question and clarification," said the energy secretary. "We now have several intelligence reports that are traced to specific individuals of Middle Eastern origin. In sharing the profile of the individuals involved, it would presumably trigger a response that would result in profiling of all individuals of Middle Eastern origin, given the nature of the intelligence. And I'm wondering is there something generic beyond that that is being recommended here, Mr. President, directly."

"I would say," said the national security advisor, fielding the question, "that under the current circumstances, given the sources and given the information, it is perfectly understandable, indeed would be..." He paused. "It would be very much the right thing to do, to inform the state and local officials of the general characteristics and nature of the individuals involved in the threat. And that may suffice for right now. But I would, if we get through this all right, without chlorine gas drifting over the White House here, Mr. President, I would very much like for us to have a meeting sometime at your convenience to discuss the overall problem caused by political correctness."

The president pondered for a moment. These, after all, were explosive issues. "I'm willing," he finally said, "to take the intelligence reports we have and base our policies over the next several days on those reports, basically accepting the period of recommendation without changing a policy that needs more thought and is already on the way. So I'd say, let's go with the practical side of it now and target the individuals based on the intelligence we have."

As had happened in the days following 9/11, a frenzied sweep of immigrants of Middle Eastern origin was about to begin. But events were already overtaking the president's ability to control the situation. As they all had feared, word of the attacks had somehow leaked to the press. A cable news network had gotten wind of rumors that al Qaeda was targeting a nuclear power plant in the tristate region around Manhattan. An attack was imminent, the network reported, airing a video montage of an airplane smashing into the facility and a mushroom cloud rising. Panic had broken out in the community where the plant was located, and people were fleeing their homes. The panic had quickly spread to other bedroom communities and to some parts of Manhattan itself.

The president and his advisors watched the TV reports in horror. "Mr. President," said the FEMA director. "I don't believe that we can ignore this. You've got millions of people evacuating, clogging the highways. And in one county alone, you've got 35,000 schoolchildren, you've got all the nursing homes and hospitals that would have to be evacuated 'cause the fear factor is so great around that plant."

"What should we do?" asked the president. The FEMA director spoke deliberately. "I think—I think at this time, based upon what we're dealing with there, and also in Virginia, I would encourage you to field an emergency declaration for the protection of the public health and safety and support resources to each state that's impacted by this. And then activate the federal response plan team in Washington in the Emergency Operations Center so they can be ready to provide those resources."

The White House press secretary now spoke up for the first time. "I think," she said, addressing the president, "that at some point in the near future, the country will expect to hear from you, sir. This has now taken on a whole new dimension with people hearing reports that they know were from us, that they know that the National Security Council is in session, that there's been no word from the White House at all, except to confirm that there have been threats, and I think that we need to take this fully by—"

"I haven't heard any specific threat against this nuclear power plant," snapped the president, interrupting. "Let—let—let—let me just—let me just make it clear," he continued with uncharacteristic hesitation. "I think we are no longer responding to specific threats. We're responding to what the news media has put up as a threat. Perception has become reality. We're responding to the panic that's already taken place in New York, which is unfortunate, but is real and we're dealing with it. I think we need to go ahead and put into effect the air cap to the extent that need be over certain nuclear facilities, the ones we think are the most vulnerable on the East Coast. I believe we need to shut down general aviation and announce that for the next three days it will be shut down, or the next two days. I'll leave it up to the director of homeland security as to the time."

"May I ask one more question, sir?" said the White House press secretary. "These are the most, ah, serious steps the country has taken since 9/11. The first time we've shut down aviation since 9/11. The first time we've seen people fleeing in fear. Ah, do you want to announce these steps *yourself* and then turn it over to the secretary of homeland security and the attorney general to answer the questions?"

"No," said the president. "I'm not confident enough we're doing the right thing. I'd rather it be the secretary."

"I think it would be reassuring to the country at this point to see your face, and see you taking charge, and see you dealing with this problem," she pressed.

In the end, she succeeded in convincing the president to appear at the 10:00 A.M. press conference. His statement, carried live by all the television networks, was brief: "The United States and its intelligence agencies have received credible warnings that terrorists are planning to attack targets in the eastern United States sometime in the next several days. Some of the threats are general, some are specific, but we are taking them all seriously. Rest assured we are doing everything in our power to prevent any such an attack. First, let me emphasize there is no specific attack against nuclear facilities in New York, New Jersey, or Pennsylvania, or any nuclear facility anywhere in the nation. As a result of this information, I have directed the secretary of homeland security to elevate the threat level against chemical and petrochemical industries to threat level red. The rest of the country is being elevated to threat level orange, and we will work with state and local authorities to implement all necessary security measures. I have been in touch with a number of governors, including the governors of Virginia, New Jersey, and New York, and we will continue to work closely with state and local authorities as we work this out. In the meantime, we will try to provide as much information as possible to the media and the public, and in the meantime, I urge caution and calm throughout the country."

After the press conference, the president was visibly nervous. He had just gone out on a limb with the American public. What if he was wrong? "The credibility of the American government is at stake here," he lamented. "I'm going to ask the director of the CIA and the head of the FBI and homeland security [if they are satisfied with their] own intelligence now."

"There's analytical capability there, sir," answered the homeland security secretary. "We do not collect, by and large. We're into the analysis and dissemination."

The president pointed a finger at him. "Mr. Secretary, I'm going to ask you to stand behind it. The CIA and the FBI have been doing this for a long time. You're going to be reporting on their behalf, but it's going to be your credibility as well as mine."

"I understand, sir," said the DHS head in a low voice. Just then a flustered-looking aide dashed up to him, thrusting out a sheaf of documents. The homeland security secretary scanned the first page, his expression changing. "Mr. President," he said. "My staff has just advised me that a charter jet on an IFR flight plan from Detroit to Harrisburg, Pennsylvania, has disappeared off the radar while on descent. There's no further information at the moment, but Three Mile Island is right upriver."

6

TERRORIST GAMES: THE
FIRST RESPONDERS

HAD THE PRESIDENT SUCCESSFULLY FOILED THE ATTACKS? Or was the East Coast a post-apocalyptic contamination zone?

Phil Anderson, the in-house terrorist expert at the CSIS, was called on to outline the plot he had devised, which went something like this: A point man acting alone had set up a front company—a real estate investment trust—incorporating in Delaware, renting office space, hiring a secretary and a law firm to front for the company. The real estate investment trust claimed to be planning major housing developments in the United States and needed to survey building locations, conducting due diligence inspections. The point man established a pattern of chartering aircraft, typically from charter services based in Los Angeles, which has the highest density of walk-in charter companies. He did this over a period of months to build a credible business profile. When his credibility was firmly established, the front company contacted the air charter service, indicating that real estate site selection was narrowed to three possibilities—one in eastern Pennsylvania, one in western Maryland, and one in southern Virginia. To make the final choices, four six-passenger luxury jets would be rented for one day, with pickup in Atlantic City or in Detroit.

The terrorists would commandeer the planes and head for the targets. Target 1, which was to have been hit by two planes, was a huge refinery in the New York–New Jersey area. It distributes refined products to the East Coast via pipeline, produces hundreds of thousands of barrels per day, and has a multimillion-pound-per-year polypropylene plant. The refining complex also includes aqua ammonia chemical operations and is strategically close to New York City. The second target was a petroleum terminal. It was selected due to its proximity to Washington and the fact that its destruction could disrupt fuel flows along the East Coast. Target 3 was a chemical company in Virginia, which stores and distributes chlorine aqua ammonia, sulfur dioxide, EDA (ethylenediamine) and is strategically located.

The Three Mile Island and tristate nuclear power stations were never targeted because the hardened concrete containment chambers around the reactors are designed to withstand the impact of an aircraft. That the first hijacked charter flight crashed near Three Mile Island was merely a coincidence. The hijackers had simply lost control of the plane. The order to ground all aviation immediately had prevented the other three planes from taking off.

Luck had favored the fictional administration. Intelligence had been off by a critical twenty-four hours, since the strikes started on February 3, and if not for the fortuitous crash of the first jet, thousands of lives might have been lost. The other attacks were prevented, but at an enormous financial cost. For days the panic on the East Coast basically shut down the economy, and the net result was that the United States was once again plunged into recession. Al Qaeda had not managed to kill anyone, but the group had terrified 100 million people, set back the nation's economic recovery for the entire quarter, and disrupted commerce to the tune of tens of billions of dollars. As the president put it, it became an exercise of fear, where perception, for the public, was reality.

The exercise also exposed uncertainty over how well the Department of Homeland Security's alerting system worked, especially for the private sector and for state and local governments. "It's clear that that is a major problem that we have to work through," said John Hamre, the president of CSIS. "There was also clearly a tension at the table between the perspective of prevention and the perspective of consequence mitigation. As the president kept saying, we're in a twenty-year war and we're in the middle of a two-day fight. How do we not get pulled apart and jerked around by terrorists, who really can create all the damage they want by getting us to react to uncertainty? If their goal was disruption, they got us to do their work for them."

It was not just top-level Washington officials who were testing their limits through terror simulations. All across the country, during the eighteen months that followed the strikes on the Pentagon and World Trade Center, hundreds of drills were being conducted at all levels of government and law enforcement, covering a whole host of diabolical possibilities. Dirty-bomb simulations rained ersatz radioactive fallout on Baltimore and New York. Mock plague epidemics were let loose on Seattle and Chicago. Suicide bombings and smallpox exercises were staged in Los Angeles. Hijackings were rehearsed in Washington, D.C., and St. Louis, and Special Ops units stormed nuclear installations. The point of the rehearsals was to probe for weaknesses in the country's emergency response programs, to ensure that every contingency had been thought of beforehand and that the next time tragedy struck, we would be better prepared. "Don't be afraid . . . BE READY," extolled the banner headline of a new homeland security website unveiled as part of Tom Ridge's infamous duct-tape Get Ready program. "Make a Kit of Emergency Supplies. Make a Plan for what you will do in an Emergency. Be Informed About what Might Happen" counseled the ready.gov site, which included handy icons titled Biological Threat, Chemical Threat, Nuclear Blast, and Radiation Threat. Judging by the sudden surge in nationwide duct tape sales, a great many anxious Americans had taken the empowering advice to heart. Whether the preparations actually made anyone safer was a matter of some dispute, but at least they made citizens feel less helpless and provided the illusion that they were doing something to help protect themselves.

Many of the hundreds of terrorist drills being conducted throughout the United States in 2002–2003 had a similar placebo effect. Like ordinary citizens, local government officials needed to feel as if they were doing everything in their power to combat terror. Drills satisfied this need, particularly for the so-called first responders. First responders, as the name implies, are those who would respond first to any catastrophe, natural or man-made. They are police officers and firefighters, paramedics and physicians, hazardous material disposal teams and specialists from the Centers for Disease Control, National Guard units and SWAT teams, municipal maintenance workers and utility company employees, and various state and federal emergency management personnel. The list of players is as broad as their roles: to restore power or drinking water, to dispense medical attention and life-saving pharmaceuticals, to put out fires and dig for bodies through rubble, to cordon off areas and evacuate people—in short, to save lives and minimize the damage and suffering caused by any terror attack. First responders perform many of these duties on a daily basis: firefighters put out blazes; police officers respond to violent attacks; ambulance drivers rush victims to hospitals; municipal workers patch streets; and utility employees restore electricity after ice storms or hurricanes.

But rarely, if ever, are first responders all called on to do their jobs at the same time and on a massive scale that taxes all their resources, whether that means handling hundreds of dead or injured, marshaling dozens of ladder companies at once, or summoning an entire city's supply of ambulances. Such efforts require careful coordination, almost military precision, and rapid reaction. Yet there is no real way to prepare for tragedies on the scale of 9/11 or even the Oklahoma City bombing. First responders have to wait for terrorists to strike and then clean up the grisly mess afterward. If they die, as had many of those brave public servants responding to 9/11, they are immortalized as heroes. But otherwise they are largely ignored, underfunded, and unappreciated.

After 9/11, first responders throughout most major cities took it upon themselves to practice for the next terror strike. Either independently or with meager federal assistance, they devised various terrorist scenarios to test their response capabilities. Their training wasn't dramatic to observe; it didn't compete for the public's attention with military strikes on Afghan terror camps, or touch a national nerve the way expanded police powers did. First responders don't get a lot of press or hype, and so they don't receive a great deal of congressional funding. But if there ever is another 9/11, it will be anonymous firefighters and medics, unheralded beat cops and hazmat teams, and not the high-flying FBI or press-savvy homeland security officials who will come to our rescue. For this reason, their drills and preparations are as important to the overall homeland security effort as other initiatives that garner much more media attention. These are the public servants who will be called on to save our children, spouses, coworkers, and friends. I wanted to know if they would be up to the task, so when I heard of one such first-responder exercise in Denver, I asked for permission to observe.

We had been told to go to the Starbucks in Republic Plaza, at the foot of Denver's tallest office building, a gray granite tower that rose fifty-six stories against the mountainous backdrop of the Front Range. It was a little after seven on an overcast Sunday morning when I arrived, and already a dozen police officers were inside the coffee shop, outnumbering the patrons, who looked up from their newspapers with puzzled if somewhat sleepy expressions.

Scores of public safety officials were milling around outside, on the 16th Street promenade across from a big Barnes & Noble bookstore. They were distinguishable primarily by their uniforms: the blue-on-brown of the county sheriff's office, the red jumpsuits of the hazmat unit, white-shirted EMS paramedics, plainclothes Denver PD detectives in Day-Glo orange vests, and a visibly agitated SWAT commander in black military fatigues.

The square outside Republic Plaza continued to fill with a rainbow of official colors. A red fire truck pulled up, followed by an orange and brown one from the Denver FD. "What frequency are they on?" asked one firefighter from the suburban Arvada FD. "We don't have a frequency for them," said his colleague. "Do we go to channel 2 or 4?" another firefighter wanted to know. "No idea," someone shot back in frustration. "But we'll probably need to monitor [channel] 3 as well."

The confusion among the different fire brigades was palpable—and very realistic. At the World Trade Center and the Pentagon on 9/11, many of the first responders hadn't been able to communicate with one another. They had incompatible radio equipment and different service providers. Some operated at 800 megahertz, others didn't. Some used Nextel, while still others had short-range walkie-talkies. If the cops couldn't talk to the firefighters, and the firefighters from different counties could not communicate with one another, much less with the paramedics or SWAT units, vital information such as orders to evacuate a building in danger of collapse couldn't flow freely. Simulations like this were designed to flag such problems before they became life-threatening, as they had been on 9/11. Nor were tangled communications isolated to Denver or New York. Crossed wires were very much a nationwide issue. A report by the Council on Foreign Relations, one of the nation's most prestigious think tanks, had pegged the cost of implementing interoperable communications across the country at $7 billion over five years.

Interoperable communications were not solely to blame for some of the early confusion among first responders in Denver. To make the scenario more realistic, no one in the city had been told what this mock attack would entail. That would have precluded the element of surprise, which is among the most potent weapons in the terrorist arsenal. The fact that there were now four hundred first responders waiting within a few-block radius of the target already ate into the realism. To give away more would defeat the entire purpose of the war game. Only the make-believe terrorist had been issued detailed instructions, floor plans, and a script to follow, which included this reference in the equipment list: "Neon colored squirt gun (will be issued), nasty disposition."

Trouble was, the terrorists/actors—the SWAT team from the

nearby Rocky Flats nuclear facility—were a no-show, and last-minute stand-ins needed to be found. Lieutenant Frank Conner, who had painstakingly planned this exercise for months, was not pleased. In true Hollywood fashion, production was delayed while Conner, a former bodybuilder (the 1988 Mr. Denver, no less) patiently coached the replacements. Conner heads Denver's elite tactical SWAT unit. A short man with a kind, intelligent face, thin sandy hair, and an earnest smile that belied his deadly profession, he spoke in calm, even tones and might have passed for a high school chemistry teacher if not for his vein-bulging forearms and the quiet confidence that came from knowing that he was a veteran of many a bloody siege, including the tragedy at Columbine High School.

"Before 9/11," he explained, "almost all our emergency drills centered around natural disasters like tornadoes or avalanches. We in the police played a backup role in those events and needed to devise an exercise with the police department as a lead agency to practice our coordination abilities. So we cooked up this little scenario."

Conner had some experience with security planning; he had put together the security details during the pope's 1993 visit, the G-8 summit of leading industrialized nations in 1998, and the trial of Oklahoma City bomber Timothy McVeigh. But he'd never devised a terrorist scenario before, been forced to think on both sides of the law enforcement divide. It proved a tricky business, akin to playing chess against oneself: coming up with a strategy and then turning the tables and trying to defeat it with the next move. The lieutenant was thus understandably anxious that everything proceed according to plan, and already there was a glitch. Instead of the scripted eleven terrorists, he would have to make do with only six understudies.

At last, at 7:45 A.M. a welcomed announcement crackled over the police radios: "Be advised, the terrorists are in place. Repeat, the terrorists are in position." Finally everyone was ready. Coffee cups were put down, muscles tensed. Observers picked up their notepads, medics readied their stethoscopes. "Here we go," said C. L. Harmer, the mayor's press secretary.

A frantic 911 call formally launched the exercise. "Gunmen have entered the building," it began. "They're shooting with assault rifles. A number of people are bleeding, including the guards. The location is the Republic Plaza building on 370 17th Street."

At this stage, the Denver PD was to respond as if a routine bank robbery were in progress. A mobile command center was already set up a block away, on the corner of 16th and Broadway, and I wandered over to see what was going on. The street was lined with dozens of white Chevy Yukons and black Dodge Durangos. The big SUVs belonged to various SWAT units, whose guns, body armor, and cumbersome equipment were too heavy for the suspensions of most cars. FBI-issue blue Crown Victoria sedans occupied one corner of the street along with a large Ford F650 truck containing heavily armed Special Operations teams from nearby Jefferson County. It seemed as if every law enforcement agency in Colorado was waiting for the "bank robbers," and more Colt .45s and HK-53 assault rifles were being bandied about than I had ever seen in one place outside of the military. Of course, in a real scenario all these black-clad warriors would be off with their families on a Sunday, at church, picnicking, or sleeping off a hangover. Now their cell phones and pagers would be beeping with urgent calls to duty, and they would be racing to the scene of the crime, sirens blaring. But I'm being unfairly picky. The point of the exercise wasn't to see how fast they could get here, but rather how everyone would work together once in action.

The plot thickened with the next 911 call, this time from the bank robbers themselves. They were not, as it turned out, bank robbers after all. "We are the ACME terrorist group," they declared in a huffy manifesto. "We have taken complete control of this building. We are to negotiate the release of Ramzi Youssef, and unless he is released we will start killing the people in this building. We have explosives planted in this building that we will use if necessary."

Now, there was a name from the past. "Why him?" I asked Conner. "He's serving a life sentence in Canyon City, near Colorado Springs," he said. "I wanted to make everything as realistic as possible, so I suggested to FBI supervisor Ron Knight that we use him. He's an al Qaeda terrorist."

"I know, I know," I said breathlessly, and eagerly told Conner the story of how Fariscal had broken up Youssef's cell in Manila and helped get him convicted for his role in masterminding Bojinka and the 1993 bombing of the World Trade Center.

At the mobile command post, there was now a flurry of activity. The FBI had been contacted and had pronounced ACME a legitimate and known terrorist group. "They are extremely knowledgeable with the use of explosives," said an analyst. "They have also been training with the use of chemicals. Consider this a most dangerous situation."

It was now a little after eight in the morning. The training exercise had begun in earnest. SWAT units began creeping toward Republic Plaza like bulky ninjas, ducking behind statues and shrubbery and racing across streets in low crouches. Firefighters donned their yellow flame-resistant suits and air canisters, and paramedics from fourteen ambulances unloaded their stretchers and gear. An elderly couple paused to take in all the commotion. "What's going on?" the woman finally asked. "Terrorism training exercise, ma'am," said a sheriff. "Oh, good," she said. Turning to her husband, she added, "Let's go, dear." Her nonchalance took me by surprise. Presumably it wasn't every day that terrorists took over downtown Denver, and I had expected the exercise to generate more curiosity with the general public. Had a drill of this scope been conducted in D.C., traffic would have been at a standstill. Thousands would have squeezed behind police barricades to watch. Scores of reporters would have turned out. There probably would have been more television cameras than SWAT teams, and highlights of the day likely would have made the network evening news. But here people passed by without so much as a second glance. There was virtually no rubbernecking from motorists, and the only local media representative I spotted was a cub reporter from the *Denver Post*. Perhaps what should have been surprising was that people thought of terrorism at all in Denver. Colorado, with its snowcapped mountains and dusty plains, seemed far removed from the East Coast, much less from the troubles of the world. The culture was markedly different here, more self-reliant and wary of the state. I could see how some Midwesterners could say, "It's not our problem. Let them worry about it in the Big Apple."

Inside the mobile command post, however, there was no passing indifference. District commanders worked the radios, and SWAT team leaders and the Republic Plaza's building managers hunched over blueprints of the high-rise. "I have been able to talk to a number of floor wardens," the building manager from Brookfield Properties explained. "The terrorists have gathered a number of the hostages on the nineteenth floor. This is where most of the gunmen are."

Brookfield is a New York–based real estate giant. Publicly listed, it owns and manages more than 46 million square feet of office space across the United States and Canada, including the Republic Plaza and two squat, black smoked-glass towers right next door that form Denver's World Trade Center complex. Brookfield's Denver properties alone are valued at over $2 billion, so the company has a sizable investment to protect. Three senior Brookfield security executives—all retired NYPD officers—had flown in from Manhattan to observe the exercise, and while the SWAT teams deployed I tried to engage them in what turned out to be a largely one-sided conversation. "We've done a lot of things since 9/11 that I can't talk about," said one. His colleagues were just as tight-lipped. "You can say we have made many security upgrades, but I won't be more specific," said another. None wanted his name to appear in print. I couldn't blame their reluctance to speak.

Brookfield offers a good example of how much of the costs of homeland security are going to be borne by the private sector, by airlines, industrial and energy conglomerates, real estate developers, and the like. Government initiatives are bound to grab the headlines, but private business will inevitably bear the brunt of the burden: extra security guards, surveillance cameras and software packages, smart ID cards, perimeter fencing and secure gates—all these expenditures will affect the bottom line. Office towers are prime targets, not only for aerial assaults, but for countless other plots. Boiler rooms can be broken into and pathogens can be introduced into water and ventilation systems. Trucks laden with explosives can be driven into lobbies. Incendiary bombs can be detonated to trap tenants on upper floors.

Given all this, if Brookfield was discreetly shoring up support columns, installing expensive scrubber air filtration systems, and putting in biometric tamper-proof locks in its utility rooms, it naturally didn't want the bad guys to get wind of the added layers of defense. If it wasn't adding any of those costly countermeasures, company officials probably didn't want tenants thinking that monetary issues outweighed safety concerns. That would hardly constitute good PR. For the corporate security guys, I can only imagine that my presence constituted what you would call a lose-lose situation. Still, the mere fact that Brookfield had volunteered its building for this exercise could only mean that at headquarters, they took terrorism very seriously.

Another scripted 911 call interrupted the proceedings. It was from a tenant hiding on the thirty-seventh floor. Of the Plaza's tenants—employees of insurance companies, law firms, accountants, and so on—130 people had volunteered to play themselves for the drill. "There are two terrorists guarding what appears to be a box with jars of liquid on the Tremont side of the building," whispered the caller.

Word of the mysterious liquid set in motion a frenzy of activity on Tremont Street. Two large red tents were hastily erected. Sections of copper piping were grafted together and attached to large portable pumps that in turn were connected via a thick hose to a fire hydrant. These were the decontamination shower units. Each cost $60,000, the fruit of a bill sponsored by Senators Sam Nunn, Richard Lugar, and Pete Domenici that released some $1.5 billion in federal grants to equip first responders across the country. Fifteen million dollars of that funding had made it to Denver thus far, and some of the money was being used to pay for this exercise. (Another $3.5 billion in first-responder federal grants were in the pipeline, so more would soon be trickling Denver's way.)

As the tents were going up, members of the South Metro hazmat brigade blocked off sewer intakes and drains and installed blue 500-gallon bladder bags to contain the showers' toxic runoff. "You don't want to contaminate the sewer system," said Fire Chief Roderick Juniel, watching his crews with an air of paternal pride. The entire setup took less than fifteen minutes, and hazmat crews in gray protective Tyvek spill-suits were soon ready for the first victims. It was now 8:50 A.M. Three SWAT teams and a tactical paramedic unit in full body armor were gingerly making their way up the Plaza's stairwells, as radios crackled with reports of heavy fighting and casualties. An elite FBI counterterror unit in desert-camouflage chemical suits, respirators, black Kevlar vests, and military helmets was preparing to head to the thirty-seventh floor, looking eerily like an outtake from a second Gulf War embeddee.

"This is a great opportunity to test our communication," said Juniel. "Not just between us, but between the police department and the FBI." Prior to 9/11, one of the most frequent complaints was the lack of cooperation between rival agencies, especially the FBI, which was seen as secretive and aloof. "As a result of 9/11," Juniel continued, "they're much more willing to share information with us, particularly about hazmats."

But the communications were not at all to Lieutenant Conner's liking. "I call one of my terrorists," he said, "and ask how the negotiations are going. He says no one's called him yet." In the excitement, negotiators had forgotten to call the hostage takers—an unlikely omission in a real terrorist scenario. But a hostage crisis would also be an extremely unlikely outcome to any al Qaeda attack. That sort of thinking was more in line with the old-style terrorism that has plagued Europe for the past thirty years. Groups like the Provisional Republican Army, better known as the IRA, the Basque separatist ETA of Spain, various PLO splinter organizations, the Algerian Islamist Group, Iranian-backed Hezbollah, and Abbu Sayyaf occasionally took hostages or used terror as a negotiating tool for the release of prisoners or territorial claims. The strategy is one reason why terrorist strikes in Europe, Asia, or the Middle East have always been limited in scope and scale. You can't murder three thousand innocent civilians and expect the government to agree to your terms. Al Qaeda was a different breed of animal. Osama bin Laden and his followers are not interested in negotiating with the United States.

As in any true emergency, the Red Cross had arrived, bringing a much-welcomed cantina truck that dispensed free coffee, juice, and snacks. Natural disasters were also more in the Colorado Red Cross's league, and it was probably the first time that customers in bubble bio-chemical space suits had ever formed a line for its raspberry Danish.

Glen Grove, the team coordinator for the hazmat units in Adams and Jefferson counties, let me try on one of these suits. They come in four styles, Levels A through D, with Level A offering the greatest protection. On the principle that safe is better than sorry, I chose to model a Level A suit. Grove plunked a large green duffel bag on the floor. Stamped on the sides was WMD, an acronym that by now most Americans know stands for "weapons of mass destruction." Grove started pulling out its contents: a self-administering syringe with atropine serum, boots, a $3,500 self-contained breathing apparatus, and a $2,000 vapor-resistant suit made by Du Pont. "Sit," he instructed. A beige, fire-resistant balaclava went over my head first. That was followed by a Lexan face mask and hood, which fit so snugly that I thought my head was being squeezed in a vise. Only once an air tank similar to those worn by scuba divers was strapped onto my shoulders could I start putting on the suit. It was made of surprisingly thick material designed to be tear-resistant, a nylon fiberglass weave that crinkled as it creased. It had a built-in Quasimodo hump in the back to accommodate the bulky oxygen tank and respirator, and a large rectangular hood of clear plastic. The special zipper was double lined so as not to allow contaminated air to seep in.

Preattached black rubber gloves formed an integral part of the hermetically sealed suit.

As Grove dressed me—it was a two-man job—he reminisced about the frantic days following 9/11, when mail laced with an unusually potent strain of anthrax killed five people and contaminated another twenty-two. Americans, back then, started seeing the toxin everywhere, and his units were being called out a dozen times a day. "It almost killed us," he recalled. "We were getting hysterical calls, like white powder had been found on the conference table of a real estate office. No one thought that maybe it was sugar or coffee creamer." He laughed. "They were convinced that al Qaeda was targeting them. Now, why would al Qaeda attack real estate salesmen in suburban Denver?"

The Centers for Disease Control and Prevention in Atlanta had faced the same problem writ large. Its labs processed over 5,300 hoaxes and false alarms in the early weeks of the crisis. One such prank had brought much of New York's subway system to a stop. Someone had left a bag of sticky white powder in the Canal Street station. Before long, trains in Lower Manhattan were halted, according to a report in the New York Times the next day, and hazmat units in Level A suits were setting up decontamination showers. The suspicious substance turned out to be cornstarch.

Over time, the panic and the crank calls subsided. "It was a knee-jerk reaction, like the early phobia with AIDS," said Grove, a friendly and thoughtful man. Still, that experience with mass hysteria had served as an invaluable lesson on the perils of false alarms, which could completely overwhelm hazmat units and prevent them from responding in time to a real case. Still other lessons had been picked up. "If you need to test an entire building," said Grove, "start with the computers. The spores collect there because of static electricity. It will save you a lot of time. You learn with experience," he added with a wry smile.

Already there have been tremendous strides with chemical detection equipment. Infrared spectrometers, once the size of rooms, can now fit into suitcases, although the miniaturized devices remain pricey, at $50,000 a unit. Recently invented were colormetric tubes in glass vials and thin sheets of M8 paper that change colors like early pregnancy tests when exposed to certain toxins. By 2003 military field monitoring units that had taken between thirteen and twenty-four hours to detect anthrax, plague, botulinum toxin, and *Staphylococcus enterotoxin B* during the first Gulf War could positively identify these toxins in thirty minutes. Scientists at Pennsylvania State University were developing new genetically engineered plants that could detect harmful agents. Under a $3.5 million Pentagon grant, researchers were studying a small flowering plant in the mustard family, the *Arabidopsis thalania*, which glows or fluoresces under ultraviolet light when exposed to chemical agents, according to a report in the *Homeland Defense Journal*. At Rockefeller University, biologists were working on a promising bacteria-eating life-form that replicates inside the anthrax germ to destroy it.

A California company, PointSource Technologies, had just developed a device that shot a laser beam through water to scan for microorganisms like *E. coli* or anthrax. First used at the 2003 Super Bowl in San Diego, eventually utilities around the country will be able to deploy the system to sound the alarm if terrorists try to tamper with drinking-water supply and distribution systems.

"The impetus for homeland security is going to act a little like NASA during the space race and unleash all sorts of technological breakthroughs," said Grove, adjusting my respirator.

"Just breathe easily," he said. I took a deep breath, and nothing happened. It was terrifying, as if my lungs had hit a wall. For a split second I saw nothing but blackness. "Oops," apologized Grove. "Forgot to turn it on."

Oxygen came, but I was still frazzled. Plus I sounded like Darth Vader every time I exhaled. Grove finished zipping up the suit. My faceplate started steaming up. My mind raced. What if the respirator failed? By the time they got me out of this monkey suit, I'd be dead. What if the zipper got stuck? Then I'd never get out. My eyes must have been bugging out, because Grove steadied me with a gentle hand. "Take it easy," he said soothingly. "It's strange at first, but you will get used to it. When you feel comfortable, try to take a step."

After a minute the initial panic passed. Moving was another story: Every step felt distended and heavy-limbed. With two pairs of gloves on, manipulating even the simplest objects was difficult. And my vision was blurred; it was like looking out of a steamy fishbowl. How could people work in this outfit? Go into so-called hot zones filled with lethal viruses or chemical agents? Climb forty flights of stairs? Fight a fire?

My respect for first responders suddenly soared. I had been offered the briefest glimpse of their dangerous, claustrophobic profession, and all I could think of was getting out of the damn suit.

Back at the Republic Plaza, some sixty-five SWAT team members and a hundred firefighters were already in the building. Reports were filtering down that one of the terrorists had been shot, and there were twenty civilian hostages on the nineteenth floor. Crews in Level B suits were sweeping the tower's lobby with a Geiger counter that looked like a relic from the Cold War. I'd seen such old-fashioned devices before in Chernobyl, but this particular one was set to crackle and click only if readings exceeded twice the background radiation. Some radiation always occurs naturally, explained the operator, especially at high altitudes and around natural emitters like granite, and no one wanted civilians to freak out, thinking they were glowing if the machine clicked and hissed constantly.

Near the elevator banks, a black object about the size of a lunchbox stood on the marble floor. A thick antenna sprouted from one side and a clear plastic receptacle cup was on the other. In the middle, an LED displayed a stream of numbers. There was also a small red siren light on top, like you see on police cars. This was a so-called sniffer, of the type the Metropolitan Transit Authority had just installed in New York's subways. The device, made by RAE Systems of Sunnyvale,

California, is a photo-ionization detector that measures the presence of volatile organic compounds in parts per million. It also tests the air with two electrochemical toxic sensors and can transmit the data in real time to a central monitoring station up to two miles away. Every subway station in New York, as well as hubs like Penn and Grand Central stations, now have such electronic canaries that will sound the alarm for evacuation in the event readings exceed norms. Many landmark buildings in New York and Washington are also installing them, as well as employing the services of roving National Guard units that drive around in mobile laboratories testing the ventilation systems that filter the air office workers breathe.

Police Chief Gerald Whitman strode into the lobby wearing a skeptical smile. At six-three, he towered over most of his colleagues. We watched a SWAT team storm by, all sweat and eager concentration. "They're about to be sacrificed." Whitman laughed. Apparently the script called for some unpleasant complication. Just then Whitman's cell phone rang and the smile faded from his handsome face. "Excuse me," he said. "I have to go to the airport."

Reality had intruded on our little world of make-believe. Luggage screeners at Denver International Airport had just found what they believed was explosive material hidden in a suitcase on a flight bound for Washington, D.C. The police chief raced off, bomb disposal team in tow.

Victims were now streaming into the lobby. Building tenant Mindy Romoff emerged from the stairwell with a yellow OUT OF PLAY sign suspended from her neck. A card she carried instructed paramedics that she had been shot in the chest and abdomen, had a perilously low pulse rate, and wasn't going to make it. All in all, she was pretty frazzled. "I've never had a gun pointed at me before," she said of her encounter with the SWAT teams on the seventeenth floor. "Or had anyone yell 'keep your hands up.' Really scary."

Suddenly, at 8:52, strobe lights on the high lobby ceiling started flashing and a loud siren wailed in short, piercing bursts. "Explosion, explosion," shot from the police radios. A huge fireball had erupted on the twentieth floor, shattering windows and rocking the entire structure. Had this been for real, debris would have been raining down on the streets and walkways around the building. Collateral damage would have been evident on neighboring towers. And everyone in the SWAT unit that had just stormed the twentieth floor would have been dead.

"We have many people killed and injured here," the police radios echoed. "We are trapped and can't go down so we are headed for the roof." The explosion posed an unanswerable challenge for the exercise's participants. Firefighters couldn't try to contain the spreading blaze as long as terrorists were shooting at them, and SWAT teams couldn't take out the terrorists, who were protected by a wall of fire. Hundreds of people were trapped above the twentieth floor, and the bad guys still had chemical or biological agents in those jars on the thirty-seventh floor. A chopper was dispatched to try to evacuate people from the roof, but the delicate maneuver was abandoned as too dangerous when the pilot complained that he couldn't fly the craft properly in his bulky chemical suit. "These suits aren't designed for law enforcement," said SWAT commander Conner. "The stuff was designed for hazmat crews," he said of the protective gear. "The gloves are too bulky to wrap your finger around a trigger. The suits are Day-Glo orange and have a built-in alarm that sounds if you are immobile for forty-five seconds. For firemen and hazmat crews, those safety features are life-savers," he explained. "But we operate in stealth, and for us it's like having a huge target painted on your chest."

The problem wasn't isolated. According to a comprehensive report by a well-known California-based think tank, the RAND Corporation, first responders polled around the country complained of similar shortcomings in their equipment. The protective gear, communications equipment, and safety devices many used were simply not adequate for counterterror duties, the study concluded.

Far from being irritated, Conner was pleased to run into such technical snafus that highlighted the urgent need for more specialized equipment. "If everything goes smoothly," he said, "the exercise has failed. I want the mistakes to be made here, not in real situations."

Victims and wounded police officers were now being evacuated from the building, and I joined Mindy and the other casualties hurrying through the emergency exits in the basement loading docks. There EMS personnel were performing triage next to a Dumpster that from the smell of it hadn't been emptied for some time. People who could ran up the steep garage ramp. Others were carried. Everyone was met at the street level by Jim Olsen, decontamination expert, who wore a green Level B chemical suit with bright orange boots and waved what looked like a speed gun over us. Known as an APD 2000, it scanned for sarin, mustard, and VX gases. Some of the volunteer victims had been asked to wear bathing suits under their street clothes, and these unfortunates were now thoroughly scrubbed down in the two decontamination showers before being loaded into the waiting ambulances.

Everything seemed remarkably realistic, if perhaps a tad too speedy and orderly. Time lines had been severely compressed during the exercise. Sweeping floors for pathogens normally takes hours if not days, certainly not minutes. Fires would have been allowed to burn while terrorists were still in shooting positions, and only the FBI SWAT unit, with its chemical suits, would have been deployed if there was a real danger of contaminants present.

The other missing ingredients, the panic and chaos that inevitably accompany any disaster, are always limiting factors in simulations. That is one reason why the instructors at the new homeland security school at a decommissioned military base in Alabama that Lieutenant Conner had attended recently subjected students to live exercises with real VX gas. "If one-tenth of one drop touches your skin, you are dead within fifteen minutes," Conner recalls being told just before being sent into a room full of the nerve agent. "Your first instinct is to freak out. To worry that your suit will rip, or your respirator will fail. But then as minutes pass and you are still alive, you slowly realize that you can function under these conditions and perform the tasks that are assigned to you."

In a real situation, the chaos would have been most evident at the joint operations command post, where contradictory or incomplete reports would likely frustrate decision making. I walked back over to the command post to see the burgeoning cooperation everyone spoke of in action. The mobile police and fire command trucks were parked beside one another, a good sign.

Outside the trucks, district commanders from various fire, police, EMS, FBI, emergency management, mayor's office, and city engineering and health departments were conducting joint briefings every thirty minutes.

10:30: "We've got guys trapped on the twenty-first floor." "We are conducting a structural survey to determine whether the building is sound." "There are numerous victims, but we don't have a count yet." "We have one terrorist in custody and we are interrogating him."

11:00: "All casualties removed from the nineteenth floor." "There is still a hostage situation on the thirty-eighth floor." "Two more suspects have been killed." "The fire has been contained to the twentieth." "Another officer is down." "Denver General is treating eight victims." "The media want a briefing."

While the district commanders still huddled, I saw a man off to the side wearing a World Trade Center Task Force cap. He was intently watching the proceedings, scribbling periodically in a notebook, and occasionally nodding in approval. "Michael Fagel," he introduced himself. He was a former New York firefighter, had spent three months working at Ground Zero after September 11, and now toured the country on contract for the Justice Department, observing preparedness exercises. He'd seen a hundred so far. "I'm impressed by the interagency cooperation here," he said. "There's no rivalry like [we have] in New York. These people are all talking to one another. I just saw a drill in Texas where the police and fire chiefs weren't even on speaking terms, for God's sake. That was a bloody disaster. But these folks are on the ball," he declared.

The drill ended anticlimactically at 11:45, when the building was declared in danger of imminent collapse and ordered evacuated. Two of the original six terrorists were still alive and holed up on the thirty-seventh floor with their mysterious jars of liquid, but everyone seemed pleased that it was over. As the last firefighters and SWAT personnel emerged from the Republic Plaza, drenched in sweat and exhausted from lugging their heavy gear up and down fifty-six flights of stairs, Police Chief Whitman returned from the airport. "False alarm," he said when I asked him about the bomb threat. A physics professor from Colorado State University, it turned out, had neglected to declare faraday cells that resembled blasting caps in his luggage. They were innocuous and used in research, but had triggered the EDS scanning machines. "Poor guy is going to have some explaining to do when the plane lands in D.C," Whitman said with a laugh.

"Well," he said, "I guess we'd better go. The building is about to collapse on us. I sure hope those two remaining terrorists go down with it."

7

GERMS AMOK: BIOWARRIORS IN THE ER

THE EXERCISE IN DENVER HAD ENDED IN TRUE HOLLYWOOD fashion: with an irresistible invitation for a sequel. As the credits rolled, fifty-six stories of steel, glass, and concrete would have rained down on Colorado's largest population center in a spectacular display of gravity. Amid the cascading debris—the mangled office furniture and computers, shattered water coolers and conference room tables, the thousands of legal files let loose like oversize confetti—would have been the contents of two jars of mysterious liquid crashing toward earth. Dispersed by the sheer power of millions of tons of pulverized cement, the liquid would be suspended, like a lethal aerosol, in the cloud of dust that would envelop downtown Denver, drifting with the prevailing winds toward neighboring office towers, the new Coors Field football stadium, and eventually settling on one suburb or another. In this alternate scenario, instead of breezily going off to lunch at the Hard Rock Café down 16th Street after the exercise, many of us could be dead within days. Business executives from those leafy suburbs would get on planes for meetings in New York or Los Angeles. Truck drivers passing through on the highway would roll down a window and carry the contaminated air to the next state. Within weeks the engineered microbes—if they were of a strain that, unlike anthrax, was contagious—would have been carried to every corner of the country. Then all hell would break loose.

That was precisely what happened when federal authorities ran a series of simulations to practice defending against bioterror. Strains of mock smallpox and plague were loosed in New England in an eerie simulation called Dark Winter. In a May 2003 scenario involving simultaneous attacks, Seattle and Chicago had participated in a five-day bio-drill that involved 8,500 people from a hundred local, state, and federal agencies. A dirty bomb rained radiation down on Seattle and a plague strain in aerosol form was released in Chicago. A 200-page script was prepared for the $16.5 million joint exercise, known as TOPOFF II, complete with real explosions, smoldering wrecks, stand-ins for the president, VP, and press secretary, and realistic movielike sets. For all the camera-ready drama, broadcast breathlessly by all the networks, officials flunked almost all of the drills, according to declassified excerpts from a secret December 2003 White House report. In Seattle, confusion over which direction the radioactive plume was being carried by winds prevented the timely evacuation of residents in harm's way. In Chicago, medical shortages and poor coordination also failed to arrest the spread of the biological agent. The exercises exposed weaknesses in communication and cooperation among federal, state, and local authorities. Distribution of medical stockpiles was found to be erratic and faulty, while existing laws were proven grossly inadequate at forcibly containing epidemics.

Denver had been the site of the first bioterrorism exercise ever held in the United States. It was staged by FEMA and the Justice Department in May 2000, even before the September 11 attacks made preparing for weapons of mass destruction a national priority. Three area hospitals had participated in the $3.5 million federal drill, which drew 600 volunteer actors, and was known as TOPOFF I. The more ambitious sequel, TOPOFF II, had played out to much greater media interest. But I preferred the original production, which was less constrained by the post-9/11 political imperative to showcase to the public how much progress was being made in emergency preparedness, "so that politicians could shine for the television cameras," as one health official put it. The Denver TOPOFF had had no such external pressure. It received little scrutiny from the national media and did not need to look good for the press. In other words, it was the most realistic reflection of what would actually happen if a biological agent was surreptitiously released in a large American city. There was one other reason why the Denver TOPOFF drill was critical: The lessons learned from this May 2000 exercise formed the priorities of America's post-9/11 bioterrorist preparedness programs. From official Department of Justice reports, time lines prepared by the Colorado Department of Public Health, media briefings, CDC postmortems, and interviews with participants, I was able to piece together how events had unfolded during that critical first exercise. The story went something like this.

The Denver Center for Performing Arts was packed for the May 17 matinee performance. *Blue's Clues* was playing to a full house of children and parents. Sometime in the second act, according to a detailed record of the exercise compiled by Disaster Relief.org, a canister of mock plague bacillus was secretly pumped into the theater's ventilation system. The aerosolized agent drifted out the air ducts over the main hall and swirled slowly around the stage and orchestra seats. Updrafts sent the trillions of microscopic germs into the balconies and boxes, where they filled the little lungs of toddlers and lodged in the bronchial passages of their parents.

The bacillus permeating the theater was the deadliest of the three plague variants: pneumonic. Pneumonic plague is transmitted by tiny droplets in the air. It can be contracted by inhaling in the vicinity of a coughing carrier or simply by breathing in an area contaminated by bioterrorists. In A.D. 541 pneumonic plague killed more than half the world's population. Along with its bubonic and septicemic cousins, both transmitted by fleas and rodents, the disease wiped out a third of Europe and claimed another 13 million victims in China in the fifteenth century. In its weaponized variant, of which the Soviet Union was a leading manufacturer, it has no taste or smell, and no one attending that morning's show at the Performing Arts Center would have had any way of knowing that they had just been exposed to the deadly virus.

For several days after the May 17 release of the aerosol nothing happened, the National Symposium on Bioterrorism noted in its study of the exercise. No one felt ill; the three hospitals participating in the drill did not know what toxin to look for, were not even aware that the exercise had begun and that the microbes were already working against them. This was the way any bioterrorist strike on America would start: silently and without warning.

The first signs that something was amiss manifested themselves early the third day. Patients (played by volunteer actors) started trickling into emergency rooms, complaining of headaches, fever, and coughs. They were treated for flulike symptoms and sent home. No one had picked up on the clues, and the three participating hospitals did not exchange information; otherwise, someone might have noticed the spike in people coming down with the flu in May. Here was another example of the inherent advantage of bioweapons: misdiagnosis. Medical professionals are trained to look for the most obvious explanations, and most bioagents present the same initial symptoms as common ailments. So no one is searching for exotic causes. In a spot test run at a Pittsburgh hospital in February 2000, for instance, only one out of seventeen doctors correctly identified the early symptoms of smallpox. The others prescribed cold medicines, falling for what physicians call the Zebra syndrome—if an animal has four hooves and a mane it is by definition a horse; only if you look beyond that initial assumption will you discover that the beast also has stripes, and may be something different from what it appears to be. Medical practitioners, however, are not taught to take that second look, because if they did, the whole healthcare system would get bogged in costly minutiae. So the disease buys itself precious time to incubate and spread.

Another day of the exercise passed, and on a Thursday the patient-actors returned, this time with chest pains, shortness of breath, nausea, and septic shock, according to the Johns Hopkins Center for Civilian Biodefense Studies. Many brought props: (fake) chest X rays and watery, bloody sputum samples.

Scores of healthcare workers would have been infected during routine examinations when patients were told to cough. Karen Nerger, a registered nurse at Aurora Medical Center, did not wear a mask while assisting a patient in the ER wing. Had the scenario been real, she would have inhaled the *Yersinia pestis* plague bacterium. Within five days, the mother of two would have been dead.

By Friday afternoon, several hundred mock patients were seriously ill. Swedish Medical Center reported its first virtual "death" that evening. The Health Department was notified. Shortly afterward, Aurora and Denver Health Medical Center—Colorado's largest hospital—also reported virtual "deaths." By this time, health officials obviously knew something was wrong, but they were unable to identify the origin of the fatal illness.

Events now started taking a momentum of their own. Saturday morning broke to find four hundred new "patients" exhibiting flulike symptoms. The governor's and mayor's offices were alerted to a possible epidemic. Swedish Medical and the other hospitals convened crisis management teams called Incident Command Systems. By afternoon reports began filtering in that patients were exhibiting similar symptoms in Pueblo. Hospitals throughout the city were soon swamped. Traffic jams started, as people from the suburbs (other actor/volunteers), frightened by media reports of a strange illness, drove into town to get checked. Eight hundred people lined up in front of the ER entrance outside Swedish Medical, banging on the doors.

The hospitals were ill-equipped to deal with the deluge. They did not have enough beds, staff, or supplies on hand, and were turning people away. "It was kinda scary, it really was," Nerger told *NurseWeek Magazine*. "We had never dealt with this serious of a drill, with not having enough staff, enough ambulances, the families demanding to see their loved ones, staff members getting infected, and the biological agent spreading so fast."

By noon the scenario's death toll had risen to twenty-five, according to a study of the exercise by the Colorado Department of Public Health. Still no one knew what illness they were dealing with—only that it was apparently contagious and deadly. Autopsies were being hastily conducted and the Centers for Disease Control in Atlanta was notified that samples were on the way. At 6:00 P.M., the governor and mayor declared a state of emergency. FEMA was mobilized. It set up a command post in a bunker on the outskirts of town. But as it turned out, cell phones didn't work there because of the bunker's thick concrete walls. "Nobody could reach me," Stephanie Denning, Denver Health Medical Center's director of public relations, complained in a report on the exercise. "In a disaster situation," echoed Sara Spaulding, the public affairs officer at Swedish Medical, "I'm not tethered to my [desk] telephone. The only tether is my cell phone or pager, and we couldn't use them in the bunker."

Thus the main communications hub was effectively incommunicado. Precious time was lost while a new, cell phone–compatible command post was found. By then Washington had taken charge of the emergency, and arguments between federal and local officials erupted over what to tell the public. Local officials favored full disclosure; federal authorities worried that releasing incomplete information would cause national panic. Conference calls with up to forty people from local, state, federal, and various health agencies degenerated into chaotic shouting matches over jurisdiction and procedures. The jurisdictional disputes grew so acrimonious that even months later, many involved were still bitter when recalling the squabbling.

"My job is to disseminate information," said Spaulding, "but in this case, there were federal and state agencies saying I couldn't do it—*they* were going to talk about it, and they would get back to me. Meanwhile our hospital was overrun with thousands of worried virtual citizens, sick citizens, and worried and sick staff. In reality," she added, "I would not have waited, because I have a responsibility to my patients and to my community to get out the information that I have."

At 7:30 P.M. the CDC lab in Fort Collins, Colorado, confirmed that plague was the cause of the deaths. Fort Collins, one of sixteen CDC centers across the country, has over 1,200 strains of plague in its refrigerated inventory and is the national repository for that particular germ. It is a heavily guarded compound, behind armed sentries and barbed wire, and tucked away discreetly in a mountainside about two

hours north of Denver. Dr. May Chu, one of the senior researchers in
its ventilated, subterranean labs, showed me what the Black Death
looked like under a microscope. Green actually, and surprisingly be-
nign: a phosphorescent constellation of cute little ivy-colored stars,
like something from a planetarium slide show.

By late Saturday afternoon, casualties had risen to 32, with 516
confirmed carriers. In Washington, senior officials were being called in
to work from their Virginia country homes; the president was demanding hourly updates and mobilizing teams of experts. No one
knew how this outbreak had started. Was it naturally occurring, or the
work of nefarious forces? The president wanted answers, and, above
all, the White House needed to make sure this outbreak did not spread
to the rest of the country. Back in Denver, now that they knew what
they were dealing with, medical personnel hastily donned masks and
gloves, while nurses and doctors scrambled to find antibiotics. Like
many bioagents, plague can be cured with simple medicines. The
problem was that there were not enough doses of antibiotics to go
around. Hospital supplies were exhausted within an hour. Pharmacy
owners were called at home and rousted out of bed to get what they
had in their stores. But their stocks, too, were used up almost immediately. The governor's office tried to requisition what little was left in
surrounding counties for rationing, but there simply wasn't enough.
Without antibiotics, several nurses on the night shift refused to go to
work. At Denver Health, orderlies called in sick, and hazardous waste
began piling up.

"In a real bioterrorism situation, we probably would see more staff
refusing to come in when we called them," Janet Shepard, the director
of emergency services, told *NurseWeek Magazine*. "We found that
some would rather stay home with their families than come in to help
for $19 an hour and probably die of a horrible infection like the people
they just saw on television."

Staff members who did show up were put on duty round the
clock—six hours on and six hours off—and were not permitted to
leave for fear that they might spread the disease. Some tried to escape,

raising legal issues of whether individuals could be forcibly quarantined. At Aurora, families of sick medical personnel demanded to see their relatives. Some pushed their way past guards and also needed to be quarantined. Colorado has no legislation on the books to forcibly restrict people's movements. Even words like "quarantine" have all but disappeared from the popular lexicon, a historical remnant of a bygone era. Could guards shoot infected patients trying to flee the hospital? Could patients be shackled to their beds? No one knew what to do to contain the disease.

The hospitals were now perilously low on ventilators and running out of food and facilities to house the growing influx. Isolation rooms were filled to capacity. "It hit me when I saw that every bed was full, that the hallways were full, we had no more resources, and we had to tell the command center that we couldn't take any more," Shepard recalled. "All our staff had been tapped out by the second day."

An urgent call was sent to Washington for penicillin, ventilators, and an additional two thousand medical professionals. It was apparent that Denver was losing control of the situation. "What became very clear, very quickly," Denning later wrote, "was that if you didn't manage it well at the very beginning, the numbers increased exponentially. What you did at the front end had tremendous effect at the back end."

At 1:00 A.M. Sunday, local health officials received word that several patients in Los Angeles had also manifested flulike symptoms. To prevent the spread of the disease, the mayor urged residents to stay inside their homes and wear masks if they needed to venture outside. He also ordered the airport closed. But it was too late.

By 9:00 A.M. 900 people were hospitalized in Denver, and 130 more victims had died overnight. More cases were being reported in L.A. and in Atlanta, as well. Outside Swedish Medical, 1,200 virtual patients, some played by actors, sought assistance, and police were dispatched to control the unruly mob.

"Some of those were really sick," recalled one scenario participant. "Others were what we called the 'worried well.' However, while they were all standing in line, the plague victims were coughing on the worried well, probably infecting them. So the public health message was, 'If you don't need to be out, stay home. If you are not exhibiting any symptoms, don't go anywhere.'" Few heeded the advice. Tens of thousands of people were evacuating, taking their families to isolated country houses in the Rocky Mountains. The main arteries out of the city were choked with traffic. There were accidents and reports of violence.

Two hours later, Governor Bill Owens ordered the entire state locked down. He placed travel restrictions in fourteen metro Denver counties and called out the National Guard to enforce the lockdown. But again, it was too little, too late. Plague reports surfaced in Dallas and Pittsburgh. By 1:00 P.M. Sunday, 270 people were dead, and there was a new problem: The city morgues were overflowing. The Denver metro morgue handled 270 cadavers annually, not daily. The morbid issue of what to do with the contaminated bodies arose. Refrigerated Safeway trucks had to be requisitioned. The bodies were piled in the tractor trailers, while officials argued over what to do with them. The infected corpses were a clear health hazard. Should they be buried? Burned? Family permission was needed for cremation. Yet there was no time to find people in the growing chaos and civil unrest. If city officials acted on their own, they could expose the municipal government to lawsuits. And what would they do if they had 2,000 or 20,000 casualties to dispose of? Dig mass graves? Take over the county incinerator?

By now 1,020 patients were hospitalized, 390 of whom were in critical condition, breathing only with the help of ventilators. Help was on its way, Washington promised. Push packs of antibiotics kept in a federal stockpile in Maryland were put on a military transport and rushed to Denver International Airport. In 2000, the federal government did not keep huge stockpiles of medicines because so many deadly diseases like plague and smallpox were considered eradicated. A good chunk of the entire national reserve of penicillin would have been on that plane, leaving unanswered the question of what federal authorities would have left should the disease spread out of control. In late afternoon, the penicillin plane finally arrived from Washington. But trucks carrying it got bogged down en route in traffic from the airport. The distribution of the push packs quickly became a nightmare. Stampedes broke out at the distribution points. People fought to get to the head of long, savage lines. National Guardsmen had to protect the stash with live ammo. The federal government could get the medicine to Denver, but what happened afterward was chaotic and disorganized. Federal officials were also unable to locate surplus ventilators on a weekend, and hospitals throughout the country were reluctant to part with theirs since the epidemic was spreading. Thus no new ventilators came with the push-pack shipment or were to be expected.

By the close of the exercise on Monday morning, the death toll had reached nearly a thousand, with almost four thousand patients listed as critical. Cases of pneumonic plague were now being reported in a dozen states and as far away as Tokyo and London. There was no longer any way of containing the outbreak.

"There were ominous signs at the end of the exercise," Thomas Inglesby of the Johns Hopkins Center for Civilian Biodefense Studies noted in his official report. "It is not clear what would have happened if it had gone on. Disease had already spread to other states and countries. Competition between cities for the national pharmaceutical stockpile had already broken out. It had all the characteristics of an epidemic out of control."

The results of the Denver TOPOFF were filed away in some dusty federal archive, where they languished, largely unread, until September 11 put germs at the top of the political agenda. Hastily dusted off and widely circulated, the newly important TOPOFF conclusions became the inspiration for Project BioShield, a $5.6 billion fund to research and develop better bioterror remedies outlined by President Bush in his 2003 State of the Union address. The most urgent recommendation of the TOPOFF drill was the dire need to upgrade the national pharmaceutical repository to store enough emergency medical supplies for every single man, woman, and child in the country. Known as the Strategic National Stockpile, or SNS, the repository became part of the Department of Homeland Security on March 1, 2003. It consists of ten secure, climate-controlled warehouses in different parts of the country. Each SNS site stores twelve prepackaged 50-ton push packs of emergency medical material—including antibiotics and smallpox and anthrax vaccines—that can be delivered anywhere in the United States within twelve hours.

But are we safer? Better prepared? Have the lessons of the mistakes committed during TOPOFF I, many of which had been repeated in the May 2003 TOPOFF II sequel, really sunk in? The following month I went to Denver's largest hospital to find out what progress had been made. Dr. Stephen Cantrill presided over the trauma ward at Denver Health Medical Center and had participated in TOPOFF. He was a slight, focused man in his late fifties, who favored bow ties and Brooks Brothers shirts with frayed collars. What would happen, I asked Cantrill, if today ten thousand patients suddenly presented symptoms of a biological attack? "Ten thousand!" he exclaimed, exasperated at the absurdity of the question. "A thousand cases would completely overwhelm the entire city's health system."

Despite many strides since 9/11, Denver, like most major American cities, was still ill-prepared to deal with a mass epidemic. Of the 4,000 employees at Cantrill's hospital, for instance, only seven had been vaccinated against smallpox. The number struck me as disturbingly low. But, in fact, it was in line with the national average, a serious blow to President Bush's bioterrorism preparedness program, which had been launched with great fanfare in late 2002. Bush had bravely received the first immunization—ten pinpricks to the upper arm—to kick off the drive, which called for as many as 10 million first responders to get smallpox vaccinations eventually. During Phase 1 of the plan, 500,000 health workers should have been vaccinated by midway through 2003. But by the June deadline, a mere 39,452 had gotten the shots, and a vaccine intended for the general public was still not ready.

Part of the problem was the side effects of the live but weakened virus in the vaccine, which health workers derisively called "calf pus." Recipients could come down with flulike symptoms and, in extreme cases, go blind or suffer kidney failures, or heart attack. The vaccine only killed in one or two or three out of a million cases, but it regularly made recipients feel like death for several days afterward. For wrongheaded administrative reasons, worker's compensation insurance did not cover the time lost while recovering from the severe cold many people developed after getting the shot. Naturally, this did not sit well with unions. There was also a period where immunized health workers could pass the virus on to others, which meant they could not be exposed to patients with weakened immune systems. In other words, they had to stay home without pay. No one was especially keen on the prospect of a two-week unpaid vacation, and many in the medical community grumbled that while Washington seemed willing to throw hundreds of billions of dollars at reconstructing Iraq, the administration was scrimping on a few weeks' salary for first responders at home. Not surprisingly, the national program had precious few takers and was faltering.

And then there were the contentious and often contradictory guidelines dictating who should get the shots. Dr. Cantrill, for example, had 180 paramedics, 160 nurses, and 45 MDs on his emergency ward staff. Should the MDs be first in line because they had advanced degrees? Were nurses' lives worth more than those of the 100 orderlies who were just as likely to contract the disease in the line of duty? Was it just to vaccinate paramedics but not ambulance drivers? The federal program created a potentially discriminatory, nonegalitarian hierarchy, and Cantrill, like many other hospital administrators, wanted no part of it. "We decided it wasn't fair to vaccinate some people while leaving others exposed," he said. "So we only immunized those health workers who would give everyone else shots in case of emergency."

That left some states, such as Arizona and Nevada, with fewer than fifty vaccinated health officials. There were other reasons why the immunization program had stalled. In an April 2003 report, investigators from the Congressional Accounting Office revealed that the government had grossly underestimated the cost of administering each vaccine. Officials had initially pegged the price tag at $13 a dose, when in fact it could run as high as $265 per person, prompting the need to allocate an additional $100 million in federal funds to state and local health agencies. Federal authorities, according to the report, also delayed in distributing a new type of needle that is safer to use for those administering the vaccine, reducing the risk of needle-stick injuries that health workers worried would expose them to the live *vaccina* virus. All in all, the report concluded, haste to implement the program without adequate consultation or forethought had contributed to its initial failure.

Like a good many people who worried about terrorism for a living, Cantrill devised grisly terrorist scenarios in his spare time. One of his favorites involved the blistering agent VX gas. "Less than a drop of it coming into contact with your skin is lethal," he said. "So if I was a terrorist, I'd brush it on to the banister in some busy place like Grand Central Station." Thousands of commuters would grasp the handrails and become contaminated and fall sick later at the office or on the subway, before authorities even realized that something was wrong. By the time they zeroed in on the source, thousands more would have come in contact with the lethal toxin. "At least a chemical attack is easier to diagnose because patients rapidly drop dead, unlike with germs, which can take weeks to incubate," Cantrill said wryly.

As he spoke, I noticed a large chart on one of the emergency room walls. "Bioterrorism Preparedness & Response," it read in bold black print. "Learn the Clues—Know the Signs."

The chart was divided into different columns: anthrax, botulism, brucellosis, plague, Q fever, and ricin were itemized in one; smallpox, SEB, T2 mycotoxins, tularemia, viral equine encephalitis, viral hemorrhagic fever, and glanders and melioidosis in another. Beneath each entry was a lengthy checklist grouped under major symptom categories: dermatological, gastrointestinal, neurological, respiratory, ocular, systemic, and "other."

"It's an indispensable tool," said Cantrill, nodding to the chart.

Behind him, a young man bled from a stab wound, while an elderly patient with a broken leg was being asked if she was allergic to any medications. These were the types of injuries most common to emergency wards, he explained. The vast majority of doctors in the United States had no experience dealing with biological outbreaks; they had never seen exotic cases of, say, brucellosis, much less diagnosed them. But if patients complained of headaches, chest discomfort, and wheezing, if they had a high fever and were nauseous, and if they were losing weight and experiencing back pain, they might be suffering from something much more severe than a bad case of the flu. They may, according to the chart, have been exposed to tularemia. "Before 9/11," said Cantrill, "I don't think anyone would have even thought of making the connection."

Making the correct diagnostic connection is critical because many bacterial and viral agents have relatively brief incubation periods during which the disease can be arrested. Health workers have a brief window of opportunity to treat viruses before they reach their full-blown, mortal stage. In the case of smallpox, for example, it is usually ten days, although the Soviets developed a particularly virulent strain of the virus, known as India One, that cut that critical treatment window period by half.

Inhalational anthrax moves even faster, incubating within two to five days before going into a latent period that can fool those exposed into thinking they had suffered from forty-eight-hour flu. But the *Bacillus anthracis* bacteria quietly germinates, spreading to the lymph nodes, then the bloodstream, and finally the inner recesses of the lungs. By then your skin turns blue, you lose the ability to breathe, and you essentially choke on your own blood, according to a gory web posting by the *Journal of the American Medical Association*. And a little anthrax goes a long way. A 1993 study by the Congressional Office of Technology Assessment concluded that 100 kilos of inhalational anthrax (as opposed to the less virulent powdered form, which killed five people in 2001) released in ideal conditions from an aircraft over Washington, D.C., could infect two million people and claim the lives of 125,000.

Equally troubling is evidence found in Afghanistan that al Qaeda had been trying to weaponize anthrax prior to the 2001 U.S. invasion. Documents seized at its Derunta camp, run by Egyptian chemist Midhat Mursi, included directions on how to purchase *Bacillus anthracis* bacteria and inventories of equipment needed to grow seed stocks. According to the *Washington Post*, Khalid Sheik Mohammed, the architect of the 9/11 attacks who was known inside al Qaeda as "the Brain," was arrested at the home of a Pakistani microbiologist with access to production materials and facilities. As of early 2004, the microbiologist—along with Mursi and several other top al Qaeda biochemical weapons specialists—was still at large.

If there is a silver lining to the anthrax cloud, it's that it is not so easy to weaponize. First one would have to acquire seed stock, which was fairly simple before 9/11. "All you needed was a fake letterhead saying you were a research institute," said Cantrill. "And you could order it by mail from a microbe bank." That, of course, is no longer the case, although plenty of other means of acquiring seed stock fraudulently remain. A November 2003 report by the inspector general's office found that security was so lax at university laboratories that in one research facility located right next to the stadium of a football-crazed college, doors were left unlocked during night games for fans to use the rest rooms. Terrorists waving "Beat State" signs could simply saunter in and steal the cultures they once mail-ordered. Federal authorities were supposed to have screened security at 1,653 labs that used pathogens by the end of 2003. According to Senator Joe Lieberman, however, virtually no labs had been certified by the deadline. So there are still gaps in biosecurity. But even if one manages to obtain the bacteria cultures, fermenting them in nutrient baths into sufficiently large quantities requires sophisticated equipment and know-how. So does the process of milling down the spores into the trillions per gram needed for a fine-mist aerosol that can retain its virulence when dispersed. (This is one reason why officials immediately discounted al Qaeda as the culprits behind the anthrax letter attacks of 2001. The spores were so finely milled as to almost certainly be the work of a U.S. scientist with access to military equipment. Similarly, home-grown lunatics are also presumed to be behind the ricin-laced letters sent to the Senate in February 2004.) Then there is the question of choosing the right strain out of the 1,200 varieties of anthrax. Microorganisms are notoriously finicky about things like sunlight, temperature, moisture, and humidity changes, and developing a specific strain that can survive in different weather conditions takes a practiced hand. "It's not something you concoct in a basement laboratory," Cantrill agreed. The problems faced by the Aum Shinrikyo cult are testimony to difficulties inherent in weaponizing anthrax. Despite having spent $10 million on a secret lab of its own, the Japanese sect tried and failed on eight separate occasions to disperse aerosols of anthrax and botulism in the Tokyo subway system. Finally members gave up and switched to the easier-to-produce sarin gas used in the 1995 attack that killed twelve people and injured over five thousand.

Against the possibility of an anthrax release, Denver Medical kept a three-day supply of antibiotics on hand for its hospital staff. The city itself had a cache of 38,000 doses. The rest would come from the SNS push packs. At least anthrax is not contagious, as smallpox and plague are. "If I were al Qaeda," said Cantrill, "I'd send twenty terrorist martyrs infected with smallpox or pneumonic plague to crisscross the country on as many domestic flights as possible." Acting as human biological bombs, the martyrs could infect thousands of fellow passengers in the closed, cramped microenvironment of the planes, which would act as flying incubators. The unsuspecting passengers would then transmit the bacteria or virus to family, friends, and coworkers. Within a month 75 million people could be infected. (Apparently the Department of Homeland Security is of a similar mind. According to a front-page article in the February 1, 2004, edition of the *Washington Post*, fears that al Qaeda would attempt to release a biological agent on board a passenger airliner prompted the January 31, 2004, cancellation of British Air flight 223 from London to Washington.)

This was scary stuff, uncomfortably close to home. What's more, no contingency, no amount of planning could either predict or forestall the panic that would almost certainly accompany any outbreak on a national scale. All reports pointed to the unsettling fact that while sufficient quantities of antibiotics and vaccines were now stock-piled, getting them into the bloodstream of every single American—in twenty-four hours, no less—would still be highly problematic, downright chaotic, and require the mobilization of every single law enforcement officer and health official in the country, and probably the military, as well. Federal officials could get bulk drug shipments to every state. How state and local officials would break up the shipments into smaller packages to distribute to every small town, rural commu-nity, and county was still somewhat fuzzy. And no amount of training or rehearsals could prepare either the American government or the public for an operation on that scale.

THE NEW COLOSSUS

"WE'RE RUNNING A MARATHON AT
FULL SPEED."

—*Department of Homeland Security official*

8

BUREAUCRATS ON THE BARRICADES

I T HAD TAKEN SEVERAL MONTHS, AND MANY SUPPLICATIONS, but I finally was granted an audience at the Department of Homeland Security.

I wouldn't be seeing Tom Ridge, but I didn't care; only a handful of outsiders had been admitted to the new DHS headquarters at the naval intelligence complex on Nebraska Avenue, and I felt a little like the Lewis and Clark of the Washington press corps, intrepidly exploring a rare piece of virgin government territory in our nation's media-trodden capital. Wangling an invitation certainly hadn't been easy. "We're just not ready to receive visitors," I had been politely but firmly rebuffed the first time I had called, some seven weeks after the department was formally inaugurated on March 1, 2003.

That DHS was up and running at all was in itself a major feat. Public Law 107-296, otherwise known as the Homeland Security Act of 2002, had enacted the new superagency on November 25, 2002, leaving a scant three months for the new department to assume direct control over twenty-two federal agencies and merge them all into one cohesive unit. These fiefs ranged from relatively natural fits like customs and the Coast Guard to more disparate entities with vastly different functions, such as FEMA and the Lawrence Livermore National Laboratory. In all, some 186,200 employees throughout the United States reported to work at DHS on the morning of March 1, 2003. They belonged to eighteen different unions that had to be brought on board (and to heel) and worked on over 650 separate computer systems that needed to be integrated. Their ranks were drawn from the Departments of Justice, Commerce, Energy, Agriculture, Treasury, Transportation, Defense, and Health and Human Services, and the new DHSers manned everything from the Federal Computer Incident Response Center to the biohazard testing grounds on Plum Island, New York.

Five separate directorates administered the new agency's main missions. The huge Border and Transportation Security unit grouped customs, the Coast Guard, the TSA, and the INS to safeguard our shores, skies, and land borders. The Emergency Preparedness and Response Directorate teamed up federal agencies like FEMA and the Strategic National Stockpile to rush vaccines, and coordinate assistance and grants, to first responders such as the firefighters and medical personnel I'd met in Denver. A Science and Technology Directorate coordinates all research and development of potential homeland security technologies, and the Information Analysis and Infrastructure Protection Directorate, the intelligence arm of DHS, comprised analysts from the CIA, FBI, DIA, and experts on industrial security from the civilian sector. An office of personnel management also had directorate status, but was chiefly responsible for in-house administrative and accounting issues.

A budget of $36.7 billion—the gross domestic product of some small nations—funds DHS's disparate operations, which on an average day include screening 1.5 million airline passengers, inspecting 57,006 trucks and shipping containers, and making 266 arrests and 24 drug seizures. Every day DHS reviews 2,200 intelligence reports and cables, issues a dozen information bulletins to as many as 18,000 recipients, and trains 3,500 federal officers from 75 different agencies. It deploys 108 patrol aircraft, has a fleet of over 100,000 vehicles, operates 238 remote video surveillance systems, and stands watch over 8,000 federal facilities and pieces of critical infrastructure. The fuller scope of its activities actually sprawls over four single-space pages of text, and that is only a sampling that DHS has chosen to put on its website to give taxpayers a taste of what they are getting for $100 million a day in security spending.

This new colossus was billed as the largest government overhaul since the creation of the Pentagon in 1947, and I had naively expected something suitably impressive at the Nebraska Avenue Complex headquarters (or NAC, as it was called in accordance with official Washington's passion for acronyms). NAC was discreetly tucked away between American University (AU) and a local television station (NBC) in a quiet residential neighborhood far removed from the imposingly columned federal buildings downtown. With its quaint, redbrick colonial structures, NAC can easily pass for a small college campus—or a large reform school, if you factor in all the barbed-wire fences, guardhouses, no-trespassing notices, cameras, and heavy, hydraulic vehicle barriers that prevent unauthorized individuals from entering and classified materials from exiting.

"Building Three," said the guard, issuing me a plastic-laminated entry pass. I wandered down the main road, past some landscapers making a racket with their leaf blowers. Buildings 18, 11, 22, and 5 were plainly visible, but not 3. The landscapers were not much help. "Maybe that way," said one with a noncommittal wave of his rake. That led me down Intelligence Way to the intersection of Cryptologic Court, which seemed a fanciful name for what was essentially a service entrance to a dark, dank courtyard dominated by an industrial-size power generator. The only thing missing was a couple of Dumpsters overflowing with garbage, and the Dickensian tableau would have been complete. This couldn't be it. "Yeah, just down there," said a passerby emerging from beneath a brick archway with an eleven-foot clearance that led to a narrow fire lane forking off from the desolate courtyard. The little alley is barely wide enough for a car, much less for a motorcade, and at the end of it was a plain, dull gray steel door, like what you might see at the side entrance of a warehouse or a seedy after-hours club. A small plaque is affixed to the unpainted wall: The Department of Homeland Security.

First impressions, it has been said, count. And I could now see why DHS officials had such trepidations about showing off their new digs. So much hype had surrounded the department's creation, so much press had been devoted to the sometimes wobbly warnings it issued, and Ridge's rugged, scowling features had become such a familiar sight on the evening news that you couldn't help imagining thousands of security professionals toiling away at some Pentagon-size complex. My own expectations had been raised further by the hundreds of people I'd met out in the field over the past year and the way they spoke of DHS, with that larger-than-life mix of awe and contempt that soldiers in the foxholes might reserve for the Joint Chiefs of Staff.

From this vantage point, though, where perception met reality in a dark alley, DHS seemed cruelly cut down to size; more like a minor, and ill-favored, bureaucratic outpost than the largest federal employer outside of the military. That DHS could be both at once spoke volumes about how cynically the political process in our nation's capital can work at times.

It is well known in Washington that the Bush administration was never overly enthusiastic about the idea of forming DHS, which was first floated by Democrats including Senator Joe Lieberman. Its very notion ran counter to the Republican mantra of fighting against "big government." Its inception could spark fierce bureaucratic turf wars that would test loyalties: Treasury would have to give up customs, the Department of Transportation would have to relinquish the Coast Guard, and so on; and none, of course, would do so without a serious fight. Getting DHS going also posed considerable public relations risks. Any reorganization on this scale was bound to be fraught with hiccups. The administration would open itself up to criticism for the growing pains—especially perilous with elections coming up. And once up and running, it could lose control of the whole thing. Congress would have much greater oversight over DHS operations than if it had remained as a small, relatively anonymous policy unit within the protective confines of the White House. Politically, creating DHS had major downsides.

Yet the public was clamoring for the government to take action on terrorism, and creating DHS would certainly give the impression that the administration was doing all it could to prosecute the war on terror—not only abroad, but at home, as well. What's more, Congress solidly backed the idea of streamlining all domestic counterterror measures into a new, efficient clearinghouse, so there would be no opposition from that traditional quarter of mischief. And there was one other added benefit: If something went horribly wrong and America woke up one morning to another 9/11, Tom Ridge and DHS could take the fall.

So while DHS did not start as a project near and dear to the president's heart, ultimately it was born of political expediency. But was it for real, or simply a paper tiger, as some cynics were already suggesting, a way of appeasing Congress and the public without substantially changing the status quo? "Homeland Security," said Senator Hillary Clinton at a speech in Manhattan on the eve of the department's formal unveiling, "is a myth written in rhetoric, inadequate resources, and a new bureaucracy. Homeland Security is not simply about reorganizing existing bureaucracies. It is about having the right attitude, focus, policy, and resources, and right now we are lacking in all four." I would have been inclined to dismiss Senator Clinton's remark as the partisan and preparatory salvos of her 2008 presidential campaign, except that the department's wholly inadequate headquarters did give me pause. It was spectacularly, even suspiciously, out of character for status-conscious Washington, almost like an afterthought, as if someone said: *Oh yeah, them—stick 'em in the storage room in the basement and keep them out of my hair.*

The saga of NAC's selection as the department's headquarters had generated only passing interest from the national media, which was otherwise preoccupied with whether to go to war in the Gulf again. But it did have a few soap-operatic moments. According to legend—actually Newschannel 8, a local ABC affiliate—a low-level

White House aide had been put in charge of finding DHS a suitable home. With war in Iraq high on the agenda, nobody at the cabinet level paid much attention to the real-estate search. Left to his own devices, the junior aide dispatched scouts to scour locations around the capital while Ridge temporarily set up shop at NAC with a skeleton staff of about 150 people. According to Channel 8, Ridge was not involved in the site search or even kept in the loop. (Like his boss, Ridge was said to be charismatic and popular internally, but not a detail man.) A modern office complex capable of accommodating up to 17,000 workers in a secure, high-tech environment was needed. NAC did not fit that bill, but several sites in northern Virginia did. With less than a month to spare before the department's March 1, 2003, unveiling, the search had been narrowed to two locations, one in Tysons Corner and the other in Chantilly, both—coincidentally—solidly Republican Virginia suburbs. Naturally, this did not sit well with Washington's Democratic city officials, who stood to lose hundreds of millions of dollars in tax revenues from the move, not to mention prestige. It would be the first time since the creation of the Pentagon that a cabinet-level agency was housed outside of the capital, and while the Pentagon was a convenient hop across the Potomac River, Chantilly and Tysons Corner were a forty-five minute drive from downtown—or an hour and a half if traffic was backed up during peak hours, which it almost always is. The mayor of Washington, its congressional delegate, and Democrats on the Hill howled at the slight. Congressman James Oberstar went so far as to tell Channel 8 that "the proceeding opens the door to questions of the integrity of the process."

On January 24, Chantilly was selected as the future home of DHS. There were a lot of long faces at City Hall in Washington, but the deal appeared to be done. Then Ridge dropped his bombshell. One day before the department officially opened its doors, he nixed the move to Virginia and announced that DHS would be staying at NAC after all. Why he plunged into the fray at the last moment is unclear. The *Washington Post* speculated that the prospect of sitting in traffic jams had something to do with it. A DHS official told me Ridge wanted the department to have the higher visibility that came with proximity to all the other institutions of state. Whatever, the last-minute reversal would have profound repercussions on DHS's organizational structure. The congressionally backed plan of having thousands of employees from the twenty-two DHS agencies under one roof would have to be scrapped in favor of a far leaner operation, more in keeping with what the White House originally had in mind. (Conspiracy theorists, of whom there is no shortage in D.C., grumbled that the whole real estate dustup had been staged all along to achieve this downsized goal.) The end result was that the overwhelming majority of new DHS employees were going to stay sitting at their old agencies. Of course, all this opened the door to doubts about whether the scattered workforce defeated the streamlining purpose of the new department.

My own doubts about whether DHS had been dealt a bad hand were not dispelled when I announced myself on a clunky old phone that hung next to its gray door. The reception area measured a hundred square feet, without room for even a chair. It had a cheap suspended ceiling of yellowed acoustic tiles and was decorated with a badly mounted blown-up photo of Ridge walking with Bush, both striding purposefully toward the mutual goal of keeping us all out of harm's way. The only other adornments were a large red sign that said NO CELL PHONES, WIRELESS PDAS, OR 2-WAY PAGERS BEYOND THIS POINT and an elevator door. I deposited my mobile phone into one of the little post-office-box–style lockers, pocketed the key, and waited for someone to come get me. I was supposed to meet an assistant secretary from the Information Analysis and Infrastructure Protection Directorate, and we had had to reschedule three times already because he kept getting called away to the Hill.

The little lobby was a veritable hub of activity. People came and went, ducking past each other like well-trained submarine crews accustomed to working in confined spaces. Ten minutes went by, and the guards forgot about me, so I just soaked in the atmosphere. A pair of slick officials dressed like Wall Street types presented their CIA credentials. Someone from the Secret Service marched in, sporting the ubiquitous buzz cut, starched white shirt, and dark Brooks Brothers suit. The Secret Service is now part of the Department of Homeland Security, and apparently not happy about it. An FBI agent, his laminated ID card dangling from his neck, stowed his Blackberry and cell phone, probably one of those $3,000 models made by General Dynamics that scrambles the signal for secure calls. Notably, the FBI is not part of the new department, which to an outsider not versed in Washington politics might seem silly, since that means that DHS has no counterterror intelligence-gathering capability of its own. "Counterterror," Paul Bremer, our viceroy in Iraq, once told me, "is 80 percent intelligence." The loss of that all-important capability is a severe handicap for DHS, especially for its Information Analysis Directorate, which, being born blind, would forever need to rely on the Bureau for information.

The FBI's own counterterror program was having troubles of its own. It was on its fourth chief since 9/11 and had lost a good deal of influence to the CIA, which had been put in charge of the Terrorist Threat Integration Center, a new body that reported to the director of Central Intelligence that many said was a precursor to a separate domestic intelligence agency. Logically, the TTIC should have been part of DHS. That Ridge had been fended off so easily was a clear sign that the new department did not enjoy the political support of some power brokers at 1600 Pennsylvania Avenue. The lack of clout was reflected in many ways. In May 2003, for instance, John Mintz of the *Washington Post* reported that Ridge ceded control of investigations into terrorist financing from the Secret Service to the Justice Department. Enraged at the loss of their traditional brief, some senior Service officials almost mutinied. In another humiliation, only twenty-two of the ninety-two FBI agents in a cybersecurity unit that was transferred to DHS opted to come on board, because remaining at the Bureau gave them higher status. Concerns over DHS's tooth-lessness, according to Mintz's searing article, were having serious repercussions for the department's ability to recruit top-flight per-sonnel. Fifteen prominent members of Washington's intelligence community, including the military's spy satellite mapping chief, Lieu-tenant General James R. Clapper, had turned down offers to head DHS's downgraded intelligence analysis directorate, and one thirty-three-year CIA veteran, Paul Redmond, resigned shortly after testify-ing to Congress in a June 2003 hearing that his office had been able to attract only twenty-six analysts. Part of the problem, he said, was that there was not enough space for more analysts at NAC. Also, DHS computers were not secure or able to receive classified data. Why? The Bush administration had decided, days before DHS's for-mal launch, that the new agency shouldn't have the same rank as the CIA or FBI in processing intelligence about terror threats. In ruling that DHS could neither collect its own data nor "routinely thrust it-self into the minutiae of analyzing raw intelligence," the White House had effectively defanged the department's Information Analy-sis and Infrastructure Protection section. Which begged the ques-tion: What exactly *was* that section supposed to be doing?

I had planned on asking the directorate's assistant secretary, Bob Liscouski, just that, but twenty minutes had now elapsed since our interview was to have started, and I was still languishing in the makeshift lobby. Ridge had just come in from a taping of the *Tonight Show* (or maybe it was *Letterman*), a couple of bodyguards in tow. He was shorter in person than on TV, but looked even tougher, which was also misleading. Ridge was adored by his staff. Despite the fierce pugilist appearance, he is said to be a conciliator, not a fighter—good for interdepartmental affairs, bad for going up against Washington heavyweights like Ashcroft over the division of resources. I noticed that he didn't have to check his cell phone at the door. The privi-leges of rank, I guessed.

I used the house phone to leave several increasingly anxious messages with Liscouski's staff and passed the next fifteen minutes leafing through a trade magazine called *GSN: Government Security News*. A very thick pile of GSNs lay on the floor, the flap copy reminding readers that time was running out to subscribe. The lead story was devoted to DHS's 2004 budget and Congress's decision to approve an extra $1 billion for the department over and above what President Bush had actually requested. (This was notable since it usually worked the other way around; Congress cut.) There was a piece on improvements needed for facial-recognition systems that DHS planned to implement to screen foreigners at borders and a front-page feature on how DHS must choose between "flat" and "rolled" fingerprints for its databases. Most of the magazine, however, was devoted to ads. Northrop Grumman took out a full page praising its laser technology and how it would work wonders protecting passenger jets from shoulder-fired missiles. ADT trumpeted its selection as the prime security provider for the Port of Oakland, bragging that "a port that processes nearly one million containers a year can't afford to make the wrong security choice." Several firms touted their radio frequency ID hardware and encryption services. And page after page was devoted to every surveillance camera system under the sun.

Dozens of homeland security magazines like GSN had sprouted since 9/11, hawking the wares of contractors eager for a piece of DHS's $36 billion budget. Washington's influence-peddling industry had also quickly seized on the opportunity to cash in on the boom. In the eighteen months since 2002, registered counterterror lobbyists had multiplied fivefold in the district to 799, according to the *New York Times*. Their cruder pitches, wrote the *Times*, included wooing potential clients with promises of "securing your piece of the homeland security pie" and advice on how "to avoid the land mines and find the gold mines of homeland security."

Special interests took up the cause in Congress, as well. One lawmaker from Missouri infamously slipped a last-minute provision into the homeland security bill to benefit his campaign donor Philip Morris, according to *Newsweek*. What exactly the tobacco giant has in common with counterterrorism is anyone's guess.

Several of Tom Ridge's former aides had become lobbyists post-9/11, as had Tim Hutchinson, former Republican senator from Arkansas and brother of DHS undersecretary Asa. Asa Hutchinson headed the big Border Protection and Transportation Security Directorate. (A meeting Tim Hutchinson had arranged for an Arkansas client with his brother in D.C. was strictly "social," the undersecretary assured when word of the get-together was leaked to the *Washington Post* by a rival lobbyist.)

Special interests are the engine of the Washington economy, which boasts even more lawyers per capita than journalists, so there is nothing unusual, unforeseeable, or even unpatriotic about the scramble for security dollars. It is, in fact, pretty tame compared to what goes on at the Pentagon. If the lobbyists can be accused of anything, it is false advertising. Regardless of how juicy $36 billion sounds, the security pie is neither thick nor savory. In fact, there is precious little money to go around. Why else would officials at NAC have been sharing desks and telephones? DHS's $36 billion budget is a misleading number, something the Enron accountants might have cooked up. It sounds great at press conferences and allows the president to say that he is spending large amounts of money to keep us safe. In reality, the sum does not represent a dramatic increase over pre-9/11 outlays. It simply lumps together the existing budgets of the twenty-two federal agencies that comprised DHS. Between them, the Coast Guard, customs, the INS, FEMA, and the Lawrence Livermore National Lab accounted for $29 billion of the $36 billion. Granted, TSA and its roughly $5 billion annual budget were new expenditures, but most of the other agencies had gotten only 10 to 15 percent raises, and some even less. Which was why I had kept hearing about money woes and equipment shortages wherever I went. The truth of the matter is that homeland security is a shoestring operation, so much so that worried Democrats in Congress kept trying to throw more money at it.

———

"Wait, wait," shouted the guard, running out after me. Because an hour had elapsed and no one was answering the phone, I had given up on my interview, returned my pass, and was starting to head for home. An effusively apologetic aide hobbled out on crutches to greet me. Last-minute scheduling problems, he said, begging forgiveness. He couldn't get to his desk and was trying to wrap everything up before the place emptied out for tomorrow's Thanksgiving holiday. I followed him up the stairs to Building 18, a three-story brick-and-brown-clapboard structure that DHS had recently taken over from the Navy. The expansion was encouraging. After all, the NSA had started humbly, as well—with one closet and some cardboard boxes—and today has its own closed city in Maryland with 80,000 denizens, fast-food courts, banks, gyms, fire and police departments, and retail stores.

Posters were tacked up on some of the walls of the second floor of Building 18. "Information leaks can trickle a flood of security" warned one, while another cartoon depicting a fairy-tale wolf eyeing an unsuspecting pig with a predatory gleam admonished: "Don't let your guard down. The threat is still out there."

We waited for the assistant secretary, Bob Liscouski, in the conference room. He had started his career as a cop in Philadelphia and had spent the better part of the 1990s as Director of Information Assurance at Coca-Cola in Atlanta, protecting Coke's secret formula. He was a runner, I could see, when he finally strode in, and he had a detective's hard eyes. I gave him a brief synopsis of my research by way of introduction and threw in a few quick anecdotes from the front lines: bioterrorism exercises, boarding ships, Hady Omar's unfortunate ordeal. "Too bad, but it's gonna happen," said Liscouski after listening to a thumbnail sketch of Omar's incarceration. "Shit happens." He shrugged. "There's going to be collateral damage. You're going to have to give up some things if you wanna live.

"I don't want to tell you how to write your book," he continued. "But it seems to me you are going about it the wrong way, looking at things from the context of different brush strokes. We at DHS are the big brush and have the ability to look at the big picture." Liscouski certainly didn't lack confidence. "I don't think you understand the complexity of what we are trying to do," he declared, having sized me up and evidently found me lacking. He whipped off his suit jacket and strode to the blackboard. On it he drew a box divided into thirteen squares, each representing different components of our critical infrastructure: water, energy, telecoms and so on. For the next ten minutes, he worked on a matrix, explaining the role of vulnerability assessments. I put my pen down—always a bad sign. This stuff was chapter 1. We had only thirty minutes allotted for the interview. I tried to move the tempo along. "What are you doing about it?"

"We don't do the doing," said Liscouski. "We do the coordinating. Our role is to look at the big picture of what is really threatened and determine how to protect it." I asked for an example. Liscouski said that for security reasons he didn't want to go into specifics. "What about the chemical industry?" I pushed. Survey after survey showed that the fifteen thousand chemical plants in the United States were probably the most vulnerable pieces of infrastructure in the nation. According to the Environmental Protection Agency, more than one hundred of these plants could each endanger up to a million lives with poisonous clouds of ammonia, chlorine, or carbon disulfide that could be released into the atmosphere over densely populated areas by a terror attack. The military ranked a strike against the chemical industry as second only to biological warfare (and ahead of nuclear devices) in the total number of mass casualties it would produce.

Not surprisingly, following 9/11 a push was made to curtail some of these risks. Democratic senator Jon Corzine of New Jersey, whose state was home to 9 of the 111 most vulnerable factories in the country, introduced a bill to police chemical producers that passed unanimously in Senate committees and quickly garnered White House

support. Tabled as the Chemical Security Act, it sought to codify parameters for site security, ensure the safer transport of toxic materials
(a single rail car filled with 33,000 gallons of chlorine could kill up to
100,000 people), and establish a timetable to shift away from the use
of the most noxious chemicals. Some jurisdictions are already doing
that voluntarily. In Washington, for instance, the water sewage treatment plant switched from chlorine to another slightly more expensive but less dangerous bacteria remover in 2002. The changeover
cost the average Washington water consumer 75 cents, but reduced
the risk of terrorist hijackings by eliminating hundreds of chlorine
tankers rumbling through the capital region. Other municipalities,
especially in environmentally conscious California, already had such
similarly strict codes on the books. A 1999 ordinance in Contra
Costa County, according to the Wall Street Journal, led refiners like
ChevronTexaco to replace chlorine with alternative disinfectants
and ammonia with water-based substitutes.

The Chemical Security Act seemed set to sail through the national legislature, but as the memories of 9/11 grew dimmer with the
passage of time, the petrochemical industry launched a well-
coordinated and well-financed campaign to scuttle the legislation.
Led by the powerful American Petroleum Institute, the Journal reported, lobby groups bombarded senators, congressmen, and the
White House with thousands of letters, position papers, and reports
on the adverse economic impact of the act. Chlorine and its deriva-
tives went into products that accounted for 45 percent of U.S. GDP,
they argued. The backyard BBQ gas grill would disappear. The American pastoral would forever be altered. Ultimately, the campaign
proved successful. The White House cooled toward the idea of regulating chemical security. The seven Republican senators who had en-
dorsed the bill in committee withdrew their support. And $5.5
million in petrochemical campaign contributions helped to ensure
that Republicans took the Senate in the 2002 midterm elections and
that the Chemical Security Act died without a vote. In its place, a
new bill introduced by Republican senator James Inhofe of Okla-

homa proposes that chemical factories be self-policing and that the government have no oversight or enforcement powers over safety regulations.

As a result, two years after the lessons of 9/11, virtually anyone could still gain entry into thousands of these sites across the country, and to prove it, 60 *Minutes* sent several camera crews in November 2003 to trespass at plants that produced some of the most hazardous materials, making it clear they could have blown a hole in any one of them. The 60 *Minutes* segment had caused quite a stir in Washington. Liscouski, though, appeared unmoved. Was DHS working on any mandatory security codes for unprotected chemical plants? At a minimum, fencing requirements, cameras, lights, guards? "Our job is not to regulate," he said. "By regulating, we could be missing out on important gaps. Not all chemical plants produce materials with the same levels of toxicity. Regulating is not our role," he repeated. The EPA did it. So did the FDA. Why not DHS? I pressed.

"We are not going to turn this country into a fortress," Liscouski snapped. "I have every confidence that the private sector will act responsibly," he added. "That they will do the right thing on their own." That was quite a leap of faith, given the slew of recent corporate scandals at Enron, Tyco, WorldCom, and Adelphia. And it also flew in the face of reality. The *Economist*, in its August 2003 issue, published a survey of 331 large corporations; it found that security spending had risen by only 4 percent since 9/11, and much of the increase was chalked up to higher insurance premiums. Only one in five of the companies said its spending would continue to increase. "Left to themselves," noted Steven Flynn, a homeland security scholar at the Council on Foreign Relations, "factory owners will do nothing. They have no incentive to. If factory A, say, spends a million dollars on security upgrades, its products can't compete with factory B down the street, which spent nothing. And yet if terrorists blow up factory Z on the other side of the country, factories A and B will suffer equally, since the whole industry will go down the drain. Only legislation can level the playing field."

Liscouski started to glance impatiently at his watch, so I knew my time was up. I still had no clear conception of what his Infrastructure Protection division actually did, other than draw Venn diagrams, and I must have made my frustration plain. "We've sent people to two dozen chemical plants we've determined are the highest risk," he finally said. "To shore up security?" I asked. "No," he said, getting up to leave. "To advise them on what their vulnerabilities are."

"So you're taking the cautious, go-slow approach," I remarked, perhaps a little too snidely. Liscouski stopped in his tracks. "If you think that, then I've just wasted my time talking to you. We are running at full speed," he snapped. "We are running a marathon at full speed."

9

THE SCIENTIFIC SENTINELS

N OT EVERYTHING AT THE DEPARTMENT OF HOMELAND SECU-
rity needs fixing. DHS has accomplished a great deal in a short
period of time and on a shoestring budget. But like many reporters, I tend to focus more on the negative. After all, writing that
something works well isn't going to get you on the front page; expos-
ing major malfunctions does. And yet there have been success stories
at DHS. One of the biggest also happened to involve one of its least-
known divisions: the Science and Technology Directorate.

Science and technology are what America does best. Our counterterror analysts may be relative neophytes, but our engineers, design-
ers, and researchers are seasoned professionals. America's technical
capabilities are unparalleled. We unraveled the genome. Our military
arsenal is the world's most advanced. We have been to the moon and
now are going to put people on Mars. Our communications expertise has made the world a global village. And we have produced more
Nobel laureates than any other nation on earth. Tapping that vast
reservoir of knowledge to discover better ways to protect America
from terrorists is the responsibility of the Science and Technology
Directorate.

The directorate occupies the fourth floor of a nondescript government building a few blocks from the Air and Space Museum. It is a
low-key address with no nameplate over the door, just far enough off
the beaten path to ensure anonymity to the hundred-odd scientists
and technicians who work there, poring over blueprints, technical
manuals, and top secret prototypes.

It is so low key, in fact, that I had trouble finding it. The security guards at the federal building next door had never heard of it; nor had anyone at the heavily guarded parking lot across the street. You can't blame them. The S&T Directorate was a brand-new creation, less than a few months old in spring 2003, and had just moved in. "Yeah, you're in the right place," said the uniformed guard, when I finally stumbled on the correct entrance. "Take the freight elevator right around that corridor," he instructed after I'd gone through the ubiquitous metal detector and had my credentials checked.

The lift rattled open on a long, empty hallway freshly painted psychiatric-hospital white. It seemed completely deserted and, with its heavy 1950s architectural details, felt more like the gloomy set of a Hitchcock film than a cutting-edge hub of twenty-first-century technical wizardry. Handwritten sheets of paper flapped from the doors, acting as makeshift nameplates until the printers and sign makers could lend a greater air of permanency to the start-up directorate.

Eventually the ghostly hallway spilled into an open space of more modern design, with new carpeting and a maze of shoulder-height cubicle partitions such as one might encounter in a large insurance company. Dr. Parney Albright's corner office was cramped, windowless, and unadorned save for the large table of elements that hung next to his door. He still didn't have a business card or formal title, and was waiting for Congress to confirm his appointment as assistant secretary of homeland security.

But if the Science and Technology Directorate had a founding father, he was it. A trained physicist with a penchant for Tom Clancy novels, he was trim and youthful, despite a bushy mane that was as white as the walls around him. My first impression was of a man who was modest and open—in other words, a rare bird in our nation's capital. If anything, Albright looked a little tired. Everyone, he said, careful to spread the credit around, had put in long hours to get the directorate up and running. "People were in till ten o'clock almost every night," he recalled. Just the logistics of starting what amounted to a billion-dollar research and development agency were daunting.

Staff had to be hired and budgets drawn up. Office space needed to be found and furnished, phone lines installed, and computers hardwired. Then there was the mind-boggling minutiae of setting up pension plans (fill out QLE form SF-3102 within 30 days, SF-1152 for spouse, SF-2808 for children under 22 within 60 days), FEHB healthcare (fill out forms SF-2823 and SF-2809 for dependents), life insurance (SF-2817 to elect option B or C coverage, unless otherwise specified, in which case fill out SF-2819 and TSP-3.) Security clearances needed to be obtained from the FBI and Secret Service, and salary disbursements had to be determined in accordance with existing GS pay scales (9 through 15, but that's a whole different batch of forms). And all that needed to be accomplished before a single piece of security hardware could be tendered, tested, or purchased.

The directorate itself was loosely modeled after the Pentagon's Defense Advanced Research Projects Agency, which worked on all the military's cutting-edge technology and had given the world such innovations as the DARPANET, whose civilian version became better known as the Internet. The CIA also had a Science and Technology Directorate. Its history was rich with the design of microscopic bugs and cameras that could fit into toiletries kits and concocting not-so innocuous poisons to kill the likes of Fidel Castro. Albright himself had done a stint at DARPA, and it was tempting to think of him as something of a younger, fitter version of James Bond's celluloid quartermaster, Q—only the gadgets he was developing had the very real-world role of keeping Americans safe from terror.

Some of the stuff coming out of Albright's shop did seem straight out of the movies: 3-D computer screens similar to one used by Tom Cruise in the futuristic thriller *Minority Report*; thermal imaging cameras that could tell if a person was stressed by measuring the blood flow around the eyes (coming soon to an airport check-in counter near you); and software programs designed to spot abnormal behavior by individuals in large crowds. Prototypes of the 3-D computers were already being used by the Department of Homeland Security's intelligence division. "The analysts love them." Albright beamed. "Data is displayed in digital spheres, which they can access or sift with a twist of the hand."

The thermal imaging cameras were also operational. "They're based on the fight-or-flight principle," he explained. "When you are frightened or nervous, the body pumps extra blood to vital organs, especially the eyes. The cameras can detect that." Of course, he added, the technology could not distinguish the source of anxiety. Someone afraid of flying, going through a nasty divorce, or simply having a really bad day would trigger the alarm just as a terrorist traveling on false papers might. "It's another tool to help determine whose bags should be searched. No one is going to be hauled away to jail based on it."

The behavior-spotting software was still in an embryonic stage. "We've hired psychiatrists to interview veteran police, Secret Service, and customs agents to try to determine what tips them off about suspicious behavior." With experience, many of these officers develop finely honed instincts, and Albright was trying to teach the computer this sixth sense. El Al screeners operate on such gut feelings, which is why they interact so much with passengers. If they keep you talking long enough, eventually they will be able to tell if anything is not on the up-and-up. How a machine would ever be able to replicate this most human quality was quite frankly beyond me. But I could certainly see the merit in automating some aspects of passenger screening.

In the fall of 2003, DHS was testing one such prototype. It was intended to verify that foreigners entering the United States were not carrying false papers or bogus visas (as some of the nineteen 9/11 hijackers had) and to ensure that they leave the country when their visas expired (as some of the nineteen hijackers had not). When I went to see Albright, it was being field-tested at Atlanta's Hartsfield-Jackson International Airport, and, if all went well, would be implemented nationally in 2004.

The US-VISIT pilot program in Atlanta showed great promise, he said. Booths at passport control are equipped with finger-scanning equipment and small unobtrusive digital cameras. Arrivals from every country that required visas to the United States (all but twenty-eight mostly western European nations) place two index fingers on an ink-less fingerprint reader, while the small digital camera snaps their photo. Their biometric features are then compared via computer software to stored algorithms of the fingerprints and photo encoded on their visa. If they match, they are legitimate visitors who already have been cleared through interviews with consular officials. The whole process takes only fifteen seconds and—most important—does not discriminate against one ethnic group. It is fair because everyone has to submit to it, whether from eastern Europe, Latin America, or the Middle East. It doesn't single out Pakistanis, Saudis, or Egyptians any more than it does Poles, Czechs, or Argentineans. So a Muslim visitor's first experience in America isn't racial or religious profiling. The system also keeps track of when people leave the country, making certain that the person who leaves is the same person who entered and has not switched documents with someone. An automated central mainframe collects the names of those overstaying their visas, a frequent occurrence in the past where illegal immigrants simply got lost in the system.

Although the US-VISIT program is not foolproof—terrorists traveling on Canadian or western European passports can still get in—there would be less need for lengthy and unpleasant interrogations at the border, and it will be far more difficult for extremists to scam their way into the country because biometric features don't lie. And after all, keeping extremists out of the country is far and away the single most effective tool against terror, far more efficient than all the Patriot Act legislation and measures combined. (The US-VISIT pilot program uncovered numerous visa frauds and led to several arrests of individuals matched against an FBI criminal database. It was deemed so successful that on January 4, 2004, it was implemented at 115 airports and 14 seaports. An additional 50 of the largest land border crossings were to be added by December 31, 2004, and every port of entry to the United States was to be outfitted with the biometric readers by the end of 2005.)

Surveillance, biometric, and data mining technology amount to around 10 percent of the directorate's activities. "Don't worry, we have no intention of sifting through your grocery list," Albright said, poking fun at the Defense Department's defunct TIA program. Most of the hardware he was developing was of a less intrusive nature: radiation portals that can distinguish between different isotopes, chemical sniffers to detect toxic agents in subways, citywide biological pathogen sensors, and countermissile defenses for commercial airliners.

Although the Pentagon already has all these gadgets in its considerable arsenal, one can't simply slap military hardware on civilian planes or in subways. One of the biggest obstacles is false alarm rates. Military gear is expressly designed to sound the alarm at the drop of a hat. "Better safe than sorry" was the Army adage when it came to many of its early warning systems. "If a chemical sniffer in Kuwait or Iraq goes off," Albright explained, "the GIs put on their gas masks. If it turns out to be a false alarm, they just take them off, and no big deal." (Viewers of the Iraqi invasion were treated to many such spectacles by reporters trying to talk through their hastily donned masks.) The margin for error in a domestic, civilian setting, however, is vastly less forgiving. "If a detector goes off in the New York subway, we are going to have a major public health event, not to mention a potential for panic."

The same holds true for the electronic countermissile defenses used by the Air Force, which eject pyrotechnic flares as decoys to distract heat-seeking missiles. "There'd be so many flares popping off that the airspace over JFK would look like the Fourth of July," Albright said with a chuckle. The flares could set off brush fires and rain down on refineries. They are simply not suited to civilian life, so another more environmentally friendly system, perhaps using lasers and other sorts of infrared jammers, must be found. Maintenance is another serious issue. Military antimissile systems need to be serviced every three hundred hours. At that rate, airlines would have to spend upward of $100 billion over a decade to service the systems, which is simply financially not feasible, even if the federal government picked up the initial $10 billion tab to install the systems aboard all seven thousand planes in the U.S. commercial fleet.

So there are still so many kinks to be ironed out that Albright was not rushing headlong into missile defense. The idea of outfitting every passenger plane with countermeasures, however, has gained considerable currency on Capitol Hill in the wake of an August 2003 scare, when undercover FBI agents arrested three men in the Newark airport plotting to smuggle a shoulder-fired missile from Russia through the port of Baltimore. The Newark incident prompted the Department of Homeland Security to earmark $120 million toward developing a civilian antimissile prototype. But the allocation did little to appease some lawmakers, who worried that the process was taking too long. "The danger of an airliner being shot down by one of these missiles is now staring the Homeland Security Department in the face," warned New York senator Charles Schumer, who along with Senator Barbara Boxer of California was pushing Albright to fast track the plan. "The fact that DHS is planning to take at least two years to develop a missile defense prototype verges on the dangerous."

Albright wasn't about to be pressured, however. "A lot of things need to be carefully thought through before we start asking taxpayers to cut those kind of checks," he said. "I'm trying to avoid the rush to failure. In engineering, not getting it right the first time ends up costing very heavily. We could do more harm than good if we move too fast."

The brewing flap over civilian antimissile systems offers a good illustration of one of the most pressing problems clouding the entire counterterror effort: deciding what risks can be deemed acceptable before reaching for budget-breaking solutions. After all, over the past thirty years, only twenty-four civilian airliners, mostly in war-torn African countries, have been shot down by shoulder-fired missiles. Statistically that means one has a greater chance of getting struck by lightning or winning the lottery—or both—than getting shot down by an SA-7 Strela missile. What's more, bigger airliners like the Boeing 747 or the Airbus A380 can take a hit from a shoulder-launched missile and still land safely, according to Bill Sweetman, an aerospace analyst who has written over twenty books on military craft. The SA-7 uses heat-seeking technology to home in on the hottest part of an aircraft, the exhaust from its engines. Unlike the smaller Boeing 737, however, the engine pods of the big commercial planes are hung at a sufficient distance from the wing and fuel bladders that even if they are hit, the blast will not cause structural damage to the wing or ignite the fuel tanks. Several of the giant C-5 military cargo planes and a big Boeing operated by DHL courier service had been hit by SA-7s in Iraq and managed to land safely. So by design, large long-haul craft are relatively immune to SA-7 attack, but not to a multiple missile attack that knocks out several engines.

True, there are a lot of SA-7s out there, perhaps as many as a half million, including the Anza MK-1, Ayn as Saqr, and Hongying-5. And whether of Russian, Chinese, or Egyptian manufacture, they are readily available for a few thousand dollars in the better-stocked Third World arms bazaars. Just a single strike from an SA-7 would do untold damage to the already fragile airline industry. But terrorists would first need to smuggle the weapon into the country, no easy task since it is almost six feet long—not something you can slip under your coat. Then they'd have to learn to use it properly, also no easy task since they cannot train openly. What's more, the missiles have a very limited range, require split-second timing, and are wildly inaccurate even in the hands of a trained professional. According to various SA-7 manuals I found on the web, even in perfect conditions the manufacturers estimate only a 25 percent chance of striking the target. That hit ratio only went up to 35 to 40 percent on the newest generation SA-18s, which are not in wide circulation. The SA-7 also has fail-safe systems—if you fire too early (at less than a 500- to 800-yard range, depending on the model), the warhead does not activate but bounces off the target harmlessly. Shot too late, the missile self-destructs after seventeen seconds of flight. So there is a narrow window of opportunity at takeoff and landing that most amateurs with only rudimentary knowledge of the weapon will miss. That is exactly what happened in Mombasa, Kenya, in November 2002, when al Qaeda operatives shot twice at an Israeli Arkia Airlines 757. "They were too excited and trigger-happy," Tal Imberman, an Arkia pilot I had met in Tel Aviv, had told me. The first warhead was fired too early, at around three hundred yards, and by the time the terrorists had reloaded—it takes a trained crew six to ten seconds to change the warhead and thermal battery—the plane was out of the weapon's two-kilometer range. "Buckshot fever," said Milton Bearden, a retired CIA agent who had armed Afghan rebels with Stinger missiles during the Soviet invasion. "We saw it a lot with the Muj [freedom fighters], until they got used to the weapon."

"I've fired one," said my Israeli friend Einav, when I asked him about the botched Mombasa attempt. "They're pretty much useless unless used in great numbers." A single shooter is unlikely to bring down a commercial jetliner, Einav said. Two or three would even the odds, however. On January 15, 1973, the PLO splinter group Black September had gone several steps further, circling the approach to Rome's Leonardo da Vinci Airport at Fiumicino with twelve SA-7 missiles. The target was Israeli prime minister Golda Meir, who was arriving to meet the pope. The Mossad had gotten wind of the operation and by the time Meir's plane was on its final approach had discovered and neutralized ten of the twelve shoulder-fired missiles, killing several of the terrorists during brief but brutal on-site interrogations designed to learn the location of the other shooters. Two remaining SA-7s, however, had eluded the security agents, according to a 1990 memoir by former Mossad agent Victor J. Ostrovsky. With less than a minute to spare before Meir's plane was in missile range, an astute Mossad man noticed something odd about a roadside food-concession cart. It had three smokestacks instead of one, and smoke was coming from the central stack only. The other two stacks consisted of holes drilled in the cart's roof with SA-7s pointing at a dot in the sky that was the prime minister's El Al plane, now fifteen seconds from missile range. The quick-witted Mossad agent, in a feat worthy of a Hollywood thriller, drove his car at full speed into the cart, literally toppling the SA-7 plot to save the day.

But even after that close call, the cost and technical difficulties in adapting military countermissile defense to civilian use were so considerable that the security-obsessed Israelis didn't outfit El Al with countermissile defenses. Instead they simply put out the rumor that they had. "A little disinformation," Einav chuckled. "And for a long time it worked." After the 2002 Mombasa incident revealed that Israeli airliners were in fact undefended, Ariel Sharon's government began studying ways to equip El Al's fleet of Boeings with the devices in 2004. But that was a mere thirty planes. In the United States, Einav argued, there were seven thousand planes in the commercial fleet and far more pressing vulnerabilities in commercial aviation in areas such as improper cargo screening. Only 2 percent of cargo on passenger planes is being screened, which seems silly when little old ladies are being made to take their shoes off for security. "As priorities go," he said, "shoring up security for airborne cargo is to me much more important. It's also a lot cheaper and technically less complicated to achieve."

So, is it worth spending $10 billion—more than twice the FBI's entire annual budget, almost a third of the total spending on all twenty-two federal agencies comprising the Department of Homeland Security—on countermeasures that most likely will never be needed? Does the threat justify the cost? Until recently this last dilemma has resided primarily in the cold domain of insurance actuaries and corporate attorneys, who weigh the bottom-line impact of adding product safety features against the potential liabilities of going without them. But since 9/11, such ghoulish calculations have entered the political discourse, where mathematics is often pushed aside by emotions and electoral considerations. Politicians, if they had their way, would protect everything. But not only is that impractical, it's financially impossible. So what should be protected? Power plants or water treatment facilities? What is more vulnerable? Cyberspace or public spaces? Should we spend more money shoring up security on commuter trains or shopping malls? Someone has to draw up priorities, decide whether we can risk leaving some areas unprotected, while devoting our limited resources to others. Unfortunately, DHS, as of early 2004, hadn't done that, according to a congressional report by the House Select Committee on Homeland Security, which criticized the department for lacking "a comprehensive threat and vulnerability assessment to set priorities and guide strategy."

The absence of such a plan is causing a growing, although still largely unpublicized, rift in Washington. On one side stand elected officials. "Legislators want to be seen by voters as doing everything possible to keep America safe," said former CIA counterterror chief Vincent Cannistraro, "regardless of expense."

On the other side, career security people like Albright, Cannistraro, and Einav know that the very notion of trying to design a zero-terrorist-risk environment is dangerously futile and that resources have to be marshaled prudently or we could spend ourselves into bankruptcy, as had the Soviets, and still be vulnerable.

Threat management, ultimately, is a mathematical equation: Which countermeasures give taxpayers the biggest bang for the buck? One such cost-effective measure is an early warning system against biological weapons such as smallpox or plague, and Albright volunteered to show me how it worked.

We went to the Mall in Washington, not too far from his office. Since the Mall—with its monuments, Million Man or Mom marches, and proximity to the White House and Congress—is such an obvious target, Albright didn't think national security would be compromised if he disclosed that sensors had been placed there. "It's a no-brainer," he said. "But don't get any more specific about the location."

It happened to be an unusually windy November day. Gusts had been clocked at 44 mph, and limbs were being torn off trees. Ideal conditions, in other words, to disperse any kind of aerosolized weapon. This was fitting, since the United Nations that very morning had released an intelligence report warning it was "just a matter of time before al Qaeda attempts a biological or chemical terrorist attack."

We made our way to a white rectangular box about six feet tall. It had an antenna and a black snorkel sprouting out the top that sucked in air at the rate of one hundred liters a minute, but otherwise it was indistinguishable from the utility panels scattered throughout the Mall. Wayne R. was waiting for us there. (For security reasons, Albright asked that his full name not be disclosed.) He serviced the air sampler, although the joggers and tourists who passed us did not give him a second glance. And that was the point. No bubble suits or gas masks or glaring white lab frocks to attract unwanted attention. He was the picture of discretion: purple stud earring, bald, an African American hipster in a black windbreaker and sneakers. No one was going to take him as the person manning the front line of our capital's biological defenses.

Wayne punched in a PIN number and opened the sampler's access panel. The PIN was automatically transmitted to a computer at the central command post, a security procedure designed to prevent unauthorized individuals from tampering with the device. Inside were two clear cylindrical tubes, each about eight inches long, and a small aluminum nozzle. These contained the primary and backup filters through which thousands of liters of air had passed, trapping any pathogens that might be present in the atmosphere. Wayne removed the filter containers, scanned them with a bar-code reader, and placed each in a labeled zip-top bag. This was done several times a day at numerous locations in Washington and in thirty other cities across the United States. "Obviously New York is one of them," said Albright. "Matter of fact, some of the samplers there are already covered with graffiti, so they blend right in. But we shouldn't be more specific about other cities. Because if the opposition knows where they are, they will also know where they are not."

A particularly nasty gust whistled past us. "I guess I'd want to duck behind that building if this thing sounded the alarm," I said, thinking I would be sheltered from any poisonous currents. "Might not help," Albright replied. Air currents in urban areas, he explained, often follow tortuous paths, swirling between structures like eddies in a river. That was why each sampler was connected to the Weather Service and a sophisticated computer program that modeled air currents in real time or at any time in the past twenty-four hours down to the city block so that the authorities could literally track every inch of the path of any pathogen release.

It cost an average of $2 million a year per city to operate the entire BioWatch early warning system, about the same price as installing antimissile defenses on just one plane. For the roughly $60 million annually that the Department of Homeland Security was paying to operate BioWatch, half the population of the United States was covered by the air samplers in the initial thirty-one cities. The relative cost effectiveness of BioWatch was one reason why the program had been fast-tracked, while officials were taking a more cautious, go-slow approach with antimissile countermeasures. In fact, Albright had started deploying BioWatch well before his department even formally existed or had a budget to spend. "Getting this fielded without funding was an interesting exercise." He smiled. Another reason for the haste was that unlike chemical weapons, lethal viral agents like smallpox or pneumonic plague are difficult to detect and highly contagious, but easily treatable if detected early enough.

That was why Wayne R. made his rounds at least twice a day. The Mall was the last pickup on Wayne's morning route, and we followed his white SUV onto the Beltway to the laboratory where the filters were tested for trace elements of about a dozen different viral and bacterial pathogens. "Anthrax is a no-brainer, but I'd prefer not to list them all because we obviously don't want the terrorists to know which pathogens we are not testing for," Albright explained.

BioWatch would not protect us against every sort of biological attack, he said. Anthrax in letters, for instance, wouldn't get picked up by outdoor air samplers. (Postal facilities had their own warning system, known as BDS, and sent all mail destined to the White House, Congress, and key federal facilities in D.C. to a special processing facility in New Jersey, where Rhodotron machines bombarded letters and parcels with accelerated electrons and X rays to destroy anthrax and render other biological agents harmless.) Nor was it clear to me if the tests were sensitive enough to pick up traces of an indoor release, as in the Denver TOPOFF scenario. Albright said he preferred not to get too specific about BioWatch capabilities and limitations, for the obvious security reasons, but allowed that air samplers in Houston had picked up a naturally occurring outbreak of tularemia in jackrabbits, so the machines were pretty sensitive. He frequently seemed to wrestle with what he could safely say and what should remain classified. "A lot of my colleagues aren't happy about my going public at all," he said. "But I think sometimes too much secrecy is counterproductive. People fear what they don't know, information that is just wrong gets out, myths start to grow."

Albright was, in fact, surprisingly forthcoming. Secrecy is something I constantly encountered with Washington officials. Sometimes, of course, they had valid reasons for keeping mum. But at other times I got the distinct impression that national security was simply a pretext for keeping blunders under wraps and not facing accountability. Security also could be invoked to avoid specific questions that might expose the fact that nothing at all has been done to remedy a problem or shore up vulnerabilities.

Albright, though, was a scientist, not a political animal with finely honed cover-up instincts, and he was just as prone to criticize his department (too bureaucratic and inefficient) as to sing its praises. "We've never had a false positive," he said of the samplers, as our van pulled up to a military facility in Maryland. The lab that tested the filters collected from the air samples was located in a single-story cinderblock structure, hidden well behind the heavy steel antivehicle barriers patrolled by MPs. Inside the lab, brown ceramic tiles covered the walls from floor to ceiling. Spare samplers were stored in one room, while large stainless steel fridges stored already analyzed samples sorted by time, date, and location.

We were issued white lab coats and ushered into a room full of expensive-looking equipment. A young technician named Tom with a goatee and a master's degree in genetics ran the diagnostic facility, which consisted of a series of workstations with Plexiglas hoods hooked up to large vacuum machines to prevent contamination. The filters resembled communion wafers—or rolling paper, a technician noted—only they had been stained black from pollution. (On the West Coast they were a rusty reddish hue from smog.) After being cleaned, they were sliced into pieces and ground with tiny glass beads to break up cells and release DNA. A reagent was added and the DNA samples were inserted into a scanner that cooked and cooled them, watching for spikes in fluorescence that indicate a polymerase chain reaction if a certain strand of DNA is present. The scanner was about the size of a Xerox desktop copier, but it cost upward of $500,000. Hooked up to a laptop, it plotted chain reactions on a graph that spiked if a pathogen was present. In the event of a hit, five more strands of the pathogen genome were tested to make triply sure there had been no mistake.

This DNA mapping had reduced the time lag for testing of biological agents from between forty-eight and seventy-two hours—the time it took to grow cultures in Petri dishes—to under ninety minutes. That leap in technology has given health authorities the critical early window to treat the viruses, break out the national vaccine or antibiotic stockpiles, and try to isolate or contain the disease before it can spread.

"We wouldn't be able to save everyone with BioWatch," said Albright. "But we sure would be able to save a lot, a lot of people."

10

COGS IN THE MACHINE

ELECTRONIC SENTINELS MAKE UP ONLY A SMALL PART OF the Department of Homeland Security's vast array of defenses. DHS, after all, is the amalgamation of more than 180,000 individual men and women who come from different backgrounds, work in different time zones, and perform a wide range of seemingly unrelated duties with the common goal of keeping America safe from terror.

Just as wars are fought by grunts and generals, cooks and captains, paramedics and pilots, homeland security is the collective effort of countless individuals. Yet the men and women manning the barricades at home are often anonymous, buried deep beneath the monolithic facade of the new DHS. Occasionally Tom Ridge or President Bush visits one of the twenty-two federal agencies that now comprise the department, and television viewers might be treated to a glimpse of someone from the rank and file, standing awkwardly in a pressed uniform on the podium next to the commander in chief. But who are these people? How have their jobs changed since being swallowed by the bureaucratic giant that is DHS? And what do they make of their new role as America's protectors? I decided to go out into the field with two of the largest agencies—both in terms of budget and personnel—that comprise DHS, U.S. Customs and the Coast Guard, to see how the transition has affected some of the 57,000 men and women securing our shores and borders.

My first stop on a foggy summer morning in July 2003 was the mammoth port of Los Angeles/Long Beach, far and away America's largest seaport, the international point of entry for nearly half of the nation's container-bound consumer goods, almost all of California's oil imports, and most of the foreign-made vehicles that plied the freeways west of the Mississippi.

Captain John M. Holmes was the Coast Guard commander at L.A./Long Beach, although he was only a few weeks from retirement. Short, slim, and silver/sandy-haired with boyish features that belied his three decades in the service, he exhibited that uniquely Californian capacity to appear both intense and laid-back simultaneously. His formal title was captain of the port, a duty that prior to 9/11 revolved mostly around responding to distress calls and monitoring vessels to ensure they didn't pollute the waters by discharging their bilges too close to port.

The events of September 11 had changed his job description almost immediately. In the span of a few hours, between the time the South Tower collapsed and ports throughout the country were ordered closed to all shipping, Holmes had been forced to embark on a new career in security. It was not something, he readily admitted, that he had much training for. "I didn't know the first thing about security," he recalled as we sat in his waterfront office and watched an oil tanker slowly glide past.

Like Baltimore and the nation's other seaports, L.A./Long Beach had been a wide-open, target-rich environment. Only the scale differed. The port was spread out over an area that had swallowed over one-twentieth of greater Los Angeles, which meant that it was about the size of central Washington, D.C. Row upon row of piers were arranged numerically and alphabetically, like the grid of streets in a planned city. As in any metropolis, this one had a skyline, with gantry cranes a dozen stories high, cloudy power-generating station smokestacks, and eerie stainless steel spires that rose like animal entrails from chemical plants. It boasted bridges, and causeways, and several prisons: one run by the INS, the other a large federal facility circled with coils of razor wire that gleamed in the afternoon sun. There were parking lots with football fields full of Toyotas and

BMWs with protective white factory adhesive on the hoods and roofs, and hundreds of oil storage tanks that from afar looked like clusters of little white mushrooms, although each was the size of an apartment building.

But what really caught my eye were the shipping containers. They were everywhere, stacked six high, 15,000 acres of little green, red, or blue boxes like the Lego building blocks my daughter played with. Every major shipper in the world was represented: Hanjin, Hyundai, Evergreen, P&O, NYK, ZIM, COSCO China Shipping Lines, Maersk, and Matson. Many had their own terminals, so that the piers were color-coordinated by carrier, so dense were the stacks of containers. The biggest ships could bring in eight thousand boxes—cans, as they were sometimes called—at a time, and the gantry cranes worked twenty-four hours a day to move the massive stacks and piles, some the size of several city blocks. The scope of the entire operation was mind-boggling: If all the containers processed here each year were lined up, they would form an unbroken chain 35,000 miles long, enough to circumnavigate the globe twice.

Perhaps that wasn't so staggering given that almost half of all the imports—43 percent to be exact—that arrived in the United States by sea container pass through L.A./Long Beach. If you own a computer, television set, or microwave oven, chances are this was its port of entry. The clothes on your back, the food in your belly, and the shoes you walk in probably had also started their American journey here. So, too, could a radioactive dirty bomb, a canister of smallpox, or a chemical weapon of mass destruction.

"We all knew that some sort of CBN [chemical, biological, and nuclear] detection system was urgently needed. But we couldn't overlook the fact that the perimeter was not even secure," Holmes recalled of the days after 9/11. He didn't know where to start. Worse, he was deluged by security services salespeople pitching every widget under the sun. "They all promised they had the answers to all my problems," he recalled. "But I didn't know what we needed, much less if any of the stuff they were peddling actually worked." So Holmes hired the

Department of Energy's Sandia National Laboratories to perform a vulnerability assessment of the port to outline security priorities. "For the first year," said Holmes, "I felt like a homeowner who was being sold a $5,000 security system for a house that didn't have locks on the doors and windows. So we had to start with the basics, locking the doors and windows: boring things like installing fences, lights, guard-houses, cameras, and increasing patrols." Miles and miles of fencing were strung along the perimeter. At the huge petrochemical com-plexes, which thanks to lobbying efforts had evaded regulation, Holmes tried to shame plant managers into upgrading security by sending out plainclothes Coast Guard officers in the middle of the night to breach defenses. "I'm not talking ninja stuff here like rap-pelling walls, just guys walking onto the premises at 3:00 A.M. unchal-lenged." Throughout the port he instituted mandatory ID checks. "There was huge opposition," he recalled. "The stevedores and truck-ers at first refused. I had to go to countless union meetings to convince them that it was for their own safety. That anyone who shouldn't be on site could be there to plant explosives."

Holmes had signs, billboards, and brochures posted throughout L.A./Long Beach that echoed the new vigilance. "Help Us Stop Ter-rorism!" one exhorted, listing suggestions as to what constituted suspi-cious behavior: "Excessive filming or photography, diving, vessels operating at night without running lights, unusually large cash pay-ments for fuel or repairs, unusual operating schedules, lights flashing between ship and shore." The list went on, admonishing concerned citizens in bold print: "DO NOT do anything other than provide in-formation. DO NOT attempt to stop illegal activity. Call 1-800-221-8724 to report suspicious activities similar to those in this pamphlet."

The new watchdog role took some getting used to, both for Holmes and dockworkers. "Culturally, it was a departure at first. Peo-ple aren't used to seeing the Coast Guard as a policing body," he said. But in many ways that's what the Coast Guard has become. Armed sea marshals, a new Coast Guard program modeled after the TSA's air marshals, now met ships many miles out at sea and boarded them to

prevent hijackers from crashing the vessels into the port's petrochemical facilities. "It made ships' crews and captains very nervous at first,"
Holmes said of the sea marshals. "They weren't accustomed to being
greeted with guns." Closer to shore, the Coast Guard played an even
greater policing role, which Holmes arranged for me to see for myself.

The crew of RB-HS boat 50 waited for me on the main dock.
Coxswain Chuck Ashmore fired up the craft's twin 225-horsepower
Honda engines and secured his gear: night-vision goggles, a Beretta
nine-millimeter sidearm, and an M-60 heavy-caliber mounted machine gun with two 200-round ammunition clips. Ashmore called out
to Petty Officer Cameron Marshburn to launch the moorings and slid
the engines into reverse. Like Ashmore, Marshburn wore his hair
close-cropped, a Kevlar bulletproof vest protected his torso, and his
dark military fatigues were crisply tucked into high combat boots.

With all the firepower and commando-like garb, I couldn't help
feeling as if I were going on a search-and-destroy mission deep behind
enemy lines with the Navy SEALs, rather than on a routine harbor
patrol. But this was the face of the new, post-9/11 Coast Guard: armed
to the teeth and ready for action. "People used to think of us as a life-
guard station," Ashmore said, gunning the throttle. "Now we've got
the big M-60s on the bow, and it takes people aback." The orange RB-
HS boat rose out of the water, kicking up a violent white wake as it
powered up to cruising speed of 40 knots. RB-HS stands for Response
Boat–Homeland Security. Six hundred of the high-speed craft had
been ordered since 9/11. They patrolled the Potomac, near the Washington monuments, the waterways around New York City, the giant
oil terminals in Galveston, Texas, and they escorted cruise ships docking in Miami, among other missions. Their crews had all undergone
special combat training at the Marine Corps base at Camp Lejeune in
North Carolina to prepare for their new role, and Ashmore, a seven-
year veteran of the Guard, seemed to relish their new tough-guy image. "People don't expect us to show up with guns. It kinda freaks
them out at first. But they realize we're there to protect Americans."

As he spoke, Petty Officer Third Class Jessica Field scanned the harbor, calling out contacts—other vessels—on points of the compass. She had a thick Boston brogue, a tough-as-nails swagger, and was attractive enough to have played the strawberry-blond heroine in any Hollywood action picture. Plus, she was rated an expert marksman on the machine gun. The port was filled with contacts: freighters and oil tankers, bulk carriers and container ships, fishing vessels and pleasure craft. A quarter of a million private boats were registered in the Los Angeles area, and because any of these could be loaded with explosives and crashed into larger ships or industrial facilities, Ashmore and his crew paid particular attention to them. "If we see anything remotely suspicious, we'll go check it out, board 'em. The owners don't like it, but that's tough. It's our job, the new reality."

Back on shore, Holmes chuckled good-naturedly at his troops' bravado. "Those kids are having the time of their life tooling around at 40 knots. Hell, if we didn't limit their fuel, they'd be out there all day." Of course, the crews of the RB-HS boats were all young, mostly in their early twenties. It was easier to retrain them than many of the service's longtime veterans who were steeped in the Coast Guard's proud ways, traditions, and traditional rivalries with other maritime and federal agencies. Some of those rivalries had emerged during the 1980s war on drugs, when the Coast Guard and customs competed openly for credit in narcotics seizures. Big busts meant press coverage, praise in Congress, and better chances for budget increases. That legacy of interagency competition still permeated relations between the different services that the Guard now worked alongside to keep America safe. "Traditionally, we're very open," said Holmes, unable to resist a stab at his colleagues at customs. "Some of the other DHS agencies, however, are not. Sometimes that causes friction."

Indeed, while Holmes had arranged for me to go out on patrol, join a boarding party of sea marshals, tour the harbor by air in the City of Long Beach's new police helicopter, visit the new radar facilities of the sea-traffic control tower, and meet with various port authorities, the one area where he could not extend his hospitality was with his DHS counterparts at customs. There he had no knowledge or influence, although the two were supposed to be working together. "The Department of Homeland Security is a big, unwieldy new machine made of many disparate parts," he said with a shrug. "Like any big merger, it'll take a while to work out the kinks."

In the complex division of labor at the Department of Homeland Security, the Coast Guard was responsible for the physical security of ships and port facilities, while U.S. Customs was in charge of securing everything the ships carried. In Los Angeles/Long Beach that was mostly forty-foot-long cargo containers, a mind-boggling number of them. How could a customs official know if any of the millions of steel shipping containers that came in and out of the port every year concealed a weapon of mass destruction? All that differentiated the containers was a nine-digit serial number and the freight company's logo. "It's not even like trying to look for a needle in a haystack," conceded Captain Holmes. "It's like looking for a needle in a pile of needles."

Unfortunately, Holmes wasn't aware of what his counterparts at customs were doing to stop terrorists from smuggling some terrible weapon of mass destruction into the country in a shipping container. (To be fair, when I later spoke with customs officials, they had no idea what the Coast Guard was up to, either.) This fact highlighted one of the weaknesses of the Department of Homeland Security unification priority. Although everyone now nominally works for the same entity, the right hand still all too often does not know what the left hand is doing. At headquarters on Nebraska Avenue in Washington, the top brass is on the same page, but out in the field that does not always translate into better lines of communication or everyone pulling together.

To get the complete picture of how both agencies were working in tandem, I had to return to Washington and apply with the Bureau of Customs and Border Protection, as customs had been rechristened to better reflect its homeland security duties, to visit its field operations. It was somewhat Kafkaesque, but my fault for naively thinking that the bureaucratic wall that for decades had separated various federal agencies had suddenly come crashing down with the creation of DHS. Jim Mitchie, an affable customs veteran with over twenty years in the service, offered to take me up to the harbor facilities in New Jersey and New York rather than L.A./Long Beach. The responsibilities of the renamed CBP were identical across the country, he said, except that in New York the stakes were exponentially higher.

Even a small nuclear bomb set off in midtown Manhattan on a typical workday could kill over half a million people and cause over $1 trillion in direct economic damage, according to a 2003 study by the Nuclear Threat Initiative, a Harvard-affiliated think tank. At the epicenter of the blast, people and structures would simply be vaporized. The shock wave would bring down buildings as far south as SoHo and north past Fiftieth Street. Tens of thousands of people would be crushed to death and sliced apart by shards of glass traveling at supersonic speeds. Even the lucky survivors would be horribly burned by the searing heat. Outside of the blast radius, millions more would be sickened by the radioactive fallout that would rain on the city's outer boroughs and suburbs. Many would die of radiation poisoning within months, while others would fail over time. Much of New York State, Connecticut, and New Jersey would need to be evacuated, and Manhattan would be uninhabitable. At ground zero, the radiation count would be so lethal as to render cleanup efforts almost impossible. The contaminated rubble would stand as a monument for ten thousand years, the half-life of some isotopes. Children in the tristate region would develop thyroid cancer at alarming rates, if not issued sufficient doses of iodine immediately. And women in the fallout zone would give birth to horribly deformed infants for years to come.

Some of this I knew from personal experience. I'd been to Chernobyl and neighboring Belarus three times, where I met kids with cancer and distorted limbs and saw the black, six-foot-long fish with tumors the size of grapefruit swimming near the destroyed reactor's cooling basin.

It was a cinematic nightmare, a fate so frightening that it had kept the Cold War from going hot for nearly fifty years. But even though the Soviet threat had abated, a new, perhaps even greater danger had arisen: that of a loose nuke getting into the hands of terrorists. In 1991 the Soviet Union had fragmented into more than a dozen nations ranging from poor to utterly destitute, some of which had inherited hundreds of intercontinental ballistic missile warheads, not to mention nuclear power stations, research facilities, and production plants where some 600 tons of nuclear materials were warehoused, according to U.S. government estimates. In the chaos, confusion, and corruption that gripped the transition from communism, no one was 100 percent sure if every warhead was accounted for. Storage facilities were poorly guarded, sometimes only with a rusty padlock and half-drunken guard. Scientists, military officers, and nuclear workers went months without pay during most of the 1990s. It was, all in all, a recipe for disaster, and Washington had rightly spent billions of dollars during the Clinton administration trying to keep a lid on the old Soviet arsenal. They'd done a remarkably good job, and, miraculously, there are no documented cases of warheads going astray and appearing on the black market.

But the genie is out of the bottle. The technology has proliferated. Pakistan, India, Israel, and other confidence-inspiring nations such as South Africa have acquired the know-how. Iran is building a Russian-engineered reactor at Bushehr that Washington worries could become a platform for a weapons program. North Korea is already frighteningly far down the pike to developing its own bomb. The father of Pakistan's atomic weapons program, Abdul Qadeer Khan, was caught selling nuclear know-how to all comers, including Libya, which fortunately has abandoned its quest to join the nuclear club. And President Bush, citing what turned out to be flawed British intelligence, used the claim that Saddam was getting perilously close to nuclear capability as one of the myriad justifications for marching on Baghdad. The real fear, though, is that al Qaeda will harness the destructive power of the atom to play out the plot of the 2002 Hollywood hit *The Sum of All Fears*, in which Baltimore is leveled by a black-market nuclear warhead. Asked during his Senate confirmation hearings as secretary of homeland security what his greatest concern was, Tom Ridge answered with one chilling word: "nuclear."

Al Qaeda doesn't even need to go to all the hassle and expense of acquiring a hard-to-come-by warhead. It can achieve many of the same destructive results by building cheap radiological dirty bombs instead. A dirty bomb uses conventional explosives—dynamite, C4, fuels, old mines, home-brewed fertilizer-based concoctions, whatever—to disperse radioactive materials: nuclear waste lifted from atomic power stations or mothballed reactors, radiological components of discarded medical equipment, or stolen batches of cesium, strontium, or—more ominously—actual uranium or plutonium from weapons and research labs. José Padilla, the ex-Chicago Latino gang member being held as an enemy combatant, was accused of conspiring to devise just such a weapon, although his expertise in the field of fissionable materials is questionable.

Still, there is no shortage of the stuff out there. According to a 2003 Harvard study, there are 130 civilian nuclear research labs scattered across forty often wobbly developing countries, many even now protected only by a chain-link fence and a poorly paid night watchman. And, unlike warheads, such fissionable materials have a nasty habit of disappearing off the shelf, judging by the number of seizures and arrests of would-be traffickers around the world. In August 2003, for instance, the deputy director of Russia's fleet of nuclear-powered icebreakers was caught trying to sell 2.2 pounds of uranium to a criminal syndicate. The month before, police in Thailand arrested a man attempting to sell sixty-six pounds of Russian cesium-137, a by-product of nuclear reactors, for $240,000. A few ounces of cesium isolate are enough for a small dirty bomb; sixty-six pounds could permanently contaminate half of central Washington. But it wouldn't level the city or kill everyone at ground zero. For that you need plutonium or highly enriched weapons-grade uranium, U-235, which is what Bulgarian customs officials discovered inside a lead container concealed in the trunk of a car in May 1999. The cargo, according to

U.S. Customs, was being transported from Turkey to Moldova as a "sample" to buyers in advance of a larger shipment of the same materials. The sellers, and their deadly product, are still at large.

Fortunately, fashioning a nuclear bomb from plutonium and U-235 is a fairly complicated undertaking, requiring significant know-how in implosion techniques, including explosive lenses arranged geometrically around a plutonium ball to crush it with perfect symmetry. This isn't something al Qaeda can cook up in some basement lab. The beauty of dirty bombs, however, is that you don't need significant expertise or even uranium or plutonium. The containers that once housed these elements are enough. In March 2000 Uzbek customs officials at the Gisht Kuprink border crossing discovered ten highly radioactive lead containers concealed in twenty-three tons of scrap stainless steel in a truck entering from Kazakhstan. Documents found in the truck, according to U.S. government reports, indicated that the Iranian driver was planning to deliver his radioactive cargo to Quetta, Pakistan, the traditional crossing point to the Taliban stronghold of Kandahar, Afghanistan. Strapped to conventional explosives and shipped in a cargo container to the United States, the radioactive lead, exploding with the force of molten lava once detonated, could irradiate many a city block or an entire borough, depending on how much radioactive material could be crammed inside a shipping container.

"The threat of a radiological attack on the U.S. is real, and terrorists have a broad palette of isotopes to choose from," a 2003 Pentagon-funded study by the Center for Technology and National Security Policy warned. Such a scenario might kill only a few dozen or a hundred people, the study notes, but the economic damage could be "devastating." A release of as little as 10,000 curies of radiation would contaminate an area the size of the Washington Mall. Skyscrapers and apartment buildings in the affected zone would have to be torn down and the rubble trucked away for burial. And none of this would be covered by insurance.

"We know beyond a shadow of a doubt that if al Qaeda were to put together a radiological device, they're going to use it," Cofer Black, the State Department's top antiterror official, told the Associated Press during a February 2004 conference in Jakarta, Indonesia. "They are doing everything they can to acquire this type of weapon, and we are doing everything we can to prevent it."

That includes vast increases in the 2005 budget to fund nuclear nonproliferation programs aimed at either removing or better protecting fissionable materials at nuclear facilities and research laboratories around the world, and diplomatic efforts to get nations with nuclear know-how to clamp down on their own rogue scientists. In the event, however, that the campaign fails and al Qaeda does get its hands on a radiological device, it is left to the U.S. Customs Service to form America's last line of defense. It is an eventuality the renamed Bureau of Customs and Border Protection has been preparing for ever since September 11, 2001, as I found out on my visit to the Howland Hook Marine Terminal on Staten Island.

The container ship *Jervis Bay* was a regular at Howland Hook. It had just completed its run from Karachi, Pakistan, and the United Arab Emirates via the Suez Canal with additional stops at ports of call in Italy and at Le Havre, France.

A light snow dusted its oily decks as Inspector Anthony Cirigliano wedged himself between two stacks of containers lashed to the ship's foredeck. He worked with the quiet dignity of a master of his trade, running a practiced eye over all the hinges, doors, and seals. A screw that was shinier than the others, a hinge that was oiled differently, the subtle line of a spot-weld along a corner would stop him in his tracks. Perhaps these were innocuous signs of recent repairs, but they could also be telltale signs that a container had been tampered with, that an entire door had been removed and reinstalled so as to leave the seal on the lock intact. Inspector Cirigliano knew all the tricks. He could open a container without leaving a mark, and often did so during narcotics sting operations. Of course, if he could do it, so could the bad guys. Cirigliano was a retired NYPD detective, a tall and gaunt figure, imposingly austere. He had planned on retiring from the U.S. Customs Service and maybe taking his pension to Florida. But 9/11 had given him a renewed purpose. He was no longer looking for import tax cheats or a bale of marijuana. His job was now fundamentally altered: to stop WMDs from reaching our cities and communities. So instead of sunning himself on the beach, he spent his days out in the cold on oily ship decks, his breath forming steamy little clouds around his intense features. He didn't say much, so his supervisor, Michael Hegler, did most of the talking. "He has a nose, an instinct he's developed over the years," he said of the shy Cirigliano. "You could say he's our last-line defense. But even if, God forbid, we catch something, it still might be too late. Look at where we are," he added, pointing to the Statue of Liberty and the lower Manhattan skyline beyond.

That proximity to where the Twin Towers had once stood—everyone here saw them fall—served as a daily reminder to everyone at Howland Hook not to let their guard down. Like many in the Coast Guard, customs agents took their new WMD responsibilities extremely seriously. But they also knew that international trade was America's lifeline, and they had to balance the economic effects of slowing commerce with the new focus on security. "We have to find ways of securing cargo without hampering the flow of trade," CBP commissioner Robert Bonner had told me in Washington. "That's essential for America's continued prosperity."

Narcotics syndicates rely on this economic imperative to keep trade flowing to send their loads through regular commercial channels, knowing that the odds of detection are heavily skewed in their favor. The fear is that extremist groups also would gamble on the law of averages to send through a payload of SA-7 shoulder-fired missiles or some chemical, biological, or radiological weapon. The shipping container is an ideal vehicle for such contraband because the United States is so dependent on international trade—one reason officials dubbed it the "Trojan Horse."

For the CBP, much more so than for the Coast Guard, technology and not manpower was seen as a way to balance the competing needs of commerce and security, of keeping America open to imports while closed to WMDs. Technology would eventually replace veterans like Cirigliano, although it likely will take a good deal of time before

GPS-enabled smart containers with built-in radio frequency ID sensors that sound an alarm if cargo is tampered with to catch on with shippers. (It is even more likely that smuggling syndicates will find ways to defeat the sensors, much as skilled burglars can bypass most home alarm systems.)

Technology is a double-edged sword that invariably gives one only a temporary lead over adversaries. Unfortunately, the United States lags behind in one crucial area of counterterrorism: the development of sophisticated radiation detectors that can check every single container as it enters port. These were only being tested in the fall of 2003, and there were still questions as to how experimental radiation portals such as those placed along the Canadian border around Detroit would react to the humidity and salt corrosion of a maritime environment. Nor can existing portals be placed on a gantry crane, the most logical location to automatically screen every incoming container without slowing down traffic, because the machines are delicate and cannot withstand a crane's shaking and jerking motions. Current portals also have limited ranges and need time to perform their calculations; containers, vehicles, or, ideally, entire ships can't move past them faster than a few miles an hour. Then there is the question of calibration: Portals must be able not only to detect radiation spikes but also to identify isotopes—the source of the radiation, whether it is harmless, naturally emitting granite, or weapons-grade uranium. No one piece of technology incorporates all these criteria, and Dr. Albright's shop, along with the Department of Energy, is working feverishly to develop and test a prototype of a radiation detector that does. But it is going to take time. In the meantime, customs agents are improvising with antiquated detection gear that was never designed for its current role.

For now, customs officials are screening only for radiation with rudimentary handheld devices on containers flagged by the new National Targeting Center in Reston, Virginia. The center is a post-9/11 creation and a way of increasing the odds of detection in the United States' favor. Its supercomputers, manned by 130 analysts, assign numeric values based on 167 criteria to determine whether a shipment is suspect and should be searched. Anomalies the computer searches for include whether the product being shipped is indigenous to the country of origin. Is it financially viable to ship such a product in the first place? What countries was it transshipped through? How established are the shipper, broker, and importer? And so forth. Cargo that scores above a certain threshold gets earmarked for inspection. Naturally, terror groups probably can fool the computers at the National Targeting Center or, at least, route their shipments in such a way as to make detection moot. "Say you don't want to advertise the fact that your point of origin is Karachi," explained an intelligence official in Washington. "You ship it from Pakistan to Lagos, Nigeria, where you change consignee. You forward it to Lisbon with a reputable shipper, and then to San Juan, Puerto Rico, as bonded freight. It goes straight through to Chicago, where it can explode right in the customs warehouse for all you care. You've reached the American heartland."

Of the *Jervis Bay*'s 501 containers, 84 had scored high enough to merit a closer look and radiation scan. Cirigliano didn't like the look of another eight containers, which made a total of 92. That was almost a fifth of the shipment, considerably above the national average for screened cargo, which had increased from 2 to 5 percent in 2003. Still, that means that 95 percent of containers enter the United States without any sort of physical inspection whatsoever.

At Howland Hook, physical inspections took place inside a large, smoke-filled hangar. Customs inspector Bill Heleman sat in a small, brightly lit booth, staring at an X-ray image of one of the shipping containers flagged from the *Jervis Bay*. The image looked like something you might see at your dentist's office, only it was projected on a computer screen and outlined the ghostly white frame of a forty-foot container, with darker, denser spots showing like cavities. "Those are supposed to be wallets from India," Heleman said, pointing at an anomaly on the X ray on his screen. "But that looks like something solid in a crate that shouldn't be there."

The X ray he was looking at was in fact not an X ray but a far more powerful gamma ray, emitted by a pellet of radioactive cobalt inside a box that runs on tracks on the other side of the container. Known as a VACIS, or Vehicle and Cargo Inspection System, it was an oversize version of the screening devices introduced at airports throughout the United States that allows customs inspectors literally to see through walls of steel, and it came in two varieties: older-generation fixed models that could process fifteen containers per hour, and faster, $1.3 million mobile units that use cesium-137 as their radioactive source, are grafted to the back of large utility-truck chassis, and could screen thirty.

Speed versus security was the primary equation that customs had to balance, and the more they could automate the process, said Heleman's boss, Chief Inspector Kevin McCabe, the more smoothly it would run. To that end, the number of VACIS machines that could screen entire containers without opening them had been tripled, from 45 deployed mostly along the drug routes of the southern borders before 9/11, to 135 by January 2004. VACIS technology, in fact, had been specifically designed for the war on drugs, not terror. The machines had a serious blind spot that could permit terrorists to smuggle in nuclear devices. A source explained it to me in some detail. Customs officials knew about it. They only hope that al Qaeda didn't.

Still, it was far cheaper and quicker to X ray high-risk containers than to crack them open, and only when Heleman noticed an anomaly on his screen did he order the boxes searched by hand. This was done in one of the hangar's loading bays by National Guardsmen called up to help relieve the manpower shortage, although stevedores later repacked searched shipments, at a cost of $800 per container. Coffee beans crunched underfoot as the Guardsmen sliced open cardboard boxes containing cheap wallets. The beans were remnants of a seizure from the day before that had netted 400 kilos of cocaine hidden in coffee sacks, but everyone appeared unmoved about the haul. "We used to get so excited when we made a drug bust. Guys would come in on their day off and stay late for free," said McCabe. Now, of course, the stakes were exponentially higher. If a drug shipment slipped through—and, unfortunately, many if not most did—it wasn't the end of the world. If a nuclear device went off in Times Square or Chicago, however, that would be a different story. "9/11 completely redefined our job, and you could say that every day we don't come across a weapon of mass destruction is a good day."

While McCabe spoke, a small black device about the size of a beeper hummed incessantly, skidding from the vibrations across Heleman's desk. "Shut up," he finally muttered, and turned the pesky device off. This was one of the infamous PRDs, or personal radiation detectors, that were causing so much trouble. Customs had hastily bought eight thousand radiation pagers after 9/11, at a cost of $1,300 apiece, and then issued contradictory directives to not use them, use them, not use them, finally settling on using them in tandem with more sophisticated backup detectors.

Here in the Staten Island terminal, customs agents wore the radiation meters on their hip and waved them at passing containers. "They're set to vibrate or ring and measure spikes on a scale of one to nine," Heleman explained. A reading of 1 indicated a negligible 7 microroentgens per hour, essentially harmless background radiation. "Nine means run like hell."

His own PRD had been continuously humming in vibrate mode, because it was picking up radiation from the VACIS machine. This meant another agent had to stand a hundred yards away all day long and hold up his pager as the containers went by. The "human glow stick," one of his colleagues said with a laugh. "Not exactly an efficient use of resources."

The pagers were unreliable, had an extremely limited range, and were prone to false alarms. Twice already the Staten Island terminal had been evacuated because of faulty scares, and once a ship from Italy was sent back out to open sea under armed guard by the Coast Guard because the radiation pagers registered Chernobyl-like readings. "It turned out to be a type of ceramic tiles," said McCabe. "They emit natural radiation."

So do granite, certain marbles, cat litter, even bananas. But the battery-operated pagers could not distinguish between gamma radiation from cesium or cobalt, much less identify far nastier neutrons blasting from weapons-grade U-235. (That was one reason why police in New York City subways, who had been issued the same pagers, were constantly strip-searching cancer-treatment patients.) After a string of embarrassing false positives, Washington ordered handheld 400 Exploranium Q-135 spectrometers that could identify different isotopes, but not all ports and border crossings had them. "We're working with what we got." Heleman shrugged. "But I wouldn't say no to a nice reliable portal."

In fall of 2003 Heleman got his wish, and Howland Hook got the country's first radiation portal after ABC News successfully sent fifteen pounds of depleted uranium in a container from Istanbul through the Staten Island terminal. Customs officials argued that depleted uranium did not give off the same signature as the active kind, so the test was not fair, but the network quoted authoritative scientists saying that if the equipment customs was using couldn't detect depleted uranium, then it probably couldn't detect the real thing, either. The Office of the Inspector General seemed to side with ABC. Because of management errors, it wrote in an April 1, 2003, report, "Customs does not have a documented strategic plan to ensure proper acquisition and deployment of equipment.... most of the radiation detection is focused on detecting gamma radiation and is unable to detect neutron radiation."

ABC later sent the same batch of uranium to L.A./Long Beach. That shipment also got through undetected.

LOSING ALTITUDE

S THE GENERAL ACCOUNTING OFFICE REPORT on INADE-quate radiation detection equipment made clear, there is an urgent need for a central research and development agency like Dr. Albright's Science and Technology Directorate. Science can help protect us, but it can also give us a false sense of security, to say nothing of wasting our tax dollars on widgets that don't work. Someone needs to make sure that the technology the Department of Homeland Security will be purchasing in the coming years is the right stuff for the right job. Albright struck me as eminently qualified and conscientious.

He has, however, a distinct advantage over some of his colleagues in DHS's other departments. "Our division is a complete start-up," Albright said. "So we don't have Hutchinson's problems." Asa Hutchinson, the undersecretary for Border and Transportation Security, had inherited huge organizations with distinct traditions, rich independent histories, and hugely disparate corporate cultures. At L.A./Long Beach, as I had discovered, the Coast Guard doesn't know what customs is up to. And at Staten Island, customs inspectors haven't the foggiest idea of what the Coast Guard is doing. Responsibilities are divided, and never the twain doth meet—or rarely, at least. Hutchinson's department is supposed to change that, to get everyone on the same wavelength: sea and air marshals, INS officials and airport screeners—over 100,000 people in all. Not surprisingly, Hutchinson is spending a good deal of time in reorganization meetings where security issues take a backseat to intra-agency jockeying. At times it seems as if the creation of DHS has created extra layers of bureaucracy, rather than streamlining the process, and the frustration shows on Hutchinson's face. "We're still very much a work in progress," he told me one afternoon in his cramped office at NAC headquarters.

It is also not surprising that many in the field have little use for DHS. It means more paperwork, new ways of doing things, and less recognition, since DHS will hog the credit for any successes. Ego plays a role. "I have to take orders from a bunch of snot-noses with clipboards," said one twenty-year veteran of the customs service. True, at DHS headquarters, the officials are younger, better dressed, have fancier degrees, and often come from prestigious White House internships or have worked on President Bush's 2000 campaign. Many are attorneys, but they have little experience guarding borders or power plants. The resentment against the Washington staff is natural and yet shockingly pronounced wherever I went. "We live in the real world out here," I was told in L.A. "They're pissing in the wind to see what sticks," snorted a health worker in Denver. "They're pretty much useless," said a city official in Baltimore.

But if DHS has not gotten off to a stellar start, it isn't because the people at NAC weren't trying. For the most part, they are well-trained and well-intentioned professionals. Many put in long hours for low pay. Several I met even worked free for the first two months, before the department had a budget and payroll. The real issue was that the Department of Homeland Security has been hamstrung. It lacks political support and financial backing, and had been deliberately rushed into service before it was ready to open its doors. Ultimately, the responsibility lay at the doorstep of 1600 Pennsylvania Avenue, DHS's reluctant architect. If the power brokers in the Bush administration had never been serious about the Department of Homeland Security, they should have found other ways to protect the nation, instead of creating a "rice-paper tiger," in the words of one disgruntled security official. With respect to the stillborn infrastructure protection directorate, the administration has clearly chosen special interests at the expense of national security in opting not to push for the regulation of security at petrochemical plants.

Entrenched bureaucratic interests have also played a significant role in leaving DHS impotent in terms of intelligence gathering and analysis. That DHS is not permitted to tread on FBI turf is yet another example of the intelligence community's resistance to real reform. Astonishingly, there have been no major repercussions for either the CIA or the FBI for the catastrophic intelligence failure of 9/11. No one has been fired, forced to resign or even demoted, even as the blue ribbon panel convened to investigate the September 11 attacks pointed in its 600-page report to risk-averse agencies saddled with bureaucratic intransigence. Only the whistleblowers—those few brave field agents like Coleen Rowley and John Roberts who dared to speak out about procedural lapses and unheeded warnings—have been punished. Both agencies actually were rewarded with bigger budgets, more personnel, and better equipment. For the FBI, 9/11 has resulted in over a 40 percent funding boost over three years to just under $5 billion annually. The CIA's budgets are classified. The most recently released figures cite a 1998 budget of just over $27 billion. It is now said to hover around $33 billion.

The creation of DHS would have been a golden opportunity to fix some of the structural and cultural problems of the intelligence community, which still lacks linguists and Arabists who can speak the language and understand the mind-set of the new adversary. The post-9/11 push to hire more Middle Eastern experts has petered out by 2004 amid allegations of bias. The FBI is 83 percent white and male, according to a May 26, 2003, cover story in U.S. News & World Report. Of its 11,500 agents, only 76 speak fluent Arabic. And some of those speakers have complained that in the Bureau's insular culture, their proficiency actually works against them. The highest-ranking Arab American on the Bureau's payroll, Bassem Youssef, has gone so far as to file a racial discrimination suit in July 2003, alleging that rather than tapping his Arabic fluency and extensive experience in the Middle East, the Bureau has sidelined him from terror investigations because of his ancestry. If his suit proves true, and the Bureau treats its own Arab American agents as suspect, it risks losing a wealth of knowledge about a culture it knows precious little about to begin with.

Starting a new domestic counterterror agency from scratch could have helped weed out, or at least diminish, such ingrained biases. Commission after commission concluded that a new domestic agency should have been formed to work side by side with DHS. Many of the nation's most senior and respected security officials—including John MacGaffin, retired deputy director of the CIA, the Agency's former counterintelligence chief Paul Redmond, and John Hamre, who ran the war room simulation at Andrews Air Force Base and had served as deputy defense secretary and CSIS head—put their signatures to reports counseling that counterterror responsibilities be hived off from the risk-averse FBI, which is fundamentally an investigative policing body rather than an intelligence-gathering organization. "Our group was divided on the question whether the FBI could make this transition," Hamre testified to the 9/11 Commission investigating the intelligence failures leading up to the September 11 attacks.

But recommendations to overhaul domestic intelligence capabilities have fallen on deaf ears. Instead, the notion of revamping the Bureau's wobbly antiterror operations—now manned by an extra five hundred agents hastily transferred from organized crime or drug details—has been paid mostly lip service. "Nothing has changed since 9/11," Baltimore's outspoken police chief, Ed Norris, complained to me. "We still have cases where we call the feds to ask if they have anything on someone who we suspect might have some sort of terror ties. They say no, and it's only after we launch our own investigation that they tell us to lay off because they're already working on it. So not only are they not helping, they're hurting us by costing us valuable man-hours. Yeah," he added, "they share more information than they used to. But their first instinct is still to hoard the good stuff for themselves. That's not going to change overnight. It's cultural." (Norris was later forced to resign for alleged misappropriation of police department funds.)

Norris's grim assessment seems to jibe with a report released by the Police Executive Research Forum in April 2003, which expresses the continued frustration of police chiefs at being kept in the dark by the feds. Progress is being made, the report notes, but not enough and not nearly fast enough. Local officials need to be kept in the loop, police chiefs like Norris and Denver's Gerald Whitman told me, because ultimately they know the lay of the land and have access to far greater manpower than federal representatives. Said Norris: "I got 4,000 pairs of eyeballs in Baltimore, the feds have a couple of hundred. But unless we are told what to look for, those thousands of eyeballs are blind."

In a report read out during Senate intelligence hearings on February 24, 2004, the Bureau's own inspector general quotes a CIA official detailed to the FBI as saying information sharing was "ad hoc" and disorganized: "Information goes into a black hole when it goes into the [FBI headquarters] building." A December 2003 report by Congress's General Accounting Office was not as harsh. It praised the Bureau for making "significant progress" in information sharing, while warning that much work still needed to be done. Some of the positive steps taken by the Bureau to improve the flow of information include the creation of 84 regional task forces and the dissemination of a daily briefing to eighteen thousand law enforcement bodies across the country. Half a billion dollars' worth of new computers have been distributed throughout FBI field offices, giving agents access to the same classified databases as the head office in D.C.

But there was still much to be improved on. Addressing reporters at a January 2004 breakfast hosted by the *Christian Science Monitor*, FBI director Robert Mueller conceded the criticism. "Part of regaining the public's trust," he said, "is identifying the mistakes, areas where we have slipped, acknowledging them, and moving on." The biggest mistakes revolve around the gathering, processing, and dissemination of intelligence. Mueller acknowledged that the Bureau could benefit from and was in fact adopting some of the tactics used by domestic intelligence agencies like the United Kingdom's MI5, but he was strongly opposed to creating a new agency from scratch because the FBI's national presence and arrest powers made it a more effective force around the country.

Yet almost everywhere I went—from Washington's water authority to war gamers—the disconnect between what federal authorities know and what local authorities are told remained sizable. "If there's specific intelligence that al Qaeda is targeting water treatment plants," said the security chief of the Dalecarlia reservoir in northwest Washington, "I need to know about it. But there's no established pipeline for me to get that sort of information."

DHS was created expressly for the purpose of streamlining those sorts of warnings to the people who need to know. It was intended to be a pipeline to local officials. But the department itself knows only what the FBI chooses to tell it, and the Bureau might be tempted to withhold information to protect the identity of an informant, to safe-guard evidence, or simply not to tip its hand to a potential terrorist cell under investigation. All may be valid reasons, but ultimately the Justice Department, not DHS, is still in the driver's seat on the deci-sion to share information. This means that we are essentially still us-ing police tactics and criminal prosecutors to catch terrorists. Terrorists have fundamentally different motivations, RICO anticrime statutes don't scare them, and it is extremely unlikely that U.S. attor-neys are going to flip terror informants by threatening them with pos-session with intent to distribute. It stands to reason that any agent who has spent the last fifteen years chasing crack dealers is instinc-tively going to use the same tactics to try to track terrorists. Mueller didn't think so: "I think particularly that FBI agents are exceptionally good collectors of information. There are persons who say we collect information with the prospect of putting it in a courtroom in the U.S. and consequently we are blinded to the facts as a whole. I don't think that to be the case. If you take what we did with La Cosa Nostra, it can be an example of gathering information...and using intelligence as well as law enforcement powers." The propensity to use traditional po-lice methods, however, can explain why so few U.S. terrorist cells have been broken up in the years since 9/11. Even the successes—in Detroit, Buffalo, Portland—netted only small fry, goofballs like Ohio truck driver Iyman Faris, who had the brilliant idea to try to bring down the Brooklyn Bridge with torches and bolt cutters. Major cases such as the prosecution of alleged twentieth hijacker Zacarias Mous-saoui, have not gone so well. Nor, most notably, have any arrests been made in the 2001 anthrax attacks that killed five. And even one of the first successful big post-9/11 indictments may have been tainted. A federal prosecutor from the case against an alleged terror cell in De-troit took the highly unusual step in February 2004 of suing his own boss, Attorney General Ashcroft. In the suit, Assistant U.S. Attorney Richard Convertino alleged that Justice Department officials in Washington interfered with the case, failed to turn over evidence that might have helped the defense, compromised the identity of a confi-dential informant, exaggerated results in the war on terror, and "con-tinuously placed perception over reality."

On other fronts of the legal war on terror, U.S. counterterror ex-perts still don't have a clear grasp of how to go after al Qaeda sleepers or sympathizers, how to cut off their sources of financing or infiltrate their recruiting drives. The General Accounting Office said as much in another report that faulted the Justice Department, the FBI, and Treasury for not having a clear understanding of how terror networks move their money and for failing to make investigations of terrorist fi-nancing a high priority. This is precisely the area where Tom Ridge had ceded investigative authority from the Secret Service to the attor-ney general's office. But the Secret Service may be inherently better suited to pursuing al Qaeda's money trail; its traditional brief has al-ways been prevention, not prosecution, whether that involves stop-ping assassination attempts or breaking up counterfeiting rings. The primary goal of counterterror agencies is to prevent attacks and disrupt terror cells, not to worry about bringing them to trial later, as the FBI obsessively does. The Bureau, while making some progress toward changing its law enforcement mind-set, continues to focus too heavily on prosecution—yet another reason why its counterterror operations should have been pried from the legal bosom of Justice and subordi-nated to the prevention-oriented Department of Homeland Security.

Lack of intelligence capabilities aside, some of the early humilia-tions at the new department have been of its own making. The color-coded alert system, which had been instituted with so much fanfare in March 2002, has quickly become something of a national joke, fodder for late-night talk-show hosts. After raising it four times to the second-highest level, orange, all DHS had to show for the heightened alerts was several billion dollars in wasted police overtime and an increasingly jaded public. A red-faced Tom Ridge conceded in spring 2003 that the system needs fine-tuning. For six months, until December 21, the color system was largely shelved; instead of elevating alert levels, DHS issued frustratingly vague weekly bulletins—al Qaeda might smuggle bombs in socks, fire shoulder-held rockets at planes, target water treatment plants, bomb Christmas shoppers, attack New York, D.C., Chicago, Las Vegas, and/or Los Angeles, simultaneously or separately. The purpose of these bulletins was equally mysterious— what was the average citizen supposed to do with this information? One never hears these sorts of all-encompassing alerts in Israel: Picture an Israeli TV announcement that a suicide bomber might target Tel Aviv, Jerusalem, or Haifa in the next week or two. In Israel, warnings are either not issued at all or are accompanied by specific leads that can be acted on. For example, it might be announced that a bomber is likely female, mid-twenties, and will strike in such-and-such a neighborhood in Tel Aviv during the next three to four hours. Tel Aviv would go on alert, but not the rest of the country. Britain, during the IRA years, didn't even alert the general public. Instead, the Home Office notified appropriate authorities, such as shopping mall or subway station managers, to ramp up security. These types of actions imply specific intelligence.

America's blanket alerts ran the gamut of all possible scenarios and seemed mostly to coincide with important calendar dates: July 4, September 11, December 25, or January 1. Stung by the criticism, Ridge apparently felt compelled to justify the December 21, 2003, elevation in the threat index by warning Americans that "catastrophic attacks rivaling or exceeding the scope of 9/11" strikes were anticipated. But don't change your travel plans, he added somewhat incongruously.

It would have made eminently more sense simply to say that as a precaution during the holidays, security was being ramped up. The mixed message did little to reassure Americans that the code orange was not another instance of "Crayola confusion," as New Jersey senator Frank Lautenberg derisively dubbed the threat index. Neither did subsequent official amplifications that terrorists might use planes again, unleash chemical weapons, visit biological agents on us, or "employ other means." Such pronouncements—and equally vague joint prophecies by Ridge and Ashcroft that al Qaeda would strike in the summer of 2004—just seemed to say that DHS and the FBI have no idea what, if anything, bin Laden has in store for us—or, as some cynics maintained, they felt that we were past due for our quarterly scare. Whichever the case, such all-encompassing warnings appear to serve chiefly to cover bureaucratic rear ends on the off chance that something does happen—and ultimately to inure the general public to real threats.

"It's clear that terrorists are toying with us," said Milton Bearden, the former CIA case officer with extensive operational experience in the Middle East. "They are using chatter [intercepted terrorist communications] to send false alarms. Sort of like 'Let's make Chicago go broke this week.' With this chatter, they can ring our bell whenever they want." When real warnings do come, DHS can move as slowly as the next big bureaucracy. Take the unsettling case of college student Nathaniel Heatwole, who for inexplicable reasons took it upon himself to prove that TSA was still porous. He sneaked box cutters and other contraband past airport security at Baltimore/Washington International and Raleigh-Durham International six times, eventually planting the banned items in the toilets of two Southwest Airlines planes. This security breach was in itself not a cause for major concern. After all, of over half a billion security checks, six lapses are statistically insignificant, even expected, since no system is foolproof. What is alarming, however, is that Heatwole had sent e-mails notifying the authorities of his stunt and where the cutters were stashed. No one acted on the messages, and it was only five weeks later, during routine maintenance of the planes, that the cutters were discovered and made public. Only then did the TSA and FBI sweep into action, launching investigations and threatening to throw the book at the college kid who made everyone look foolish. How Heatwole's e-mail warning sat unheeded for five weeks in some DHS computer has never been explained.

To be fair, eight months is too brief a period to judge an undertaking the size of DHS. It is very much still "a work in progress," as Hutchinson has said. But if the more glaring problems of 2003 still persist after eighteen months, that would be a different story. With Bob Liscouski's Infrastructure Protection department, I suspected the handicaps are structural and can never be fixed; other issues, such as lack of space, would be resolved over time.

And yet, as the reversal on chemical plant legislation has demonstrated, time is working against DHS and the entire homeland security effort. "Time is our greatest enemy," said Captain Holmes. The farther 9/11 sinks into distant memory without what officials called "a second event" to remind Americans that the threat is still out there, the more likely we are to become lackadaisical and lower our guard. "It's human nature," Holmes said with a shrug. Vigilance requires hardened discipline that can be born only from an immediate sense of threat; without it, constant attention is difficult to maintain. The military ramped down after the Cold War. Even the perennially paranoid Israelis allowed themselves to relax a bit during the short-lived détente that followed the Oslo Peace Accords. But are we risking complacency prematurely?

"You're losing altitude," said Offer Einav, when I caught up with him again nearly a year after we had first spoken in late 2002. We met at one of those frightfully expensive Washington steak houses on lobbyist row, and Einav was barely recognizable in his banker's suit and designer eyewear. He was in town for a security conference, but even these events were being held less frequently by late 2003 as the terror gold rush waned. "Americans have a short attention span," Einav complained. "You think just because there hasn't been an attack in two years that the danger has passed. That shows a clear lack of understanding about the nature of terrorism."

Einav was still busy with U.S. clients (nuclear and airline), but his biggest new gigs were in Europe, where he said the counterterror effort was more consistent and concerted. "Homeland security and the war on terror have been reduced to clichés in the U.S. The process has been hijacked to push a lot of agendas that have nothing to do with terrorism. You're not looking for solutions to fit the problem," he added, "but problems to fit the solution."

Solutions, he elaborated, invariably involved technologies and programs with little preventive value that were pushed by influential contractors. Remote threats that did not justify huge financial outlays were being hyped by lobbyists, while cheap remedies to real dangers—like cargo screening—were being shunned because they did not directly benefit entrenched interests. Throughout the country, counterterrorism was being invoked as an excuse to promote a slew of political white elephants that otherwise didn't stand a chance to get off the ground. L.A.'s intrepid mayor, James K. Hahn, for instance, pounced on the notion of terrorists striking LAX International to propose a $9.6 billion reconstruction of the airport. The stunningly expensive plan needed to go ahead, the mayor's office steadfastly maintained, for the sake of safety. That Mayor Hahn may have wanted a nice new airport for the city apparently had nothing to do with the proposal.

Meanwhile, the public could become more cynical, less welcoming to real countermeasures, more apt to roll their eyes whenever officials raised the specter of terror. Said Einav, "It's the sort of short-term thinking and disillusionment that al Qaeda is counting on. Terrorist organizations are very patient. A lot more patient than politicians or the general public. That's their inherent advantage."

Surveys bear him out. A Gallup poll released on the eve of the second anniversary of 9/11 showed that only 12 percent of respondents still considered terrorism to be the number-one issue facing America, while 48 percent said the economic recovery was the top priority. (In another Gallup poll, taken during the January 2004 code orange alert, the level of concern had increased to 21 percent.) Politicians take their cues from the public, and by fall 2003 counterterror initiatives had started falling off legislative agendas at all levels of government.

President Bush himself set the tone for the backsliding, noting in a May 2003 address to troops that "Al Qaeda is on the run. Right now about half of all the top al Qaeda operatives are either jailed or dead. In either case, they are not a problem anymore."

In the view of some, however, the message from the White House downgrading the threat posed by al Qaeda was premature. "The momentum appears to have waned," concluded a December 2003 bipartisan commission on terror preparedness chaired by Jim Gilmore, the former governor of Virginia and Republican Party boss. The United States was losing focus on terror, the commission noted, as real, everyday problems ranging from Hurricane Isabel to worries about sudden acute respiratory syndrome and flu epidemics were competing with the intangible threat of al Qaeda for the attention of federal and local officials.

There have been small signs of the slippage on almost all fronts. FBI seizures of terrorist funds were down dramatically in 2003, following the post-9/11 crackdown. In Philadelphia, city officials decided that it was no longer worth erecting security barricades in front of the entrances to historic government buildings. In D.C., the police department no longer placed its officers on costly twelve-hour shifts during warnings (although, annoyingly, police cruisers still drove around town with siren lights permanently turned on, a practice whose deterrent value against extremists may be questionable, but that certainly sowed confusion among motorists who thought that they were being pulled over for moving violations). In San Francisco, the National Guard was taken off Golden Gate Bridge duty. Down the coast in L.A./Long Beach, Captain Holmes was cutting back on sea marshal ship boardings. "At first, you just open up your wallet, but after a while you realize, holy crap, this is costing a fortune," he said. L.A./Long Beach only had four VACIS machines—or 3 percent of those deployed nationwide—to screen nearly half the country's seaborne containers. It was not nearly enough. "We have budgetary constraints," Robert Bonner, the commissioner of customs and border protection, conceded, when I asked about the shortage. At the main CDC plague lab in Fort Collins, Colorado, Dr. May Chu said her 2004 counter-terror budget had been chopped and she was gearing up for SARS instead. Indeed, the day after we spoke, she flew to Beijing to observe how the Chinese were dealing with their health crisis. In late March 2004, DHS's two largest front-line agencies—the INS, or the Citizenship and Immigration Service, as it had been renamed, and Bonner's Bureau of Customs and Border Protection—announced hiring freezes because of a $1.2 billion budget shortfall. (The DHS Office of Public Affairs, meanwhile, was advertising a $136,466 a year position for a director of the Entertainment Liaison Office in Hollywood whose principal responsibility is to make DHS look good in the movies.) Similarly, money woes forced the FBI in April 2004 to abandon plans to hire an extra 84 forensic accountants to track terror funding.

But even monies already earmarked for counterterror expenditures were getting snared in red tape and not making it out of federal coffers. The port of Charleston, for instance, was awarded a $3.7 million grant from DHS that includes $2 million designated for the purchase of a helicopter for the Charleston County Sheriff's Department. But according to the September 9, 2003, edition of the *Washington Post*, DHS later informed county officials that they couldn't buy a chopper, due to some clerical snafu, and that therefore the port of Charleston couldn't spend the $2 million allotted to it. Similar bureaucratic snafus prevented the nearby port of Jacksonville, Florida, from spending more than $300,000 of the $3.4 million allotted to it in the nationwide homeland security grant program. The freeze on funds prompted Senator Ernest Hollings of South Carolina to grumble that many of the DHS grants were simply "smoke and mirrors." He was not alone in expressing his frustration. According to an angry September 2003 report by the United States Conference of Mayors, 90 percent of 168 U.S. cities surveyed had not received any of the $1.5 billion earmarked for them in 2002 under federal security assistance programs. (What monies are being doled out don't seem to make much sense either. Alaska and North Dakota get twice as much terror funding per capita from Washington as New York. Wyoming, at $61 a head, gets four times more than California, according to a study by the Public Policy Institute of California commissioned by *Time* magazine.)

It isn't just local municipalities that are feeling the pinch. The TSA can't check airborne cargo for bombs, because there is no money to hire the estimated 27,000 new screeners required for the new procedure. There isn't even enough money for air marshals, due to a $900 million budget shortfall. Coinciding with a slew of DHS warnings about new hijacking threats, the announcement of the planned air marshal cuts galvanized Congress into finding more funding; still, several thousand airport screener jobs are slated for the chopping block, and there is talk of trimming back funds designed to help local police departments bolster security at airports by providing additional officers. At customs, internal reports indicate the urgent need for 1,600 radiation portals to be deployed at ports, borders, and airports. But the 2004 budget could afford only 120 portals. "If protecting ourselves from a dirty bomb isn't a national priority," lamented one longtime veteran of the customs service, "then we've completely lost track of what we are supposed to be doing."

By far and away, however, the greatest competition for resources with the homeland security effort is the war in Iraq. Money, human resources, and political capital that could have been used to shore up various cash-strapped DHS agencies have been spent in Baghdad.

The CIA devoted the better part of a year searching for evidence of Iraqi WMD that as of June 2004 did not exist. The Agency spent another eight months backing up Special Ops Task Force 121 tracking down Saddam. According to a detailed report by the Carnegie Endowment in Washington, the pressure from the White House on CIA director Tenet to produce proof of Iraqi mischief was so intense both before and after the invasion that CIA reports expressing skepticism about Iraqi weapons of mass destruction were sent back to Langley for more optimistic rewrites.

Astonishingly, after wasting so much time on the politically charged issue, Tenet was then asked to fall on his sword and take the heat for the WMD fiasco. "No one told us what to say or how to say it," he defended the administration in a rare public address at Georgetown University on February 5, 2004. Almost immediately afterward, President Bush praised Tenet on *Meet the Press*, saying he'd done a "good job" and that his position was safe. The pronouncement did little to appease critics who cited the mutual endorsements as further evidence of the urgent need for sweeping reforms at the politicized CIA, including the establishment of set terms of office for the director so that he would not be beholden to the Oval Office for his job. (Tenet, loyal to the end, did announce his resignation several months later, citing personal reasons.)

The focus on WMDs instead of Osama demoralized many career intelligence officers, who blame Tenet for playing office politics and not taking a firmer stand with the White House. "A tremendous amount of manpower was shifted from al Qaeda to the Iraqi theater," said one. "Entire programs were scrapped so personnel could be redeployed to satisfy administration policy toward Iraq. It had nothing to do with the reality of the threat. It was all politics." The reallocation of resources covered a wide spectrum of fields, in terms of human, financial, and technological assets, including a diversion of as much as 700 million dollars according to journalist Bob Woodward. Predator drones, which the CIA had armed with Hellfire missiles for the express purpose of taking out Taliban and al Qaeda stragglers in remote corners of Afghanistan, Yemen, and elsewhere, were reassigned to Iraq. Afghanistan itself was packed off to NATO custody. Incongruously, Germany—a staunch opponent of the Iraq offensive—was left in charge of NATO troops in Kabul, while U.S. forces decamped for the Gulf. Not surprisingly, major arrests of Taliban or al Qaeda figures fell off dramatically while Washington was otherwise preoccupied with Saddam.

The White House reprised its hunt for bin Laden in the spring of 2004. But even though there is a distinct possibility that bin Laden or al-Zawahiri, his number two, will get nabbed in the tightening noose, it's too late. Al Qaeda—the organization—has morphed into a movement, an entirely new threat.

For now, al Qaeda—the organization and the movement—are still inexorably linked, used interchangeably by the media and government officials. Yet this new animal is different. It is not a single group, beholden to a single leader. It has no centralized structure or chain of command to disrupt. No headquarters to bomb or finances to freeze. It is an ideology. And counterterrorism experts warn that it will be immeasurably more difficult to stamp out than the organization from which it has sprung.

"There was a time when al Qaeda, the organization, could have been defeated," says Matthew Levitt, a former FBI counterterrorist analyst. "But you can't strangle a movement, and anyone who tells you we will win the war on terror is either an optimist or a politician."

Unfortunately, these unsettling developments are coming as money has become an issue for America's ability to prosecute the war on terror. The occupation of Iraq is soaking up staggering amounts of funds, while generous tax cuts propel budget deficits to levels not seen since the Vietnam War. The $87 billion President Bush requested to finance the Iraqi invasion, plus the extraordinary appropriations in 2003 to fund the occupation and another 25 billion in May 2004, put the price tag on Saddam's head at well over $150 billion. That is more than ten times the allocation for ridding Afghanistan of the Taliban and roughly three times what is being spent domestically to secure the United States. Trying to preempt Democratic election campaign criticism that the Bush administration is shortchanging domestic security at the expense of Iraq, the White House announced that it would bump DHS's and the FBI's 2005 budgets by 10 percent. But that is still only a fraction of what Iraq is costing taxpayers. The FBI's entire 2005 budget, for instance, is less than one-third of the value of Halliburton's $17 billion contracts to rebuild Iraqi infrastructure. Even the modest increases in domestic security spending are not written in stone. A secret White House memo leaked to the press in 2004 lists DHS among the federal agencies slated for post-election cuts.

Aside from draining resources from the home front, the occupation of Iraq had another, equally important consequence that could ultimately affect the safety of Americans. It had vastly increased the number of people in the Muslim world who wished us ill. "By invading an oil-rich Arab country, we validated all of bin Laden's arguments that the U.S. is an imperial power that seeks to subjugate Islam," said Bruce Hoffman, a terror expert at the RAND Corporation.

Indeed, there was mounting evidence—both empirical and anecdotal—that toppling Saddam Hussein has been a propaganda disaster for the U.S. and a boon for bin Laden. "I can't imagine a better recruiting tool," said Levitt, the former FBI terror analyst. International public opinion polls seem to bear him out. According to a nine-nation survey published in 2004 by the nonpartisan Pew Research Center in Washington, support for the U.S. since the Iraqi invasion has plunged in every country polled except for Britain. "Support for America has dropped in most of the Muslim world," Vice Adm. Lowell Jacoby, head of the Defense Intelligence Agency, reported to Congress in February 2004. Favorable ratings for the U.S. among Moroccans dropped to 27 percent from 77 percent in 2000, he said. In Jordan, a key partner in the war on terrorism, those rates plummeted even more drastically, to 1 percent in May 2003 from 25 percent in 2002. And that was before horrific photographs of U.S. soldiers stacking naked Iraqis in sexually demeaning human pyramids aired on Arab television in May 2004.

By then the United States had all but lost the high moral ground of 9/11. Its intentions were viewed with deep distrust almost everywhere, even among the more moderate element of the outraged Muslim community. Between half and up to 71 percent of all respondents polled by Pew, for instance, saw the Iraqi war as primarily an attempt to control Mideast oil. Of even greater concern to U.S. officials, 82 percent of Jordanians and more than 40 percent of those queried in Morocco and Pakistan now said suicide attacks were justified. In Pakistan, according to the Pew survey, support for al Qaeda was running at 65 percent. Asked about the results, Pakistani President Pervez

Musharraf told ABC News that this was not so much an endorsement of bin Laden as "a reflection of anti-American sentiment."

Whichever way you sliced it, the results spelled trouble: Islamic extremists were bound to capitalize on the growing disenchantment with the United States. "It's the law of averages," said Beardon, the former CIA officer: As the number of Muslims with grievances against the U.S. swells, so too does the pool of potential al Qaeda recruits. Another security official likened the phenomenon to Internet spammers who send out millions of e-mail solicitations in the hope of getting a few bites. "Even if the rate of response is only a small fraction of one percent, you dramatically increase your odds by reaching a wider audience." And al Qaeda, by the summer of 2004, indisputably had a wider audience. How this unintended result of the war in Iraq will affect our ability to stay safe in America remains to be seen.

For civil liberties activists at home, the loss of momentum in the domestic counterterror effort offers some reason to rejoice. The 2003 Christmas code-orange alert notwithstanding, by early 2004 a backlash against many of the more intrusive antiterror measures was swelling. Audrey Collins, a federal judge in California, ruled that parts of the Patriot Act banning certain types of support for terror groups were so vague that they violated the First and Fifth amendments. New York's City Council added its weighty voice to the 140 municipal governments around the country that passed resolutions condemning the Patriot Act. Despite President Bush's entreaties, Congress refused to extend provisional Patriot Act laws such as the FBI's right to sneak and peek past the originally mandated deadline of 2005. One after another, states dropped out of the Justice Department's Multistate Anti-Terrorism Information Exchange, or MATRIX, data-sharing program. The implementation of CAPPS II, the computerized passenger screening system, has been delayed over privacy issues and concerns about the potential for abuse of the data collected by the system.

At the Justice Department, Ashcroft has been forced to relent on his earlier refusal to disclose the number of library record subpoenas (fifty) and to shelve plans for even more draconian Patriot II legislation. The Supreme Court dealt the attorney general another blow when, bowing to pressure, it agreed to rule on whether the president's prerogative to designate "enemy combatants" was constitutional. The administration was forced to relent and announced that enemy combatants would be granted access to counsel. The Pentagon followed suit, saying some of the 660 Taliban and al Qaeda suspects still held at Guantánamo Bay may be allowed legal representation and right to trials. As a further sign of the changing winds, the military started to release some Guantánamo prisoners. The retreat extended to the Justice Department's controversial registration program for students and visitors from twenty-five Muslim countries, known as the National Security Entry Exit System, or NSEERS, which was terminated amid allegations that it had unfairly targeted people and led to the deportation of thirteen thousand. Similarly, the Justice Department's own inspector general issued a searing report on the treatment of the twelve hundred original 9/11 detainees, such as Hady Omar, including videotape of physical abuse and a strongly worded warning that procedural safeguards needed to be instituted to prevent future blanket sweeps.

Some of the most vocal criticism of the Bush administration's handling of the domestic war on terror came from expected quarters: senior Democrats. "It makes no more sense to attack civil liberties to get at terrorists than to invade Iraq to get Osama bin Laden," opined Al Gore in a full-page ad in the *New York Times* titled "This Administration is Using Fear as a Political Tool." The ubiquitous Martin Sheen, apparently under the misconception that his role as a TV president gives him unusually keen political insight, appeared in countless print ads condemning the administration. "No more Ashcroft" became a rallying cry of John Kerry's presidential campaign. Of course, many of the front-running Democratic candidates-turned-campaign-critics conveniently forgot that they had either backed or stood silent while Patriot provisions had passed almost unanimously on Capitol Hill. (The policy amnesia also extended to support by some Democratic candidates of Operation Iraqi Freedom.)

The backlash against counterterror excesses, however, has not been confined to partisan politics. The federal terror commission chaired by Republican Jim Gilmore recommended that the White House establish a civil liberties oversight panel to determine whether terror laws infringe on basic individual rights. The Gilmore commission was especially concerned with the growing domestic use of surveillance technology such as the satellites I'd seen at Space Imaging Corp. in Denver. "It now becomes essential for the Congress to legislate and for the Defense Department to implement through clear procedures the limitations of the use of satellite imagery and other advanced technology monitoring in the United States," the commission noted in its December 2003 report, warning that "as more terrorist attacks occur, the pressure will rise to lessen civil liberties, albeit with different labels."

As the first half of 2004 passed without any of the predicted terrorist strikes, the pendulum, which had arced so intrusively in the direction of prying counterterror measures, seemed to be regaining its equilibrium. For now, many Americans have decided that our leaders had overreacted, had gone too far in laying the legal and technological groundwork for a maximum security state. An America where people could be imprisoned arbitrarily without access to counsel, where computer databases and surveillance programs tracked citizens' movements, and where people lived in fear of terrorists and the government would no longer be the same country. It wouldn't be worth living in such a place.

That is the principal lesson of the first two and a half years of the domestic war on terror. And it is one worth remembering, because as the Gilmore commission sagely prophesied, the urge to sacrifice the fundamental values that make America one of the world's freest societies will prove powerful in the years to come, for the question is not whether terrorists will strike again, but *when*.

About the Author

MATTHEW BRZEZINSKI is a contributing writer for *The New York Times Magazine* and former foreign correspondent at *The Wall Street Journal*. He is also the author of *Casino Moscow: A Tale of Greed and Adventure on Capitalism's Wildest Frontier*. He lives in Washington, D.C.